THE NON-DRAMATIC WORKS

OF

THOMAS DEKKER.

IN FIVE VOLUMES.

FOR THE FIRST TIME COLLECTED AND EDITED,
WITH MEMORIAL-INTRODUCTION, NOTES AND ILLUSTRATIONS, ETC.

BY THE REV.
ALEXANDER B. GROSART, D.D., LL.D. (EDIN.), F.S.A. (SCOT.),
St. George's, Blackburn, Lancashire.

VOL. III.

DEKKER HIS DREAME. 1620.
THE BELMAN OF LONDON. 1608.
LANTHORNE AND CANDLE-LIGHT. 1609.
A STRANGE HORSE-RACE. 1613.

NEW YORK
RUSSELL & RUSSELL · INC
1963

*First Published in 1885 and
Reissued in 1963 by Russell & Russell, Inc.,
in an Edition Limited to 400 Sets
L. C. Catalog Card No: 63–15156*

CONTENTS.

Reader, here is fuch a Book
Will make you leap before you look,
And fhift, without being thought a Rook.

The Author's airy, light, and thin,
Whom no man faw e'r break a fhin,
Or ever yet leap out of's fkin.

When e'r he ftrain'd at Horfe or Bell,
Tom Charles himfelf who came to fmell
His faults, ftill fwore 'twas clean and well.

WILLIAM CARTWRIGHT.

IX.

DEKKER HIS DREAME.

1620.

NOTE.

For ' Dekker his Dreame' I am again indebted to the British Museum. The last page of this exemplar is executed in marvellous fac-simile by Harris. In 1860 Mr. James O. Halliwell (now Dr. Halliwell-Phillipps) reprinted this tractate in some 25 copies or thereby. His Copyist did his work most perfunctorily ; his errors of omission and commission making the beautiful little book just so much waste-paper. The following are some of the more flagrant blunders—

Page 8, *line* 28, 'feelings' for 'feelings.'
„   13, „   15, onward — the whole of the margin-notes are omitted—without notice.
„   18, „   28, 'sphæte' for 'Sphære.'
„   20, „   10, 'greping' for 'griping.'
„   21, „   28, 'Trumph'd for 'Triumph'd.'
„   22, „   17, " Honor and Greatneffe wore Immortall cloathing " —dropped out.
„   23, ., 3, 'bufferings' for 'buffetings.'
„   30, „   7, 'broken starues' for 'broken statues.'
„   33, „, 26, 'the' for 'he.'
„   34, „ 26, 'thereby' dropped.
„   35, „ 11, 'tembling' for 'trembling.'
„   35, „   18, 'daly' for 'dayly.'
„   35, „   19, 'nor' for 'or.'
„   36, „   21, 'were' for 'where.'
„   38, „   15, 'for' for 'fet.'
„   38, „ 19, 'hillish' for 'hellish.'
„   42, „   10, 'though' for 'through.'
„   43, „   19, 'ruffian' for 'Ruffian.'
„   43, „   25, 'he' for 'be.'
„   45, „   9, 'At' for 'A.'
„   45, „   28, 'digestion' for 'disgestion.'
„   50, „   12, 'sale' for 'sayle.'
„   51, „   7, 'than' for 'then.'
„   51, „   24, 'tylts' for 'Iylts.'
„   52, „   4, 'perwid' for 'periurd.'
„   52, „   17, 'head' for 'bread.'
„   52, „   24, 'Tob' for 'Iob.'
„   54, „   3, 'nimicum' for 'nimium.'
„   56, „   8, "I neuer flept in a Rich lordly Roome "—dropped out.
„   56, „   9, 'I' before 'neuer' superfluously.
„   57, „   3, 'Like' for 'Little.'
„   58, „   12, 'a' before 'Methuslem's' superfluously.

All these in a slender pamphlet, and over-and-above scarcely numerable departures from orthography, capitals, italics, etc., etc.

Title-page—The woodcut of 'Dekker' in bed asleep in no way is faithful to the original. The features especially are grotesquely false. The dreaming poet's nose is in the original narrow and sensitive, in Mr. Halliwell-Phillipps' thick and gross ; the cheeks thin and worn, in the reproduction fat and bloated, and so throughout. Our admirable fac-simile (in 4°) will therefore be doubly acceptable. The late Rev. Thomas Corser, in his 'Collectanea Anglo-Poetica' (*s. n.*), has re-used Mr. Halliwell-Phillipps' woodblock, and by the kindness of the Chetham Society I am enabled to give an impression from this as used by both (page 5), to prove how utterly unfaithful it is to the original. See Memorial-Introduction on the probable likeness of the Author herein.

The original tractate consists of 22 leaves (B. Museum 39, c. 6).

A. B. G.

Dekker his Dreame.

In which, beeing rapt with a Poeticall
Enthusiasme, *the great Volumes of Heauen*
and Hell to Him were opened, in which he
read many Wonderfull Things.

Est Deus in nobis, agitante calescimus Illo.

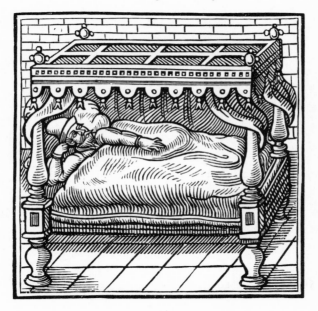

LONDON
Printed by NICHOLAS OKES. 1620.

To the trvely-accomplished Gentleman,
and worthy Deſeruer of all Mens Loues,
Maſter Endymion Porter.

Sir:

F *you aſke why, from the heapes of
Men, I picke out you onely to bee that*
Murus ahæneus, *which muſt defend mee,
let me tell you (what you know already)*
that Books are like the Hungarians *in* Paules, *who
haue a Priuiledge to holde out their* Turkiſh *Hiſtory
for any one to reade. They beg nothing, the Texted
Paſt-bord talkes all; and if nothing be giuen,
nothing is ſpoken, but God knowes what they thinke.
If you are angry, that I thruſt into your hands
a Subieƈt of this Nature; O good Sir, take me thus
far into your pardon; that it was impoſſible for me
to beget a Better: For the Bed on which ſeuen years
I lay Dreaming, was filled with thornes inſtead of
fethers, my pillow a rugged flint, my Chamber-
fellowes (ſorrowes that day and night kept me
company) the very, or worſe than the very Infernall
Furies. Beſides, I herein | imitate the moſt Courtly*

*Reuellings ; for if Lords be in the Grand Masque,
in the Antimasque are Players : So in these of
mine, though the Diuell bee in the one, God is in
the other ; nay in Both. What I send you, may
perhaps seeme bitter, yet it is wholesome ; your best
Physicke is not a Iulep ; sweete sawces leaue rotten
bodies. There is a* Hell *named in our Creede, and a*
Heauen, *and the* Hell *comes before : If we looke not
into the first, we shall neuer liue in the last. Our
tossing vp and down (here) is the Sea, but the land
of Angels is our Shoare. Sayle so long as we can
beare vp, through Honors, Riches, Pleasures, and
all the sensuall Billowes of the World ; yet there is
one Harbour to put in at, and safely to arriue (There)
is all the Hardnesse, all the Happinesse. Bookes are
Pilots in such voyages : would mine were but one
point of the Compasse, for any man to steere well by.
I doe not thinke, but euen those Courtiers, who are
most taken with the glittering of Pallaces, doe from
those glorious Enter-viewes, masques, tilt-triumphs,
& such like, (with which their eyes are so often
banqueted), reade sometimes excellēt lectures to their
soules, by a comparatiue laying those transitory Ones,
and those immortall beauties of heauen together.
The very Roofes of kings Courts, do almost draw vs
vp to / such a contemplation : For when the Paue-
ments of such Places are at the best but Marble, yet
the vpper seelings are like Firmaments of Starres :*

*There you fee the golden Embofments and curious
Enchafings : The true brauery is aboue.*

An excellent Dinner was that in France, *when
the King and Queen fate at Table, and with them,*
Thomas Aquinas *and* Bonauentura *(the two great
Schoolemen): whilft the others were feeding, one of
thefe caft an earneft and fixed eye vpon the beauty of
the Queene : at which the King wondring, afked,
why hee did fo? O (quoth he), if the great
Worke-maifter, out of a peece of clay, can mould and
fafhion fo admirable a creature as your Queen is ;
I am rapt into an aftonifhable amazemēt to thinke,
how glorious thofe Bodyes are, who are Courtiers
attending vpon his Maiefticall Throne. If I hold
the Pen longer in my hand, I fhall fall afleepe againe:
But howfoeuer I wake, or haue mine eyes clofed,
——I reft,*

Euer ready to do you feruice,

Tho. Dekker.

TO THE READER.

OVT of a long Sleepe, which for almoſt ſeuen yeares together, ſeized al my ſences, drowning them in a deepe Lethe of forgetfulneſſe, and burying mee to the World, in the loweſt graue of Obliuion / : Meeting in that drouzy voyage with nothing but frightfull Apparitions, by reaſon (as now I gueſſe) of the place in which I lay, being a Caue ſtrongly ſhut vp by moſt Diuelliſh and dreadfull Enchantments ; I did at laſt fall into a Dreame, which preſented to my waking Soule infinite Pleaſures, commix'd with In-vtterable Horrors. More did I behold thus Sleeping, then euer I could before, when my eies were wide open. I climbed to the tops of all the trees in Paradiſe, and eate ſweeter Apples then *Adam* euer taſted. I went into the Star-Chamber of Heauen, where Kings and Princes were ſet to the Barre, and when the Court aroſe, I fed vpon *manna*, at a table with Angels. *Ieruſalem* was the Pallace I liued in, and Mount *Sion* the hil, from whoſe top, I was dazled

with glories brighter then / Sun-beames. This
was my Banquet: The Courfe-meate was able
to kill mee. For I was throwne (after all this
Happineffe) into a fea Infernall, and forced to
fwim through Torrents of vnquenchable fire. All
the Iayles of Hell were fet open. And albeit the
Arraignements were horrid, yet the Executions
were ten-times more terrible. Ioyes tooke me by
the hand in the firft dance, but feares and forrowes
whipt me forward in the fecond. I muft not now
tell, what I faw, neither can I now fee fo much
as I haue told. What Muficke led both thefe
meafures, do but open my fong-Booke, and the
Leffons are there fet downe.

If the Notes pleafe thee, my paines are well
beftowed. If to thine eare they found vntuneable,
much are they not to be blamed, in regard they
are the Aires of a Sleeping Man.

Farewell. /

DEKKER HIS DREAME.

Which beeing truely Interpreted, is
able to comfort the good, and ter-
rifie the Bad.

 HEN downe, the Sun his golden
Beames had layd,
And at his wefterne Inne his
iourney ftayd,
Thus Sleepe the eyes of man
and beaft did feize,
Whileft Hee gaue light to the Antipodes :
I flep'd with others, but my Sences ftream'd
In frightfull formes, for a Strange Dreame I
Dream'd.

Signes before the laft Day.

Peace fled to Heauen (me thought),   Warre.
And as fhe went,
Her Roabe fell from her, which Warre   As before
Christs coming
finding Rent   first there was

an Vniversall Peace ; so before his last cōming, there shalbe (if not General wars) euery mans heart fighting one against another.

Into a thouſand Ragges, dying them in
   Gall,
Mix'd with Mans bloud, and charged
   the World to call
Thoſe / ſpoyles his Enſignes : then (all-
   Arm'd) beſtriding
A Canon, and with Thundring voyce diuiding
Nations Colleagu'd ; down fell the Golden Chaine
Of Sweete Commerce, linck'd both by Loue &
   Gaine :
Order ran mad, Diſorder fild his Roome,
When beating at Hell gates the Fatall Dromme,
Out-yſſued Vengeance, Horror, Inceſt, Rape,

Famine. Famine and Death, in the moſt vgly ſhape
That Hell could ſend them out in. At theſe
   Sights,
Seas threatened Shores, The Earth (in ſtrange
   affrights)
Shooke at the Center : then (me thought) one drew
From his Full Quiuer, poyſned ſhafts, which flew

Pestilence. With burning feathers of Hot Peſtilence,
Filling the wide-worlds vaſt Circumference
With blaines, and bliſters, whileſt each Kingdome
   raues,
To ſee the whole Earth but one field of Graues.

Treason. Anon (me thought), Treaſon, and
   Murther cry'de
Kill, kill ; wilde Vproares Gates flew open wide;

The Father ftabd the Sonne, the Sonne the
    Brother,
Man was not Man, till he deftroyd Another ;
Each man was both the Lyon and the Prey,
And euery Corne-field an Aceldema :
A Citty on a Citties ruines ftood,
And Townes (late peopled), now were Lakes of
    Bloud.
As boyftrous billowes, boyftrous waues confound,
So Nations, are in Nation's glories drownd.
The Turkifh Halfe-moone on her filuer   Slauery.
    Hornes,
Toffes the Chriftian Diadem, and adornes
The Sphaere of Ottoman with Starry light,
Stolne euen from Thofe, vnder the Croffe who
    fight :   Ciuill vproares.
The / Sacred Empire did it Selfe o're whelme ;
State on ftate trampled ; realm did beat down
    realme :
Religion (all this while) a Garment   Religion made
    wore,   a Strumpet.
Stayn'd like a Painters Apron, and turn'd Whore.
To feuerall Countries, till from deepe Abyfme
Vp her Two Baftards came (Error and Schifme),
She in That motley Cloake, with her Two
    Twinnes,
Trauell'd from land to land, fowing Ranck
    Sinnes,

Which choak'd the Good Corne, and from them
    did rife
Opinions, factions, black leau'd Herefies;
Pride, Superftition, Rancor, Hate, Difdaine,
So that (me thought) on earth no good did Reigne.

All this afore named (and more terrible præ-
dictions then the weake *Pen* of a filly man can
fet down), are liuely written in God's Eternall
Calendar : where his Prophet Ezechiel thus
thundereth forth the Terrors foregoing the later
Day   [Ezech. 39].
    The fifh of the Seas, Birds of the aire, Beafts of
the field, and al that creepeth on the ground,
together with all humane generations which liue
vpon the face of the earth, fhall be in an vproare.
Hils fhall bee ouerturned, Hedges broken downe,
euery ftrong wall fall to the ground.   I will call
againft them the fword from the tops of all
Mountaines, and euery man's fword fhall bee bent
againft his owne brother ; my Iudgement fhall bee
in peftilence and bloud, &c.   And I will raine fire
and brimftone.
    Marke, how an Euangelift feconds a Prophet,
with this new battry vppon the world.   When (faith
    Luk. 21.   hee), you fhall heare the fame or bruite of
warres and vproares, be not afraid, for that thefe
things muft bee.   And yet prefently the end of

the world fhall not enfue. One Nation fhall rife
againft another, and one Kingdome fhall inuade
another ; there fhall be great earth-quakes, peftilence, and famine, moft terrible Signes and tokens
from Heauen.

The latter day.

Thefe tranfitory, poore Terreftriall terrors,
Seru'd but as Heralds to found forth the Horrors
Of woes Eternall ; this, was but a Sceane
To the Great following Tragedy. So that then
(Me thought) one fitting on a Raine-bow, founded
A trumpet, which in earth-quakes Earth con-
    founded.
And then a voyce, fhrill (but Angelicall),
Full of Command and Dreade, from heauen did
    call,
To Summon the whole world to ftand to th' Barre.
Both All that euer haue beene, and now are,
To giue a ftrict account how they had fpent
That Tallent of their life, which was but lent.

We muft All be Summoned before the Tribunall
Seate of Chrift, and euery man receiue either Good
or Euill, according as he hath behaued himfelfe
whilft he liued vpon earth. Chrift taketh Account
of all his Tallents. Luke 12, 16, 19, 10. Matt. 26.

Terrors / of the later day.

The Leaues of Heauen (me thought) thē rent in
Clouds shrŭck   ſunder,
vp like parch-
ment. Out of which, Lightning brake, and
    Horrid Thunder,
Which paſh'd (in peeces) Kingdomes : whizzing
    flakes
Of Brimſtone rain'd, that Seas ſeem'd Burning Lakes :
Rocks crumbled into powder; Scalded Mountaines
In their drie Iawes, dranck riuers vp and fountaines :
Fury, with Snaky locks and Smeared hands,
(Toſſing about her eares two firy brands)
Met Wrath, and Indignation, rauing-mad,
Tearing each others fleſh, and wildly clad
In Skins of ſpotted Tygers : vp and downe
They ran, and ſpied (at laſt) Confuſion :
With whom ſwearing a League, black ſtormes
    they Hurl'd,
With whirlewind violence to cruſh the world,
And bury her in 's quick Ruines ; All the Floore
Celeſtiall, crack'd and fell downe in a ſhower
Of Bloud, whilſt the Terreſtiall Pauement burn'd,
Starres. In which the Starres to ſpent-out Snuffes
      were turnd;
Sunne. The Sun leap'd from his Chariot, and in
      feare
Moone. Of Firing, headlong ran to th' Moones
      cold Sphære,

But fhe (for all her Flouds, Ice, Frofts and Snow)
Did like a lumpe of fteele i' th' Furnace glow.
The Sun and Moone were neither Sun nor Moone,
Their Shining could be cald, nor Night nor Noone :
This Maffy, Vniuerfall, Earthly Ball,   The world
Was All one Bonfire, and it burnt out   on fire.
    All.
In an eies Twinkling, more by Fire was loft
Than Twenty Earthes ; and all their wealth e're
    coft.

Chrift / his coming in glory.

As in an Army Royall (led by a King),   A simile.
After the Canons Sulphurous thundering,
Battring downe Bulwarkes, Rampires, Parapets,
Forts, Gabions, Palizadoes, Cazimates,
Horror on all fides Roaring, Wings here flying
At Wings (like armed Eagles) ; here Troopes dying,
A butcherous Execution through the field,
Bellowing with Fiend-like threats, when yet none
    yeeld,
Though Death ftalkes vp and downe, ghaftly and
    pale,
The Victors Wreath lying in a doubtfull Scale ;
The King himfelfe, fafe guarded on a Hill,
Seeing this black day, yet ftirring not vntill
H findes fit time to Strike : then downe, amayne,
Wh rying he comes ; a glorious dreadfull Trayne

Of High-Heroick Spirits, circling him round,
Who with fwift Vengeance do their Foes con-
    found,
And flaue-like drag them at prowd Chariot wheeles,
Whilft miferies (worfe then Death) tread on their
    heeles :

So (but with greater Terror, State, and

The terrour
of Christs
comming.   Wonder)
Heauens Supreme Monarch (one hand
    griping thunder,

The other ftormes of Haile, Whirle-winds and
    fire,

Veniet splen-   Enfigns of his hot-burning quenchleffe
dore Rutilans
pulchritudine   ire) ;
Admirandus,
justis ama-   When the Worlds buildings, fmothered
bilis, Impijs
horribilis.   lay in fmoake,

(With fparkling eyes), Maieftically broke

Esay 28.   Out of his Pallace, ne're fet ope' before
And ftood like a Triumphant Conqueror,

O Death !   Trampling / on Death and Hell : About
where is thy
sting ? &c.   him, round

(Like petty Viz-royes), Spirits (me thought) all-
    Crownde,

How Christ   Shewd, as if none but Kings, had bin his
comes guarded
and attended.   Guard ;

Whole Hierarchies of Saints were then preferd,
With Principalities, Powers, and Dominations ;
Thrones, Angels, and Archangels, (all att' once)

Filling the Prefence : Then like heauen-borne
    Twinnes,
Flew fiery Cherubins, and Seraphins ;
Whilft the old Patriarches, cloath'd all <small>Patriarches</small>
    in white, <small>Mat. 13.</small>
Were rap'd with Ioy, to fee beames far more
    bright,
About the Prophets and th' Apoftles <small>Prophets.</small>
    runne
Than thofe whofe Flames were kindled at the Sun,
Martyrs (me thought), with felfe-fame <small>Martyrs.</small>
    luftre fhinde,
As Gold, which feuen times was by fire refinde :
Virgins, whofe Soules in life from Luft <small>Virgins.</small>
    liu'd cleare, <small>Pfal. 20.</small>
Had Siluer robes, and on their heads did weare
Coronets of Diamonds. Were my Fingers flint,
My Pen of pointed Adamant, t' imprint
Charaćters in tough Iron, or hammered <small>In imitation</small>
    braffe, <small>of that in</small>
    <small>Virgill.</small>
Mine inke, a depthleffe Sea ; All thefe
    (alas !)
Would be worne out, ere I one lyne fhould draw,
Of thofe Full Glories, which (I dreamd) I faw :
Nor could I write this (though it be but meane),
Did not fome Angell guide my Fainting Pen.
Gods Heire Apparent (here once made away)
Triumph'd in this his Coronation day,

In which Heauen was his Kingdome, Mercy his
    Throne,
Iuftice his Scepter, a Communion
Of Sanctified foules, the Courtly peeres,
And his Star Chamber Lords ; who now had
    yeeres
Which / neuer turn'd them Gray, by Times rough
    wether,
            Greatneffe was now, no more cald For-
The Saints in   tunes fether,
heauen inioy
all perfection. Nor   Honor   held a fruitleffe golden
    Dreame,
Nor Riches a bewitching fwallowing ftreame,
Nor Learning laugh'd at as the Beggars Dower,
Nor beauties painted cheeke a Summers Flower.
No, no, life endleffe was, yet without loathing,
Honor and Greatneffe wore Immortall cloathing ;
Riches were Subiect to no bafe Confuming,
Learning burnt bright, without Contentious fuming,
Beauty no painting bought, but ftill renew'd,
Each one had (heere) his full Beatitude.
O my weake eyes ! how did your Balls (me
    thought)
Burne out their Ielly, when they had but caught
One little-little glimpfe of thofe Diuine
And in-acceffible Beames, which did out-fhine
Hot-glowing coales of Fire ? no mortall Sight
Can ftand a Maiefty fo infinite.

That Face whofe Picture might haue As Christ was, in euery part
   ranfom'd Kings, of his body crucified by
Yet put vp Spettings, Baffulings, Buffet- *Iewes*; so will He come
   ings. glorified in all perfection, to

   Efa. 50. Ierem. 3. Math. 26. the Terror both of *Iewe*
   Marke 14   Luk. 22. and *Gentile*.

That Head, which could a Crowne of Starres haue
   worne,
Yet fpightfully was wrench'd with wreathes of
   Thorne.
                    Math. 27.   Mark 15.   Iohn 19.
Thofe Hands and Feete, where Pureft ftamps were
   fet ;
Yet Naild-vp like to Pieces Counterfet.
                                   Pfal. 77.
Thofe / Lippes, which though they had Command
   o're All,
Being thirfty, Vinegar had to drinke, and Gall.
                                   Luk. 23.
That Body, fcourg'd and torne with many a
   wound,
That his deere Bloud (like Balme) might leaue vs
   Sound.
                    Luk. 23.   Pfal. 129.   Zach. 13.
The Well of Life, which with a Speare being
   tride,
Two Streames (Myfterious) gufh'd out from the
   Side.   Iohn 19.

Meſſias, great Iehouah, God on hie,
Yet Haild, King of the Iewes, in Mockery.

Math. 2.   Mark 15.   Luk. 23.

The Manger-Cradled Babe, the Begger borne,
The pooreſt Worme on earth, the Heighth of
    Scorne.   Math. 2.   Pſal. 22.
That Lord, by his Owne Subiects Crucified,
Lo, at this Grand Aſſize comes Glorified,
With troopes of Angels, who his Officers are,
To call by ſound of Trumpe his Foes to a Bar.
Thus ſtood he Arm'd ; Iuſtice his Breaſt-plate was,
Iudgement his Helmet, ſtronger farre than Braſſe :
On his Right Arme, Truths Shield he did aduance,
    Wisd. 5.   And turnde his Sharpned Wrath into a
    Lance :
Out of his Mouth a Two-edg'd Sword did flie,
    Apoc. 1.   To Wound, Body and Soule, eternally ;
Arm'd / (Cap-a-pe) thus, who 'gainſt him durſt
    fight ?
There was no ground for Strength, nor yet for
    Flight.
At this (me thought) All Graues that euer held
Dead Coarſes, yawn'd wide-open, and compell'd
The bones of Dead-men vp with Fleſh to riſe ;
Yea, thoſe on whom the Seas did tyrannize,
And droun'd in wrackes, and which were peece-
    meale eaten,
With liuely bodies to the ſhoares were beaten :

Whom Sword, or Fire, Iibbets, or Wheeles had
    torne,

Had their own limbes againe, and new were
    borne ;

From the firſt Man God made, to th' laſt that died,

The Names of All, were here Exampli- The Generall
    fied ;   Sessions.

Emp'rours and Kings, Patriarches, and Tribes
    forgotten,

The Conquerors of the world (moldred and
    rotten) ;

Lords, beggers, Men and Women, young and old,

Vp (at a Bar ſet forth) their Hands did hold.

The Iudge being ſet, in open Court were layd

Huge Bookes: at ſight of which, All   The bookes
    were diſmaid,   of Conscience
                                         opened.
Would faine haue ſhrunck back, and   Vnusquisque
    fell downe with feare :   cernet ante
                                         faciem suam
                                         exposita opera
In ſheetes of Braſſe, all Stories written sua, sine bona
    were   illa, sine mala,
                                         &c. Item
                                         Formidabiles
(Which thoſe Great volumes held)   libri aperien-
    Charaċter'd deepe   tur, in quibus
                                         scripta sunt
                                         opera nostra,
With Pens of Steele, Eternal Files to   & Actus, et
    keepe   Verba ; et
                                         quæcunque
                                         egimus in hac
                                         Vita : illic non
solum Actus, verum et cogitationes, et intentiones Cordis, scriptæ erunt.
Ephra in lib.—De Vera Pœnitentiæ—Cap. 4.   Quid nobis miseris fiet,
cum omnia (orbi Vniuerso) palam facta, in tam aperto, tamque illus
tri theatro denudata.   Hominum nobis partim cognitorum, partim
incognitorum oculis subijcientur? &c. D. Chrysostom: Homil. 5. Ad
Roman.

Of euery Nation, fince the Earth began,
And euery Deede, Word, thought of euery Man :
Sins hatch'd in Caues, or fuch whofe Bawd was
     Night,
The Minutes of the Act were here fet right.
Great men, whofe fecret Damn'd fins vizards wore
So clofe, that none vpon their Browes could fcore
The leaft Black line (becaufe none durft) had here
A Bill of Items in particular,
What / their Soules owed for Sin, to Death and
Or, if it happened that they er'e did well,   [Hell ;
In thefe True Iournals, it as large was found,
And with rich promife of Reward was Crown'd.

The Bookes were opened, &c.   Apoc. 20.

Which done (me thought), the Seffions thus began,
Confcience the Cryer, cald forth euery Man

Cōscienee   To make appearance ; and (though to
the Cryer of
the Court.   my fight

The Numbers that were there were infinite)
In an Eies-twinkling, yet they parted were,

Triticum a   The Good from Bad, the Spotted from
zizanijs, bono   the Cleare ;
pisces a malis
seperabit.   The Wolues and Goates to th' left Hand
        howling went,
The Lambs, and Harmeleffe Sheep to th' Right
    were fent :

After this Separation, vp did rife
Heauen's Lord Chiefe-Iuftice, and this Sentence
flies
Out of his Dreadfull Breaft: O you (quoth he),
That haue my Lambs bin, and did
follow me,
As your true Shepheard, and did know
my Voyce,

The Lord-Chiefe-Iuftice his sentence on the prisoners.

As I in you, you fhall in Mee reioyce :
And now is come the day: this is the Houre
In which my Bleffings on your Heads I poure :
Beloued of my Father, Come and Take
A Kingdom layd vp onely for your fake ;
For me you haue bin Mock'd, Reuil'd,
and Beate,

Come ye Blessed, &c. Mat. 25. Mat. 5.

Mount therefore now into a Glorious Seate :
O bleffed word ! which none but he can fpeake,
O word of Loue Diuine ! when (not with
weake
But Armes Omnipotent-ftrong, fpread ope' wide)
He cries, Come, Come ! How is Man dignifide
(Being / but a Vaffaile groueling on the ground),
Next to his Kings owne Throne thus to fit
Crown'd ?
Come and poffeffe : O what fhall you
poffeffe ?
A Kingdome, whofe vaft Boundes none
can expreffe :

The excellence of that Inheritance laid vp in heauen for those that doe well.

Had all the Peebles in the world bin cut
Into Rich Diamonds, and both Indies put
Into Two Hils of Siluer, and fine Gold,
Nor all Kings hoarded Treafures downe being told,
Can this Inheritance buy, which for your Good
Is purchaft at a High Rate (Chrifts deere blood).
    Come and Poffeffe, what Time can neuer Rot,
Theeues fteale, Warres fpoyle, or Cank'rous Enuy
        blot ;
Come, and poffeffe, a State, whofe Title, Law,
Attorneys Wiles, no, nor the Scarlet Awe
Of corrupt Iudges, euer can Intangle :
No Bawling Pleader at the Barre fhall wrangle
To proue the Right of This, being Stronglier
        Grounded
Than Defcents Lineall, by which Realmes are
        Bounded.
Set at his Table, which doth Euer lie
Couered with banquets of Eternitie :
Salutations Cup ftands fill'd for you to th' Brim,
Come Drinke, where Immortality doth fwim.
    Come and Poffeffe, you bleffed, Bleft in This,
The deere Sonne giues you a Cœleftiall Kiffe
For welcome : Come you bleffed, and poffeffe
Wealth, Honor, Glories, Pleafures numberleffe.
The not-guilty Forth-with (me thought) they All were
how rewarded.   Crown'd with gold,
Set thick with Starres, and in their hands did hold

Scepters of fparkling Diamonds, which out fhinde
Sun-beames, or Siluer, feuen times being Re-finde.
The / Ioy at this, was wondrous : All the Skies
Danc'd to the foundes of feuerall Harmonies ;
Both Angels and Arch-angels loudly fung,
All Heauen was but One Inftrument well ftrung.
But They, who on the Left-hand were fet by,
(As Out-cafts) fhooke and trembled fearefully,
Like falling Towers : their Sinnes and The guilty how
    Soules were black, perplexed.
And troopes of Hel-hounds waited at their Back :
They beat their breafts, they tore their flefh and
    haire,
And curf'd that houre in which they firft drew
    aire.
And then with Grones (able to fplit in funder
Their very Soules, like trees riuen If the contem-
    through with Thunder), nation bee so
    grieuous, what
They wrung their hands, fobd, fhrik'd, wil the execu-
    & howl'd, & praid tion bee?
    Osee 10.
That Rocks and Hils might on their backs be
    layd
And they to duft be grinded, fo that they
Might from the Iudges face but turne away :
And feeing themfelues inforc'd to ftand the
    Doome,
They gnafh'd their teeth, and curf'd their mothers
    wombe ;

Ierem. 25.   They who on earth were reard (Coloſſus-
Psal. 149.   high)
Spurn'd Kingdomes, trod on Thrones, and did defie
Omnipotence it ſelfe, into baſe graues
Tombling: prow'd Monarches here tooke place
      with Slaues,
And like to broken ſtatues down were throwne,
Trampled, and (but in ſcorne) not look'd vpon.

The Iudge   Their cries, nor yellings did the Iudge
implacable.   regard,
For all the doores of Mercy vp were bard ;
Iuſtice and Wrath in wrinkles knit his forhead,
And thus he ſpake : You curſed and abhorred,
You brood of Sathan, ſonnes of death and hell,

                  In fires that ſtill ſhall burne, you ſtill
The Maledicti.   ſhall dwell ;
In / hoopes of Iron then were they bound vp ſtrong,
(Shrikes being the Burden of their dolefull Song.)
Scarce was the Sentence breath'd-out, but mine eies
Euen ſaw (me thought) a Caldron, whence did riſe

Soules tor-   A pitchy Steeme of Sulphure and thick
mented.   Smoake,
Able whole coapes of Firmament to choake :
About This, Diuels ſtood round, ſtill blowing the
      fire,   [wire
Some, toſſing Soules, ſome whipping them with
A-croſſe the face, as vp to th' chins they ſtood
In boyling brimſtone, lead, and oyle, and bloud.

Millions were here tormented, and together
(All at this Seffions doomd) were condemnd hither.
My frighted Soule (me thought), with terrors
    fhooke
To fee fuch Horrid obiects : bloud forfooke
The conduite pipes of each Exterior part,
And ran to comfort and defend the Heart ;
But the worlds Glorious Frame being rac'd in fire
And none aliue left, I had then defire
(Me thought) to fee That black Infernall Court,
Whither (in thoufands) Soules did fo refort.
The way was quickly found ; paths   Facilis de-
    numberleffe   scensus
                                    Auerni.
(Beaten with feete which thither faft did preffe)
Lay trodden bare ; but not One Path Vestigia nulla
    returning,   retrorsum.
Was euer feene from this dark houfe of Mourning.
This Flaming Kingdome hath One Ferriman,
And he One Boate : he rowes through Acheron,
Styx, and Cocytus, Riuers that in Hell
Spread all the Countrey ouer : Fogges ftill dwell
Stinking and thick, vpon them, and there growes
Vpon their bankes (in wild difordered rowes)
The / Poplar (white and black), with blafted Ewgh;
The deadly Poppy, Cypreffe, Gall, and Rew,
(Emblems of Graues, Tombes, Funerals, and
    Beeres) ;
And on the boughes no other Bird appeares,

But Schriches, Owles, and Rauens, and the fhrill
  throates
Of Whiftlers; death ftill liftning to their Notes.

Thefe Riuers of Hell, Poetically inuented,
cary a Morall and Myfticall Interpretation: for Acheron (the firft water)
fignifies Bitterneffe: Styx, a deteftation;
and Cocytus, a Sorrow or Repentance;
and are thus applyed. When foules, by
reafon of their Sinnes, are to paffe ouer
the troublefome Riuers of Death, being
tormented with remembrance of the loffe of worldly
Honors, Riches, &c., then they paffe Acheron, it is
a bitter draught: Styx is the next, for when they
fee no remedy, but they muft paffe ouer to their
laft fhore, they begin to haue a loathing of their
anteacted life: and then comming to ferry ouer
Cocytus, they mourne and howle: fo that all the
conflicts, combats, and earthly wraftlings about the
time of a Mans departure, are figured vnder thofe
Three Riuers.

A pardon for these Poeticall Fictions, may (without much begging) bee giuen, if the Curious Cen-sor makes but true vse of the Inclusiue moral, no way derogatory from Diuinity.

I hollowed to the Ferriman (me thought),
And with a ftrech'd voyce, cry'd a Boate, a boate:
Hee came at firft call, and when neere he drew,
That of his Face and Forme, I had full
  view,

Death terrible in countenance.

My bloud congeal'd to ice with a colde feare,
To fee a Shape fo horribly appeare :
His eyes flafh'd fire, grizled and fhagg'd his Haire,
(Snarl'd all in felt-lockes) : Terror and Defpaire
Lay / in his wrinckled cheekes, his voyce was hoarfe,
And grumbling, he look'd ghaftlier than a Coarfe.

This defcription of the Vgly Ferriman is but
an Argument how terrible the apparence of death
is vnto vs, at our laft voyage, which we take in
departing from the world.

By thofe who there ftood thronging on the fhoare,
I heard his name was Charon : a blacke Oare
And dirty, held he in his brawny hand,
And though 'mongft thofe who ftood vpon the
    Strond
He faw fome Kings, fome Beggers, None   Mors sceptra
    had roome   ligonibus
                                        æquat.
For Birth, or Bloud, but fate as they did come :
None gaue the Cufhions here, for there was none,
But in heaps tumbling in, All were as One :
Some thither came laden with bags of gold,
Some with braue cloath's ; then did he barke, and
    fcold,
And fnatch'd all from them, with looke fharpe and
    grim :
All Fares (he fayd) muft Naked goe   Iob 4.
    with him.

As Death hath no refpect of perfons, for the beggers difh & the kings ftanding cup of gold, are to him of one weight : fo he fpoyleth all men of all that they poffeffe ; Princes of their Crownes, Lords of their Mannors, Iudges of their Scarlet, Gentlemen of their Reuenues, Citizens of Riches, Souldiers of Strength, Scholers of Learning, Women of Beauty, Age of Experience, Youth of Comelineffe. And as they enter into the Lifts of the world, weake and vnfurnifhed ; So muft they go forth, Beaten, Vanquifhed, and Difarmed.

At / laft (me thought) I leap'd into the boate ;
Which feene, the Sculler pluck'd me by the throate
To haue his Fare firft : afking what it was,
He cry'd a Penny.   I for That did paffe :
Being glad for bought experience : I could tell,

Couetousnesse That Auarice houfe ftood the next doore
a hag infernal.   to hell.

Charon by interpretation is Ioy ; for after we
What Charon haue ferried ouer the troublefome pas-
is.   fage of death, and landed on the fhoares
of Bleffedneffe, then the Ferriman (how churlifh and terrible foeuer hee feemed at firft), hath a countenance merry and comfortable.   Charon alfo, is pictured Old, thereby fignifying Good Councell, & Sweete perfwafion to prepare for death, and that brings Ioy : For what Ioy can bee greater, than

that which arifeth out of an affured knowledge of
a fpotleffe Innocence, or of an hope that fins committed are repented and pardoned ?

Anon (to fee with what a Reftleffe Gyre
The Soule entranc'd is whirld, fome times through
    fire,
Then waues, then Racking Clowdes ; earth, heau'n
    and hell
Lying (then) all open, free and paffible)
Me thought, being in a Twinkling ferried o're,
And trembling on the horrid Stygian fhore,
I faw the Brazen gates of deepe Abyffe
In a vaft bottome ftanding ; none can miffe
The way, it is fo beaten, and fo wide
That ten Caroches (breaft-wife) in may ride.
    To it there is a Headlong bafe Defcent,
Slippery in whorrying downe, yet turbulent
Through / throngs of people dayly poafting thither,
For Day nor night are the Gates clofde Noctes atq :
    together.   Dies patet
                               atri Ianua
    As at fome direfull Tragœdy (before   Ditis.
Not Acted), men preafe round about the dore
Crowding for Entrance, yet non entrance haue,
But (like toff'd billowes) this and that way Waue :
So Here ; I afk'd the caufe, and thoufands cry'd
Hell is fo Full, there's roome for Few Hell extreame
    befide.   full.

In thruſt I 'mongſt the thick'ſt, and ſweating got :
(For all the Aire mee thought was ſulphry hot).
With much a-doe to th' Gate, where ſtood a grim
And churliſh Porter, being in voyce and limbe

Cerberus por-
ter to Hell. A Dog ; yet like the Porter of a Iayle ;
On new-come gueſts he Fawn'd and
wagg'd his taile,

But bawl'd aloud for Fees, ready to teare   [ther :
Their throats, who without bribes begg'd Entrance
I choak'd the Curre with what he crau'd, and went
On with bold ſteps to the Black Regiment.

The Feeding and Feeing of Cerberus, taxeth
thoſe in office, who wey the gift, not the cauſe ; and
haue no other language in their mouthes, but *Quid
dabis ?* yet S. Paul willeth him that hath an office,
to looke to his office : And as for taking of Bribes,
there is a direct Statute againſt it, ſet downe by the
Vpper houſe of Heauen in theſe expreſſe words,
Thou ſhalt take no bribe.   Exod. 23.

[led,
Noyſe was my Guide (mee thought) by which being
I got to th' Court where Soules were Sentenced :
Full was it of braue Fellowes and fine Dames,
Their Haire (once ſo perfum'd) all turnd to Flames.

Lucifer in his
state. The / Prince of darkeneſſe, ſate vpon a
Throne

Of red hot Steele, and on his head a Crowne

Of Glowing Adamant : as in he drew
The noyfome Ayre, flames from his noftrils flew,
His Eyes dafh'd fire, and when with dreadfull found
He Roar'd (for that's his Voyce), he fhooke the
    grownd
Of his Tartarean pallace : maffy Keyes
(The Enfignes of his Empire) held (as Stayes) :
A Canopy of Braffe aboue his head,
Which hard (to laft) in Hell was Hammered.
Thofe Keyes being Emblems of Eternall paine,
For who there enter ne're come forth againe,
Being lock'd-vp Euer : At his clouen feete
Three Iudges fate, whom I did lowly greete.

    Thofe Iudges names are Minos, Rhadamanth,
and Æacus : the Infernall King is called The infernal
Pluto.   Now, albeit by the lawes of God   Iudges.
we both beleeue, and are bound to acknowledge
Him onely to bee fupreme Lord and Iudge
both of Heauen, Earth, and Hell, yet fithence
thofe former figured Names (drawne from Poeticall Inuention) carry in them a Morall and In-
ftructiue Meaning, they are not altogether to be
reiected ; and the rather becaufe in Picturing forth
fo Terrible an Obiect as the Kingdome of hell,
and Tortures of the Damned, I ftriue to fhaddow
the Horrors of them, and to fet them off with
heightning both of Profit and Delectation.

The Iudges in their hands held Whips of Wire,

Hee will bruse them with a rod of iron, &c. Psalme 2. Dipp'd in boyld brimftone, to pay Soules their hire

According to their Facts : The King
    of Fiends

Spying me there i' th' throng, roares out and fends

Two / of his Furies (Beadles of the Court)

To drag me to him, who in currifh fort

(Like flefh-hooke-fingred Sergeants) hal'd me on :

Being there, the Iawes of Black Damnation

Thus yawnd, and bellowed : Wherefore art thou
    come

Hither (thou Slaue) ere Death fets downe thy
    Doome ?

Thou art aliue, and not a foule that drawes

Breath Vitall, by our dread infernall Lawes

Muft heere fet footing. Humbly then (mee
    thought)

With pale and frightfull lookes I Him befought,

That fince I was a Stranger, and aliue,

Hee by his hellifh large Prærogatiue

Would figne my Paffe, but to walke all the
    Rounds

Of his vaft Countries and to view their Bownds:

A yelling Out-cry all-about was hurld,

That 'twas not fit one of the Vpper World

Should be a clofe intelligencing Spy,

Of their fcorch'd fhores to make difcouery.

But the Crim Tartar, with diftorted brow
Thwarting their grumbling, held it fcorne to bow
To any wifh of theirs, and Vnder-writ
The Paffe, with toades bloud from the Witches pit,
Charging me as my foule (if ere it fell
Into his Pawes) fhould anfwere it in hell,
Not to a next World that my Pen betrayd
What there I faw. His threatning being obay'd,
From him I tooke my way, nor did I feare
To lofe my path, Hels path was euery where.

Heere / begin the Defcriptions both of the
Darkeneffe and fires of Hell, &c., as alfo of
the particular Torments affigned to euery Man,
according to his particular finnes.

On wings of hot defire I flew from thence
With whirle-wind fwiftneffe, noyfe, and violence,
Being mounted on a Spirits back, which ran
With Mandrake-fhrikes, and like a Lubrican :
Whilft round (me thought) about me there did
    roare
Ten thoufand Torrents, beating on a fhoare
Made all of Rocks, where huge Leuia-   Iob 27.
    thans lay   Efay 57.
Gaping to fwallow Soules new caft away.

The Darkneſſe of hell.

Were all the Rowndure betwixt Hell and Heauen
        One Clowd condenſ'd, & into blacknefs

The darkenesse
of Hell (no   driuen,

way to bee de-
scribed) is Not That ; no, nor the Chaos vn-refinde,

heere notwith-
standing by (When in one Bundle Darkeneſſe vp did

comparison of
others made   binde

fearefull vnto
Humane vnder- That confuſ'd Lumpe of Mixtures) being

standing by
such things   put too,   [new,

as we know. Not That ; no, nor if ſince the world was

All Nights (that euer were) might grow in One,
Neither could That : Nor the Ægyptian
Caliginous, Black vapor, which did riſe
From Caues infernall to blind Pharaohs eyes,
Clammy as if that pitch from Heauen did melt,
And glutinouſly-thick it might be felt :
Adde / to all theſe, that hideous direfull houre
When all the lamps Cæleſtiall out did poure
Their lights like ſpent oyle, dropping from their
        Sphære
(As in my dreame at firſt it did appeare) :
Not all theſe Darkneſſes together glowd,
And ten-times-ten Redoubled and Renewde,
Are half ſo diſmall as the Night infernall.
Black, Stinking, Stiffling, Poyſning, and Eternall.

    See for this Darkeneſſe Math. 22, 13. Iud. 13.
Iob. 10.   Prou. 4, 14.   Psal. 107, 10.

Horror of Hell Fire.

How then (it may be aſked) did my weake Sight
Pierce theſe thick walles of Horror, where no
    light
Euer ſhed Beame? why, on that Sorcerous Coaſt
Where Hagges and Witches dwelt was not I loſt?
My Spirit had balls of Wild-fire in his head
For Eyes (me thought), and I by them was led :
For All theſe coale-pits (faddom'd deepe as hell)
Still burne, yet are the Flames Inuiſible.

    This fire is none of that which God
      lent Man,
When (driuen by ſinne out) he from
      Paradiſe ran,

Tartarei Ignis ardor, sic nostrū materialem Ignem vincit, vt noster pictum, &c. Anselm.

Bitten with cold, beaten with froſts and Snow :
And in meere pity did that Warmth beſtow,
Teaching him how to kindle it at firſt,
And then with food combuſtible haue it nurſt :
No ; / this Red Gloomy Fornace is a Firing,
Deuouring, yet not waſting, nor ſelfe-tiring.

    Arithmetick cannot in Figures ſet
An Age of Numbred yeares to ſwell ſo Great,
As to fill vp that time when theſe ſhall dye,
Being NEVER, for it burnes Eternally,
From the Worlds firſt Foundation, to th' Con-
    founding :
Were Deluges on Deluges abounding,

Not All that Raine (able to drowne the World)
Reach'd it to heauen, nor thoufand Oceans
　　hurld
On top of all thofe Waters, can euer flake
Or quench the leaft drop of this brimftone Lake.
_{Fire without} For (which moft dreadfull is) the Flames
_{light.}　　　ceafe Neuer
To torture Soules, and yet no light feene Euer :
It is a Burning which doth Brightneffe lack,
The Coales being infinite-hot, and infinite black.
Yet through my horfe of Hell gallopp'd amaine,
Now plung'd in Boyling lakes, then vp-againe ;
Leaping into vaft Caues, where heate neuer
　　comes :
For fharper cold then Winters breath, benummes
The Aire fo ftiffe, it freezeth All to ice,
And Clowdes of Snow : whofe Flakes are harder
　　thrice
Than thofe Quadrangled Haile-ftones, which in
　　thunder
Kill Teemes, and Plough-men, and riue Oakes in
　　funder.

The / Extremities of Cold in Hell.

The Hyperborean wind, whofe Rough   <small>Simile.</small>
    hand flings
Mountaines for Snow-balls, and on 's Marble wings
Beares rocks of ice fetch'd from the Frigid zone,
Which ftuck i' th' North feas, Seas and fhoares
    were One ;
Ten thoufand wild Waues hardned in the Aire
Rattling like Ificles on his grizly Haire,
And in his driueling Beard Snow ten times more
Than e're the bald-pate Alpes in Periwigs wore,
When from his Caues of braffe (bound there in
    Giues
Of Adamant), out he whorries, and fore him driues
(In whirlewindes), Haile, Frofts, Sleete, and
    Stormes ; and meetes
With rugged Winter, whom he Roaring greetes,
Then clapping their obftreperous Squallid Wings,
Each of them on the frozen Ruffian dings
Such bitter blafts downe, that they flye in Droues
(Though fwadled all in furres) to Sweltring Stoues :
The Muffe, the Scythian, nor the Freeze-land-boore,
Nor the Laplandian Witch once peeping o're
A threfhold, left their Nofes, Cheekes, and Eyes
(Pinch'd off by his Clumzy Nailes) be made a prize
To fnarling Boreas. O yet, all this cold
(Were it pil'd vp in heapes a hundred fold,

In ftifned Clowdes to freeze ten thoufand yeere)

The effectes
of the cold
in hel. Is a Warme Thaw, to th' piercing
Horrors heere.

Hells cold fo biting, fo Inuincible,

Infufferable, inexpreffible,

That / from all cold elfe the fharpe nips doth
fteale ;

Should fire come neare it, it would fire congeale,

Till Flames turne icy Flakes, and force fire leefe

His Vertue fo, that coales Red-hot will freeze.

Here I beheld (mee thought) Soules fcar-crow-
like,

Some bound, fome hang bi' th' heeles, whofe heads
did ftrike

The Icy-knobbed-roofe, toff'd too and fro

By Gufts implacable, able downe to throw

Rampires of Braffe ; which ftill beate out the
Braines,

And ftill Renewde them with Plangiferous Paines.

Here I beheld Kennels of fat-paunch'd Dogges,

Hard hearted-
nes punished. From one to one howling in Dialogues
Of Hellifh Language, curfing that they fat

At prowd Voluptuous Tables, yet forgat

Numm'd Charity, when at their gawdy gates

She begg'd but Scraps of their worft Delicates,

Yet ftaru'd for want ; whilft they at Toafting fires

Bath'd their Ranke Guts ; and with fharpe whips
of Wires

(But nothing elfe) heated her Shiuering limbes:
They quaffing Bowles (i' th' mean time) crown'd to
　th' Brims.
And when ragg'd Souldiers, of their ┌ Souldiers
　Bodies making └ vnpittied.
Anatomies in Wounds, with chill blafts quaking
And fhrunke-vp mawes, did to their Worfhips
　come,
A Whipping-Poaft, and Halter was their Doome.
Or when Thin-pale-cheek'd Schollers held but forth
Their Thread-bare armes, and did be- ┌ Schollers vn-
　feech their Worth └ rewarded.
To pittie haplefTe Learning once fo much,
As not to fee her beg : No, they'd not Touch
A Poore bookes couer, though within it lay
Their Soules wealth, but (in fcorne) Shuffled away.
O / Diuine Vengeance ! how moft Iuft thou art !
What they Stung others with, is Now their fmart.
Bleake Agues, Apoplexies, Murres, Catarrhes,
Coughes, Dropfies, Rhewmes, difeafes that make
　wars
And in cold bloud kill Health, did here reigne rife,
And though they could not Waft, yet Worried life.
Death from his earthy hands flung here and there
Cold Snakes, and Scorpions, which did piece-male-
　teare
Froft-bitten Soules, and fpewd them vp againe
Wanting Difgeftion: And to whip Paine with Paine,

Ten thoufand Salamanders (whofe chill thawing
Puts Bonfires out), their ftarke-ftiffe lunges it were
    gnawing :
Harfh was their Muficke therefore, on no ftring
But Yels ; Teeth-gnafhing, Chattring, Shiuering.

When thus farre I was tranfported by my *Dreame*,
I called to minde (me thought) that vpon earth I
had heard many great Schollers defend, that there
was no Cold in hell. But then (turning ouer the
leaues of my memory) I found written there, that
Iob once fpake thus :—

Sebastian Baradas in 4 Euangel. lib. 10. cap. 5. They fhal paffe from the waters of Snow, to
too much Heate ; and that vpon thofe
wordes Reuerend *Bede* did inferre, that
Iob feemed to point (with his finger as
it were) at Two Hels, the one of fire, the other
of Cold. And that *S. Hierome* vpon the tenth of
Mathew, did auouch the fame thing : And againe,
Hugo Victorinus, lib. 4. cap. 13. that *Hugo Victorinus*, in his booke *De
Anima*, had fet downe, that in Hell there
was a Paffage from the waters of Snow,
to the heate of Fire, and both of thefe were Infufferable, &c. Iob. 24.

I likewife / (me thought) remembred, that the
Tom. 9, cap. 2. Author of the Booke intituled *De Triplici
Habitaculo*, (that is to fay, Of Heauen,
Earth, and Hell) being thought to be the worke

of Saint *Augu∫tine*, had the∫e wordes, There are
two principall Torments in Hell; viz., Intollerable
Colde, and Intollerable Heate. Whereupon the
Euangeli∫ts wrote, there ∫hall bee in Hell Weeping
and Gna∫hing of teeth; Teares, melting from the
eyes through the Extremity of Fire, and that of
the Teeth, proceeding from the Sharpne∫∫e of Colde.
(Math. 13 ; Luke 13).

Then called I to minde, that *Iu∫tinianus*, in his
booke *De ca∫to Connubio Animæ*, ∫ayd thus : There
is in Hell a Fire Corporeall, Inextinguible, wanting
Combu∫tible matter to nouri∫h it : It ∫hines to
Puni∫hment, not to Con∫olation. In that place
there is Colde Incomparable, Gna∫hing of teeth,
and Smoake mo∫t Horrible-Stinking, &c. And that
Haymo commenting vpon *Mathew*, ∫ung Haymo on
the ∫ame Tune, thus : That among all ^{Math. 8 cap.}
the Tortures in Hell, the greate∫t were Heate and
Cold.

My memory (me thought) among∫t the∫e mu∫tred,
An∫elmus in his *Elucidary ; Innocentius* with his
booke *De Contemptu Mundi*, with many others, all
fighting vnder the ∫ame Opinion. (Innocent. lib. 6,
cap. 4).

Againe, I tooke hold vpon the 39. Chapter of
Ecclefia∫ticus, ∫peaking thus: They are Spirits created
for Reuenge, and in their fury they haue fortified
their Torments ; when the finall Day ∫hall come,

they fhall powre forth the force and rage of him
that created them, Fire, hayle, famine, &c.

Thefe / & other Fortifications of Reading defending me, were Armors fufficient & of proofe,
that there was Cold in Hell : And that haply the
_{Bede on Iob} Infernall torments did fo change, that
^{24.}   fome times the Soules of men were
fcorched in fires, and anon as grieuoufly plagu'd
with inexpreffible anguifh of cold: yet confidering
with my felfe that it was no Pillar for Salua-
tion to leane vpon, to beleeue that there was or
was not any fuch thing, it could (mee thought) be
no offence to Perfwade it was fo, or not fo : and
the rather, becaufe it was but a Dreame.

My Mephoftophilan nag (which foam'd before
With a white frothy Sweate, by fcudding o're
The Fields of Flames), had now the Glanders got
Through fudden Cold, when he was Extreame
        hot :
Foundred he was befides (halting downe right),
So that I durft nor on, nor yet Allight ;
Myfelfe (mee thought) being almoft frozen dead.
Back therefore did I reyne his ftubborne Head ;
When quick as Thought, he gallopp'd thence away,
And came againe where Soules all broyling lay :
Vpon them fell downe ftormes of burning Speares,
Trumpets red-hot, blowing Flames into their Eares,

Each Sence, and Member, that on earth had bin
An Armour in the quarrell of Damn'd Sin
To fight 'gainſt Heauen, were (here) in Esa. 27.
    pieces rent,
And Faults weigh'd out with equall puniſhment;
  The Glutton roar'd for Cookes to giue him
    meate ;
Drunkards for Wine, to quench their ſcalding
    Heate ;
Adulterers for their Whoores, to coole
    thoſe Fires   I will exercise
Which now burnt hotter then their old   Iudgment in
    Deſires.   weight & Iustice in measure.
Some / for Caroches cry'd, ſome for their   Ierem. 25. Esay 27.
    Trayne
Of Vaſſailes to attend, but cry'd in vaine.

They ſhall cry to the gods whom they ſerued in
this life, and they ſhall not ſaue them in this time
of affliction.　Ier. 2.

Gay gawdy women, who ſpent yeares of
    Noones   Pride of wom̄e
                   (and in that
In tricking vp their Fronts with Chape- the effeminacy of men in this
    roones,   age) is heere limde, and
And powdred Haire :   whoſe Taylors   rewarded.
    ſheares did quarrell
With pride, how to cut onely their apparrell;

Whofe Backs wore out more Fafhions then their
    Wit,
Phantafticknefſe being fhort to alter it
Into fo many fhapes, as they did vary :
The loades being more then thofe when fed Mules
    carry
(In Sumpters) Great Lords things ; whofe heads
    were reard
I' th' Aire high as a Stag's, 'boue all the Heard ;
And when they rode (their Foote-men running by)
They feem'd prowd Ships in all their Gallantry,
Newly-arriu'd, full-fraighted, vnder fayle,
Slight empty cock-boates dancing at their Tayle ;
Thefe Dames, who each day in French Chariots fat
Gliftring like Angels, a prowd-bounding Trot
From foure faire Steedes drawing all on them to
    wonder,
That the Clowdes eccho'd and the Earth fhook
    vnder :
But when their Courfers tooke their full Cariere
It look'd like that Day, when the Thunderer
Struck with his Triple-fire Heauens Rider downe ;
                For (from their horfes noftrils) Breath
Phætont.
Fab., Ouid.   was throwne,
Metam. lib. 2. Hot-quick as lightning, and their Hoofs
                vp-hurld
Such Clowdes of Smoake, as when he fir'd the
    world.

O / horrid fight! Thefe (once fo much Ador'd)
In hell were drudges, fpurn'd at, and abhorr'd;
Their Painted cheekes, turn'd into Witches looks,
Bright Haire to Snakes, long Fingers into hooks,
Pearle-Chaines to roapes, their gawdy Robes to
     Ragges,
And delicate bodies, vglier farre then Hagges:
They that for Table-crums refuf'd to buy
And (for their foules) hoord vp Eternity,
Here offred worlds of Treafure, but to get
One drop of Water: (O hels infinite Heate!)
Yet not a drop was fufferd once to fall:
To quench their thirft, Diuels held out cups of Gall.

Diues the patterne of fuch vncharitable wretches,
cries out in that language: O Father *Abraham*,
haue compaffion vpon me, and fend down *Lazarus*
vnto me, that he may dippe the toppe of his finger
in water and coole my tongue, &c.   Luke 16.

Cram'd-vp in ftinking corners I beheld
Bafe Heapes tumbled together, who all   What rable
    yell'd   are in Hell.
Like bandogs tyed in kennels: High-way-ftanders,
Foifts, Nips, and Iylts, Prinadoes,   Theeues
    Bawdes, Pimpes, Panders,   Panders
                                 Bawdes.
Old funck-eyde Beldames hir'd to keepe the doors,
Till their owne Daughters were by flaues made
    whoores:

Catchpolles, and Varlets, who did poore men
Catchpolles.   fleece
(To their vndoing) for a Twelue-peny peece.
        Mongſt theſe were mingled Periur'd
Common-bail.
Petti-foggers.   common-Baile,
Light weights breede heaui- With petti-foggers, that ſet Law to ſale
nesse.   With Cauterized Conſciences ; Theeues,
        Cheates,
Tradeſmen that fed vpon the Broken Meates
Of / Oathes and Rotten-wares ; and thoſe to ſell
Car'd not for ſingle money to buy Hell.
Ten thouſand Packs (like theſe) were baſely throwne
Into a Ware-houſe of Damnation,
Good cheere in hell for sinners. Where Fire their foode was, Adders galls
        their Drinke,
And their Tobacco a ſtrong Brimſtone ſtinke.

His bread (ſpeaking of the wicked Worldling)
Iob 20. in his belly ſhall be turned into the gall
of Serpents ; hee ſhall be conſtrained to vomit out
againe the riches which he hath deuoured ; God
ſhall pull them forth of his belly ; he ſhall be
conſtrained to ſuck the gals of Cockatrices,
and the tongues of Adders ſhall ſlay him, &c.
Iob 10.

The Worme of Confcience.

The whips that lafh'd the Damn'd were fome of
    wire,
And fome of Iron; others were roapes of Fire
Knotted with ragged ftones of glowing Flint,
Which though in thoufand formes they did imprint
Tortures vpon their Soules, yet there was One,
To which all Torments elfe compar'd were None.
A kinde of Worme there was, all fpeckled
    black,
That fhot ten thoufand Prickles from his back,
Sharper then quils of Porcupines, and longer,
And further flying, and more fwift and ftronger ;
It bare a Tearing forked fting behinde,
Which in the Striking did fo ftrangely winde,
It / wounded euery way where it did Hit,
Nor could it be put by, by force or Wit :
This Worme had Teeth of needles, and lay gnawing
Both night and day, Black Soules in peeces drawing;
The more 'tis rack'd, it liues, the more it fries
In Flames, the leffe it Burns, and Neuer dies.

*The worme of
conscience.*

Our *Sauiour* fpeaking of the paines of the
Damned, faith that their Worme dieth not. *Mar*.
9. 44.

To call but this Worme to minde (amongft the
other Torments of that Infernall Lake), marke in

what paſſions one powreth his feares : Gehennam

timeo, quippe interminatam, exhorreo Tartarum vt cui nimium inſit Caloris, paueo Tenebras quoniam nihil admittunt Lucis, Formido peſtiferum VERMEM quoniam eſt perennis, &c.

I feare Gehenna, becauſe it hath no end ; Hell to
me is horrible becauſe it hath too much Fire; the Darkneſſe I tremble at, becauſe it hath no Light, the Deadly WORME affrights me, becauſe it is Euer-laſting.

Holy *Bernard* being pierced to the Soule with
the ſame Agony of Feare, thus confeſſeth it : Paueo Gehennam, Contremiſco a Dentibus Beſtiæ infernalis, Horreo VERMEM roden-tem, et ignem torrentem Fumum, et Vaporem, et Sulphur, et Spiritum Procellarum, &c.

I am (ſaies hee) afraid of Hell, I tremble at the teeth of the Infernall Dragon, the Gnawing WORME is a Horror to me, and the roaſting Fire, and the Smoake, and the Brimſtone, and the Spirit of Stormes, &c.

One / Soule, (me thought), boyling in ſulphurous flame
          Curſ'd God, and on his Rigor did
exclame ;
          Rail'd at him for Iniuſtice, and thus Cri'd,
If for my Sin thy Son was Crucified,

Why am I hell'd in Execution
In this Damnd Iayle, euer to be Vndone?
If Hee layd downe his life to fet me Cleere
From all my Debts, why am I Dungeon'd Here?
Why for a life no longer then a Span,
Am I Euerlafting damned Man?
He whom the Firft bad woman did intice,
Was but once driuen out of Paradice,
Yet hee (euen then) was Sole Monarchall Lord
O're the whole Globe: Seas did to him   Adam a
             Accord   Monarch after
                        his deposing.
In fweete Obedience : all the Beafts on Earth
As vnder his Dominion they tooke birth ;
So from him had they Names, they all did Bow
Their knees to him, and did obferue his Brow.
He loft a Garden, but an Orchard found
Wall'd in with Seas, with Sun-beames compaft round:
Where Birds (whofe Notes were neuer fince fo
    cleare)
Seru'd as Mufitians All, to tune his Eare :
A Serpent cozened Him by forcerous Charmes,
But (in his ftead) a woman fild his Armes :
A woman ! in whofe Face more Beauties fhone
Then all the Beauties after made in One :
He was Man's Maifter-thiefe, Robd him of All,
Droue him from Eden, and (fo) forc'd him Fall
Out of the Sphære of Innocence ; and yet
Thofe Crownes of Bleffings God on him did fet ;

Why / then for Sin but of a minutes date
Muſt I for Euer be a Reprobate?

Auri sacra
fames. Gods holy hunger though it oft did kill
me,
Gods holy Banquet yet did neuer fill me;
The Silke worme ne're for me wrought in her
    Loome ;
I neuer ſlept in a Rich lordly Roome,
Neuer eate Pies of nightingales Tongues, or ſate
Like Diues at my table feru'd in Plate.
My Beldame Nurſe (the Earth) when ſhe gaue
    Suck
To me, her left Breaſt ſtill ſhe forth did pluck,
Being Iuice-leſſe ; or from thence if Drops did fall,
How could I quench my thirſty Iawes with Gall?
I neuer lackeyed by prowd Fortunes wheele;—
For all the taſte of Pleaſures I did feele,
Was in the warme Embracements of my Whore :
If that were Sin, why then did Nature ſtore
My Veines with hot bloud, blowing luſtfull fire?
'Twas her Corruption, and not my Deſire.
I likewiſe (now and then) was waſh'd within
All o're with Wines; but why ſhould that be Sin,
When God the Vineyard planted, and in 's word
Bid Man drinke wine? Thou art a rigorous Lord,
(Mee thought the Hell-hound howl'd) for trifling
    Crimes
To Damne me in a World out-lengthning Times.

Say, that full fixty yeares my Glaffe did run,
More then that halfe I flept, there was won
Little to Hell in fleepe : but my lifes thread
Reach'd but to thirty, fo that I lay dead
Fifteene of thofe, and of thofe fifteene fiue
(At leaft) were childifh : O muft I aliue
Be / held for Euer in damnation Iayle
For poore ten yeares ! when I perhaps did faile
Some part of them towards Heauen ? What curfed
    waue
Threw'ft Thou to drowne me in th' Infernall
    graue ?
My Parents bleft me Mornings, Noones and
    Nights;
Were all thofe fpent in Vayne ? I tooke delights
In plucking apples from t' Hefperian Trees,
Which Eating, I grew Learn'd: adde to All
    thefe
My Priuate Readings, which more School'd my
    Soule
Then Tutors, when they fternlieft did Controll
With Frownes or Rods : fome Dayes in This were
    Spent,
So that if All my Faire-writ leaues were Rent
Out of Gods Memory, alack ! it were
A Thin Booke of the Foule : yet muft I (here)
For fowing fome Few Acres vn-awares
Of Bad Corne, reape an Endleffe Field of Tares ?

D. III.   8

At this, ten thoufand Soules (rauing-mad) Roard
That on their Heads the felfe-fame fhot was
    fcoard :
But then a Voice (tun'd to an Angels Sound)
With repercuffiue Ecchoes did rebound
Through all the Court of Barathrum, thus Thun-
    dering
Terrors that fhooke Hells Center : Ceaffe thy
    wondring
(Thou Bawling Reprobate), a recompence
Is giuen thee to the Weight of thine Offence.
For had thy yeares out-reach'd Methuflem's Age,
Thy Black lifes orrent (with impetuous rage)
Had Boundleffe, Bottomleffe, Reftleffe bin ;
So that as Thy Eternity did Sin ;
Tortured thou art in God's eternity :

Peccas Homo Thy faults to him, his rods for thee doe
in Aeterno tuo:
Punit Deus in   buy :
Aeterno suo. Nor / can he in his Iuftice pittie thofe
Who pitty not themfelues, but do expofe
Their Soules to Foule Acts, fcorning threatned
    Paine,
Like Whoores, who buy Damnation for fmall
    Gaine.
Thou on the bread thy Sins did earne doeft feede,
Not paying by the Day, but by the Deede.
    What was thy whole life but a Mutinous Warre
'Gainft thy Creator ? Euery Senfe did Iarre

From his Obedience : like to Mad-mens fwords
Thy works were wounds, and blowes flew from thy
words.
Thy Lips, Eares, Eyes, haue ftill him Gates fet
wide
To let in Blafphemy, Luft, Auarice, Pride,
And Legions of fuch Diuels.   Thou didft Dwell
Firft in a Houfe of Flefh, but now in Hell:
That was thy Partner and (as Partners _{The soule and body beeing}
doe) _{Partners, vndo one another.}
Hath thee Vndone for Euer : Thou fhalt Rue
His Ryots, Whorings, Swearings : his Diforders
Are thy damnations : euery Senfe now furders
Thy Torments, the loofe Glances of the Eyes,
The Liquorifhneffe of Tafte, the Melodies
To the Lafciuious Eare ; All, all thefe turne
To thy Perdition, thou for thefe fhalt burne
To no hand holden-vp can helpe be giuen,
The Left is Hels, the Right beat back from
Heauen ;
In flames go it Wher, and grow Green againe ;
Paine kill thee, yet thou ftill fhalt liue in paine.
On was he going, but to drowne this Voice
All Hell broke loofe, and then were heard no
Noyfe
But Vlulations, Shrikings, Horred Soundings
Of Ratling-Chaynes, and thoufand ftrange con-
foundings

Of / indistinguishable dire-mix'd Terrors :
At which (I trembling) WAKDE ; and though the
    Errors
Of my Sleepe-wandring-Soule were now left cleare,
And that my cold-hands had taine leaue of feare,
Yet my Heart panted, and my Haire turn'd white
More through the Ghaftly Obiects of this Night,
Then with the Snow of age : And yet euen then,
Collecting vp myfelfe, I read of Men
The Volumes ouer, and the World, fo well
That I found Here worfe Diuels then are in Hell.

FINIS.

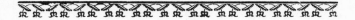

x.

THE BELMAN OF LONDON.

1608.

NOTE.

For my exemplar of the two 'Belman' tractates, I am again indebted to the Huth Library. By the liberality of the Chetham Society, I give in the title-page their admirable facsimile of the wood-cut in the 'Belman' title-page of 1608. There is a smaller and poorer one in the other. See Memorial-Introduction on the two tractates.—G.

The Belman of London :
BRINGING TO LIGHT
THE MOST NOTORIOVS
VILLANIES THAT ARE NOW
Practiſed in the Kingdome.

Profitable for Gentlemen, Lawyers, Merchants, Citizens, Farmers, Maſters of houſholds, and all ſorts of ſeruants, to marke, and delightfull for all men to reade.

Lege, Perlege, Relege.

Printed at London for Nathaniel
Butter. 1608.

The poore BELMAN of London.

To all thoſe that either by office are
ſworne to puniſh, or in their owne
loue to vertue, wiſh to haue the dis-
orders of a State amended, humbly
dedicateth theſe his Diſcoueries.

T *your* Gates *the* Belman *of London
beateth, to awaken your eies, to
looke back after certaine* Grand
and common Abuſes, *that daily
walke by you, keeping aloofe (in
corners) out of the reach of Law.*
It muſt bee the hand of your authoritie that muſt
fetch in theſe Rebels *to the Weale-publick, and your
arme that muſt ſtrike them.* I chuſe you as Patrons,
(not to my booke) but to defend me from thoſe
Monſters, *whoſe dennes I breake open in this my
diſcouery. More dangerous they are to a State,
than a* Ciuill Warre, *becauſe their villanies are
more ſubtile and more enduring. The* Belman *not-
withſtanding hath plaid the* Owle *(who is the*

Embleme *of wifedome) for fleeping in the day, as
abhorring to behold the impieties of this laft and
worft age of the worlde. In the night therefore hath
hee ftolne forth, and with the helpe of his lanthorne
and candle, (by which is figured* Circumfpection*)
hath he brought to light, that broode of miichiefe /
which is ingendred in the wombe of darkeneffe. A
monftrous birth is it, and therefore worthy to be
looked at : from monftrous parents doth it proceede,
and therefore the fight of it to be fearefull. But of
fuch rare temper are your eies, that (as if they had
funne-beames in them) they are able to exhale vp all
thefe contagious breathes which poifon a kingdome,
and fo to fperfe them into thin aire, that they fhall
vtterly vanifh, & be no more offenfiue. In this black
fhore of mifchiefe haue I failed along, and beene a
faithfull difcouerer of all the creekes, rocks, gulfes,
and quick-fands in and about it : Bee you therefore
as fecond aduenturers, and furnifh men armed with
iuftice, and well furnifhed in all points with a defire
to conquer thefe Sauages, and fend them to fet ftrong
and fearefull footing amongft them. It fhall be honour
to yourfelues, and them, and a rich benefite to the*
Republick *wherein you liue. For my owne parte
I vowe, that as I* dedicate *thefe my labours to your
hands, fo will I* deuote *my life to the fafetie of my
country in defending her from thefe Serpents : I will
wafte out mine eies with my candles, and watch from*

midnight till the rifing vp of the morning, my Bell *fhall euer be ringing, and that faithfull feruant of mine (the* Dog *that followes me) be euer biting of thefe wilde beaftes, till they be all driuen into one heard, and fo hunted into the toyles of the* Lawe. *Accept therefore of this* Night-prize *(my* Graue *and worthy* Patrons*) drawne rudely, and prefented boldly, becaufe I know the colours laide vpon it, are not counterfeit, as thofe of borrowed beauties: but this is a picture of* Villany, *drawne to the life, of purpofe that life might be drawne from it. None can be offeded with it, but fuch as are guilty to themfelues, that they are fuch as are enrold in this Mufter booke, for whofe anger, or whofe ftab, I care not. At no mans bofome doe I particularly ftrike, but onely at /* the bodie *of* Vice *in* Generall *: if my manner of* Fight *(with thefe dangerous Maifters of the* Ignobleft Science *that euer was in any kingdome) doe get but applaufe; the* Belman *fhall fhortly bid you to another* Prize, *where you fhall fee him play at other kind of weapons.*

Deuoted night and day yours,
The Belman of London. /

A Table of the principall matters
contained in this Booke.

A Difcouerie of all the idle Vagabonds in England :
their conditions : their lawes amongſt them-
felues : their degrees and orders : their meetings,
and their maners of liuing, (both men and women.)
A difcouerie of certaine fecret Villanies, which
borrow to themfelues the names of Lawes.

THE BEL-MAN OF LONDON.

Difcouering the moft notable villanies
now in *the Kingdome*.

NTRING into a contemplation
of the *Changes* of *Time* ; how
all things that are vnder the
Moone are as variable as her
lookes are : how *Goodnes* growes
crooked, & hath almoft loft her
fhape : how *Vertue* goes poorely, and is not
regarded : how *Villany* iets in filkes, and (like
a God) adored : And when I confider, how all
the pleafures of this life are but as childrens
dreames, how all the glories of the world are
but artificiall fire workes that keepe a blazing
for a time, and yet die in ftinking fmoakes :
and how al the labours of man are like the
toiling of the winds, which ftriue to caft vp
heapes of duft, that in the ende are not worth

the gathering : Then, euen then, doe I grow
wearie of my felfe: then am I neither in loue
with ỹ beautie of ỹ Sunne, neither ftand I
gazing at the dancing of the ftarres : I neither
wonder at the ftately meafures of the cloudes,
the nimble galliards of the water, nor the wanton
trippings of the wind, nor am I delighted when
the Earth dreffes vp her head with flowers ; I
wifh my felfe a *Beaft*, becaufe men are fo bad
that *Beafts* excell them in goodnes, and abhorre
all company, becaufe the beft is but tedious, the
worfer loathfome, both are the deftroyers of *Time*,
and both muft be maintained with coft.

Since then that in the *Nobleft Streames* there
are fuch *Whirlepooles* to fwallow vs vp, fuch
Rocks that threaten danger, (if not fhipwracke,)
and fuch *Quick-fands* to make vs finke, who
would not willingly take downe all the fayles
of his ambition, and caft anchore on a fafe and
retired fhore, which is to be found in no place,
if not in the Countrie.   O bleffed life ! patterne /
of that which our firft Parents lead,
The praife of
the Coūtry the ftate of Kinges (now) being but
life. a flauery to that of theirs.   O fchoole
of contēplation ! O thou picture of the whole
world   drawne   in   a   little   compaffe !   O   thou
Perfpectiue glaffe, in   whome   wee   may   behold
vpon   earth,   all   the   *Frame*   and   *Wonders*   of

heauen. How happy, (how thrice happy) is
hee that not playing with his winges in the
golden flames of the Court, nor fetting his foot
into the bufie throngs of the Cittie, nor running
vp, & downe, in the intricate mazes of the law,
can bee content in the winter to fit by a country
fire, and in the fummer to lay his head on the
greene pillowes of the earth? where his fleepe
fhall be foft flumbers and his wakings pleafant
as golden dreames. Haft thou a defire to rule?
get vp to the mountaines, and thou fhalt fee
the greateft trees ftand trembling before thee,
to do thee *Reuerence* ; thofe mayeft thou call thy
Nobles : thou fhalt haue rankes of *Oakes* on each
fide of thee, which thou mayeft call thy *Guard* :
thou fhalt fee willowes bending at euery blaft,
whome thou mayeft call thy flatterers : thou fhalt
fee vallies humbled at thy feete, whome thou
mayeft tearme thy flaues. Wouldeft thou behold
battailes? ftep into the fields, there fhalt thou fee
excellent combats betweene the ftanding Corne
and the Windes. Art thou a tyrant & delighteft
in the fall of *Great-ones?* mufter then thy har-
uefters togeather, & downe with thofe proud
fummer lordes, when they are at the higheft
Wouldeft thou haue *Subfidies* paid thee? the
Plough fends thee in corne, the *Medow* giues
thee her pafture, the *Trees* pay cuftome with

their fruite, the *Oxe* beftowes vpon thee his
labour, the fheepe his wooll.   Doft thou call
for *Muficke*? No Prince in the worlde keepes
more fkilfull mufitions : the birds are thy confort,
& the winde inftruments they play vpon, yeeld
ten thoufand tunes.   Art thou addicted to ftudie ;
Heauen is thy Library ; the *Sunne, Moone,* and
ftarres are thy bookes and teach thee *Aftronomie* :
By obferuing them, thou makeft Almanacks to
thy felfe, that ferue for all feafons.   That great
Volume is thine *Ephemerides,* out of which thou
maift calculate the predictions of times to follow ;
yea in the very cloudes are written leffons of
Diuinity for thee, to inftruct thee in wifedome :
the turning ouer their leaues, teach thee the
variations of feafons, and how to difpofe thy
bufineffe for all weathers.   If the practife of
Phificke delight thee, what *Aphorifmes* / can all
the Doctours in the world fet downe more certaine ? what rules for good diet can they draw
out more finguler? what medicines for health
can they compound more reftoratiue ? what vertues can al their *Extracted Quinteffenfes* inftill
into our bodies more foueraine, than thofe which
the earth of her owne bountie beftowes for our
preferuation, and whofe working powers are daily
experimented in beaftes for our example ? O you
Plants of the field, and you *Flowers* of the

Garden! (Natures Apothecaries, & Earths Chi-
rurgions!) your ftalkes are flender, yet you your
felues are the cheefeft pillars that vphold mans
life : what cleareneffe doth the fight receiue onely
in beholding you? what comfort does the *Sence*
of *Smelling* finde onely in your *Sauors?* and how
many that haue had halfe their bodies in their
graues, haue beene brought backe againe onely
by your facred Juices? Who therefore would
not confume his youth in company of thefe
creatures, that haue power in them to keepe off
old age longer than it would ; or when old age
doth come, are able to giue it the liuelihood and
vigour of youth? Who would not rather fit at
the foote of a hill tending a flocke of fheepe then
at the healme of Authority, controuling the ftubborne and vnruly multitude? Better it is in the
folitarie woods, and in the wilde fields to be a man
amongft *Beaftes* than in the mideft of a peopled
Citie, to bee a *Beaft* among men. In the homely
village art thou more fafe, than in a fortefied caftle:
the ftinges of *Enuy*, nor the bullets of *Treafon*,
are neuer fhot through thofe thin walles : Sound
healthes are drunke out of the wholefome wodden
difh, when the cup of gold boyles ouer with
poyfon. The Countrie cottage is neither battred
downe by the cannon in time of warre, nor peftred
with clamorous fuites in time of peace. The *Fall*

of *Cedars* that tumble from the tops of kingdomes, the *Ruine* of *Great Howſes*, that bury *Familyes* in their ouerthrowe, & the noyſe of *Shipwracks*, that beget euen ſhrikes in the heart of Citties, neuer ſend their terrors thither : that place ſtands as ſafe from the ſhock of ſuch violent ſtormes, as the *Bay tree* does from lightning.

The admiration of theſe *Bewties* made mee ſo enamoured, and ſo really in loue with the inheritor of them that the flames of my affection (were in their burning) onely carried thither. So that in ſtead of paued ſtreetes, I trod the vnbeaten pathes of the / fieldes, the rankes of trées, were to mee as great buildings, Lambs & ſkipping Kiddes were as my mery companions, the cleare fountaine, as my cups of wine, rootes and hearbes as the table of an *Ordinary*, the dialogues of birdes as the Sceanes of a play, and the open emptie medowes, as the proud and populous Cittie. Thus did I wiſh to liue, thus to die. And hauing wandred long (like a *Timoniſt*) hating Men becauſe they diſhonoured their *Creation*, at length *Fortune* lead mee by the hand into a place, ſo curiouſly built by Nature, as if it had bin the pallace where ſhee purpoſed none ſhould lie but her ſelfe : It was a *Groue* ſet thicke with trées, which grewe in ſuch order, that they made a perfect circle ; inſomuch that I ſtood in feare, it

was kept by *Fayries,* and that I was brought into
it by enchantment. The branches of the *Trees*
(like fo many handes) reached ouer one to another
and in their embracements held fo faſt together,
ẏ their boughes made a goodly gréene roofe,
which being touched by the wind, it was a
pleaſure to behold fo large a Seeling to moue ;
vpon euery branch fate a confort of fingers, fo
that euery trée ſhewed like a *Muſicke* roome.
The Floore of this ſummer-houſe was paued all
ouer with yellow field-flowers, and with white,
& red dazies, vpon which the Sun caſting but a
wanton eye, you would haue ſworne the one had
beene nayles of gold, and the other ſtuddes of
enamelled Siluer. Amazed I was when I did but
looke into this little paradice, and afraid to enter,
doubting whether it were fome hallowed ground
or no, for I could find no path that directed me
to it ; neither the foote of any man nor the hoofe
of any beaſt had beaten downe the graſſe ; for the
blades of it ſtood fo hie and fo euen, as if their
lengthes had been giuen them by one meaſure.
The melodie which the birdes made, and the
varietie of all forts of fruits which ẏ trees
promiſed, with ẏ prettie & harmeles murmuring
of a ſhallow ſtreame running in windings through
ẏ middeſt of it (whoſe noyſe went like a chime
of bels, charming the eyes to ſléepe) put me in

mind of that *Gardē* wherof our *Great Grādfyre* was the *Keeper*. I euen wept for forrow to thinke he fhould be fo foolifh, as to bee driuen from a place of fuch happineffe : and blamed him in my mind for leauing fuch a prefident behind him, becaufe by his fall, wee loft his felicitie, and by his frailtie all men are now apt to vndoe themfelues, and their pofterity, through / the inticements of women.

Into this *Groue* therefore at laft I did venture, refoluing to make it the Temple where my thoughts fhould fpend themfelues in fruitfull contemplation ; I purpofed to diuide the day into Actes, as if the *Ground* had beene a ftage and that the life which there I meant to leade, fhould haue beene but as a Play. Some of my houres fhould haue run out in Speculation of the admirable workmanfhip of heauen and of the orders which the Celeftiall bodies are gouerned by : Some of my howers fhould haue carried me vp and downe the earth and haue fhewen vnto me the qualities and proportions of the *Creatures* that breed vpon it : at another time would I haue written *Satyres* againft the impietie of the world ; At another, I would haue chaunted *Roundelayes*, in honour of the Countrie life. The reft of my time fhould haue fetched in prouifion for my body. Thefe were appointed to be my Actes,

in this goodly *Theater*, the *Muſicke* betweene,
were the *Singers* of the *Wood*, the audience ſuch
as *Orpheus* plaid vnto, and thoſe were, mountaines
and trees, who (vnles the whiſpering windes
troubled them with their noyſe) would haue
beene very attentiue. But whilſt I was ſetting
forth to runne this *Goale* ; behold, caſting vp
mine eye, I eſpied a farre off certaine cloudes of
ſmoake, whoſe vapours aſcended vp ſo blacke
and thicke into the element, as if the *Sighes* of
Hell had burſt the bowels of the earth, and were
flying vp toward heauen, to pul downe more
vengeance. Before I ſaw this, I beleeued that
this place had beene frée from all reſort : deſirous
therefore to learne who they were that neigh-
boured ſo nie, and in a ſolitarie wood, (that ſtood
ſo farre from inhabited buildings,) I ſtept forward
and came to the place, which (what by Nature
and what by Art) was ſo fenced about with trees,
quickſet-hedges, & buſhes, which were growne
ſo high, (that but for the ſmoake) it was not
poſſible to imagine how a houſe could there be
builded. There was but one path leading to it,
which (after much ſearching and many turnings)
being found, boldly went I on, and arriued at
a homely cottage : the very doore of it put me
in mind of that poore Inne of good *Baucis* and
Philæmon, where a God was a gueſt : for it was

fo low, that euen a dwarfe might haue feemed
a tall man, entring into it, fo much would it haue
made him ftoope. This houfe ftood not like
Great mens places, / alwaies fhut, but wide open, as
if *Bountie* had been the porter, and being within,
it feemd *Hofpitalitie* dwelt there, and had giuen
you welcome. For there was a table readie
couered, with faire linnen, nut-browne round
trenchers lay in good order, with bread, & falt,
keeping their ftate in the middle of the board.
The *Roome* it felfe was not fumptuous but hanfome ; of indifferent bignes, but not very large :
the windowes were fpread with hearbes, the chimney dreft vp with greene boughes, & the floore
ftrewed with bulrufhes, as if fome laffe were there
that morne to be married : but neither faw I any
bride or bride-groome, nor heard I any muficke :
onely in the next roome (which was the kitchen,
and into which I went) was there as much ftirring,
as comonly is to be feene in a Booth, vpon the
firft day of the opening of a *Fayre*. Some fate
turning of fpits, and the place being al fmoaky,
made mee thinke on hell, for the ioynts of meate
lay as if they had beene broyling in the infernall
fire ; the turne-fpits (who were poore tattered
greafie fellowes) looking like fo many hee diuels.
Some were bafting and feemed like feindes powring fcalding oyle vpon the damned : others were

myncing of pye-meate, and fhewed like hangmen
cutting vp of quarters, whilft another whofe eies
glowed with the heate of the fire, ftood poaking
in at the mouth of an *Ouen*, torturing foules as it
were in the furnace of *Lucifer*. There was fuch
chopping of hearbes, fuch toffing of ladels, fuch
plucking of géefe, fuch fcalding of pigges, fuch
finging, fuch fcolding, fuch laughing, fuch fwearing,
fuch running too and fro, as if *Pluto* had that day
bidden all his friendes to a feaft, and that thefe
had beene the Cookes that dreft the dinner.

At the laft efpying an old nymble-tongd beldam,
who féemed to haue the command of the place, to
her I ftepped, and in faire tearmes requefted to
know the name of the *Dwelling*, why this great
cheere was prouided, and who were the *Guefts*,
for as yet I faw no bodie, but this *Band* of the
Blacke Guard. In ftead of her tonge her eyes
(that had ftarted backe a good way into her
head, as if they durft not looke out) made me
an anfwere. I perceiued by her very countenance,
that I was not welcome, which afterwards fhe
confirmed in wordes, telling mée, the place was not
for mée, the feaft was for others, and that I muft
inftantly bee gon, for that a ftrange kind of people
were that day to bee merry / there. No Rhetoricke
that I could vfe had power to win her to difcouer
who thefe *Guefts* fhould bee, till at the length, a

Bribe preuailing more then a *Parlee*, fhee told mee I fhould be a *Spectator* of the comedy in hand, and in a priuate gallery behold all the Actors, vpon condition I would fit quietly and fay nothing ; And for that purpofe was I conuaied into an vpper loft where (vnfeene) I might (through a wodden lattice that had the profpect of the dyning roome) both fee and heare all that was to be done or fpoken.

There lay I like a Scoute to difcouer the comming of the expected enemy, who was to fet vpon this good cheere, and to batter downe the walls of hot pyes and pafties. Mine eyes euen aked with ftaring towards the doore, to fpie when thefe ftates fhould enter, ducking downe with their heads like fo many geefe going into a barne. At length (with bagge and baggage) they came droping in one after another, fometimes three in a cōpany, fometimes fiue, now more, now leffe, till in the ende, the great *Hall*, was fo full that it fwarmd with them. I know you wonder, and haue longing thoughts to know what *Generation* this is, that liued in this hofpitable familiarity; but let me tell you, they are a people for whome the world cares not, neither care they for the world; they are all freemen, yet fcorne to liue in Citties : great trauellers they are, and yet neuer from home ; poore they are, and yet haue their

dyet from the beſt mens tables. They are neither
old *Seruingmen* (for all I ſay they are poore) that
haue béene courtiers, and are now paſt carrying
of cloake-bags : nor young gallants that haue
ſerued in the low *Coũtries*, (albeit many of them
goe vpon wodden legges) nor hungry ſchollers,
ẙ all their life time haue kept a wrãgling in ẙ
ſchooles and in the ende are glad to teach children
their horne bookes : neither are they decayed Poets,
whoſe wits like a fooles land, hold out but a
tweluemonth and then they liue vpon the ſcraps
of other mens inuention : no nor Players they bée,
who out of an ambition to weare the *Beſt Ierkin* (in
a *Strowling Company*) or to Aɛt *Great Parts*, for-
ſake the ſtately and our more than *Romaine* Cittie
Stages, to trauel vpon ẙ hard hoofe frõ village
to village for chées & butter-milke : neither are
they any of thoſe terrible Noyſes, (with thredbare cloakes) that liue by red lattiſes and Iuy-
buſhes, hauing authority to thruſt into any mans
roome, / onely ſpeaking but this, *Will you haue
any muſicke ?* Neither are they Cittizens that
haue beene blowne vp (without gunpowder) and
by that meanes haue beene frée of the *Grate* at
Ludgate, ſome fiue times : no ; no, this is a *Ging*
of good fellowes in whome there is more brother-
hood : this is a *Crew* that is not the *Damned
Crew*, (for they walke in Sattin) but this is the

Ragged Regiment: Villaines they are by birth, *Varlets* by educatiõ, *Knaues* by profeſſion, *Beggers* by the Statute, & *Rogues* by Act of Parliament. They are the idle *Drones* of a Countrie, the *Caterpillers* of a Common wealth, and the *Ægyptian* lice of a *Kingdome*. And albeit that at other times their attire was fitting to their trade of liuing, yet now were they all in hanſome cleane linnen, becauſe this was one of their *Quarter-dinners*, for you muſt vnderſtand that (as afterward I learnt by intelligēce) they hold theſe ſollemne méetings in foure ſeueral ſeaſons of the yeare at leaſt, and in ſeuerall places to auoid diſcouery.

The whole aſſembly being thus gathered together, *One* amongſt the reſt, who tooke vpon him a *Seniority* ouer the reſt, chargd euery man to anſwere to his name, to ſée if the Iury were full : the *Bill*, by which he meant to call them being a double Iug of Ale, (that had the ſpirit of *Aqua vitæ* in it, it ſmelt ſo ſtrong) and that hee held in his hand : Another ſtanding by with a toaſt, Nut-meg, and ginger, readie to crie *Vous auez* as they were cald, and all that were in the *roome* hauing ſingle pots by the eares, which like piſtols were charged to go off ſo ſoone as euer they heard their names. This *Ceremony* being ſet abroach, an *O-yes* was made : But he that was *Rector Chori* (the Captaine of the *Tatterdemaliõs*) fpying *One* to march vnder his cullors, that had neuer before ferued in thefe Lowfie warres, pawfed awhile, (after he had taken his firft draught, to taft the dexterity of the liquor) & then began (Iuftice-like) to examine this *Yonger Brother* vpon Inter-rogatories.

The firft queftion hee demanded, was, if hee were ftalled to the *Rogue* or no? the poore *Hungarian* anfwered, yes, *He was*: then was he afked by *Whom* he was *Stalled*, and *Where*, and in *What manner* of *Complement* it was done: to which queftion the *Nouice* hauing not fo much beggerly knowledge as might make a learned reply, forth-with did the *Wicked Elder*, cõmand the yong *Slauonians* that ftood about him to diffurnifh him that was / fo vnfkilfull in the *Rudiments* of *Roagarie*, of his beft *Garment* and to carry it prefently to the *Bowfin Ken*, (that was to fay to the tap-houfe) & there to pawne it for fo much ftrong Ale, as could be ventured vpon it: Thus the chiefe *Rag-a-muffen* gaue in charge, the reft obeyed and did fo, whilft the other Suffered himfelfe to bee ftript, and durft not refift their bafe authoritie.

This done, the *Grand Signior* called for a *Gage* of *Bowfe*, which belike fignified a quart of drinke, for prefently a pot of Ale being put into his hand, hee made the *yong Squire* kneele downe,

and powring the full pot on his pate, vttered
thefe wordes, I—doe ftall thée—to the *Rogue*, by
vertue of this foueraigne Englifh liquor, fo that
henceforth it fhall bee lawfull for thée to *Cant*,
(that is to fay) to be a *Vagabond* and *Beg*, and
to fpeake that pedlers french, or that *Canting
language*, which is to be found among none but
Beggers : with that, the *Stalled Gentleman* rofe, all
the reft in the roome hanging vpon him for ioy,
like fo many dogges about a beare, and leaping
about him with fhowtes like fo many mad-men.

But a *Scilence* being proclaimed, all were hufhed;
whilft *Hee* that played the maifter - diuels part
amongft thefe *Hell-hounds*, after a fhrug or two
giuen, thus began to fpeake to him that was new-
entered into the damned *Fraternitie*.   Brother
Begger (quoth he) becaufe thou art yet but a
méere frefh-man in our Colledge, I charge thee
to hang thine eares to my lippes, and to learne
the *Orders* of our houfe which thou muft obferue,
vpon paine either to be beaten with our cudgels
the next time thou art met, or elfe to bee ftript out
of any garments that are worth the taking from
thee.   Firft therefore, (being no better than a
Plaine ordinarie *Roague*, mary in time thou maift
rife to more preferment amongft vs,) thou art not
to wander vp and downe all Countries, but to
walke only (like an *Vnder-Keeper* of a forreft) in

that quarter which is allotted vnto thee. Thou art likewife to *Giue* way to any of vs that haue borne all the *Offices* of the *Wallet* before thee, and vpon holding vp a finger, to auoyd any towne, or country village, where thou feeft we are forraging to victuall our Army that march along with vs. For (my poore *Villiaco*) thou muft know, that there are degrées of *Superiority* and *Inferiority* in our Societie, as there are in / the prowdeft *Company*. We haue amongft vs fome eighteen or nineteene feuerall offices for men, and about feuen or eight for women : The *Chiefeft* of vs are called *Vpright men*, (I my deere *Sun-burnt-brother*, if all thofe that are the *Chiefeft men* in other companies were *Vpright-men* too, what good dealing would there be in all occupations ?) the next are *Rufflers* : then haue we *Anglers*, but they feldome cat[c]h fifh, till they go vp *Weftward* for *Floŭders* : then are there *Roagues*, (ẘ liuery thou thy felfe now weareft :) Next are *Wilde Rogues*, then *Priggers* : then *Palliardes* : then *Fraters* : then *Tom* of *Bedlams* band of madcaps, otherwife called *Poore Toms Flocke of Wilde-geefe* (whome here thou feeft by his blacke and blew naked armes to be a man beaten to the world,) and thofe *Wild-geefe*, or *Hayre-braynes* are called *Abraham-men* : in the next Squadron march our braue *Whip-iacks*, at the taile of them come crawling our *Counterfeit Crankes* : in another troope are *Gabling Domerers* : then *Curtals* follow at their heeles, and they bring along with them, ftrange *Enginers*, called *Irifh-Toyles* : After whom follow the *Swigmen*, the *Iarkemen*, the *Patricoes*, and laft the *Kinchin-Coes*. Thefe are the tottred *Regiments*, that make vp our maine armie. The Victualers to the campe are women, and of thofe fome are *Glymerers*, fome *Bawdy-Bafkets*, fome *Autem-Morts* : others *Walking-Morts* : fome *Dopers*, others are *Dols*, the laft and leaft are called *Kinchyn-Morts*, With all which *Comrades*, thou fhalt in thy *Beggarly Perigrination*, meete, conuerfe, and be drunke, and in a fhort time know their natures and *Roaguifh* conditions without the helpe of a *Tutor*. At thefe wordes the victuals came fmoaking into the hall to bee fet vpon the board, wherevpon the whole fwarme fquatted downe, being as vnciuell in manners, as vnhanfome in apparell, onely the *Vpright-men* and *Rufflers* had the *Graine* of the board giuen them & fate at vpper end of the table, the reft tooke their trenchers as they happed into their handes, yet fo, that euery knaue had his *Queane* clofe by his fide.

The table being thus furnifhed both with *Guefts* and Meate, in ftead of *Grace*, euery one drew out a knife, rapt out a round oath and cryed *Proface* you mad *Rogues*, and fo fell to. They fed more hungerly, than if they had come from the féege of *Ierufalem* : not a word was heard amongft them for a long time, onely / their téeth made a noyfe, as if fo many Mils had béene grinding. *Rats* going to the affault of a *Holland* cheefe could not more valliantly lay about them, nay my Lord Maiors *Hounds* at the dog-houfe being bidden to the funerall banquet of a dead horfe, could not picke the bones cleaner : At length when the platters began to looke leane, and their bellies grew plumpe, then went their *Tongues* : But fuch a noife made they, fuch a confufion was there of beggerly tayles, fome gabling in their *Canting* language, others in their owne, that the fcolding at ten conduits, and the goffipings of fiftéene bake-houfes was delicate muficke of it. At the length, drunken healths reeled vp and downe the table, and then it would haue made a Phifition himfelfe ficke, but to haue looked vpon the waters that came from them. The whole *Roome* fhewed a farre off (but that there was heard fuch a noyfe) like a dutch peece of *Drollery* : for they fate at table as if they had béene fo many Anticks : A Painters prentice could not draw worfe faces than they themfelues made, befides thofe which God gaue them ; no, nor a painter himfelfe vary a picture into more ftrange and more ill-fauord geftures, than were to be féene in the Action of their bodies: for

fome did nothing but wéepe and proteſt loue to
their *Morts,* another ſwore daggers & kniues to
cut the throate of his *Dopye,* if hee found her
tripping : Some ſlept, being drowned ſo deepe
in Ale-dregs, that they ſlauered againe ; others
ſung bawdie ſongs ; another crew, deuiſed curſes
vpon Iuſtices of Peace, Headboroughes and Conſtables, grinding their teeth ſo hard together for
anger, that the grating of a ſaw in a ſtone-cutters
yard, whē it fyles in ſunder ẙ ribs of Marble
makes not a more horrible noyſe. In ẙ end *One*
who tooke vpon him to be *Speaker* to the whole
houſe, (bidding the French & Engliſh pox on their
yelping throates,) cryed out for ſilence, telling them
it was his turne (according to the cuſtomes of their
Méeting) to make an Oration in praiſe of *Beggerie,*
& of thoſe that profeſſe the *Trade.* Hereupon (as
if an *Owle* had happened amōgſt ſo many birds)
all their eyes did preſently ſtare vpon him : who
thus began.

My noble hearts, my old weather-beaten fellowes, and braue Engliſh Spirits, I am to giue you
that which all the land knowes you iuſtly deſerue
(a *Roaguiſh* commendation,) and you ſhall haue it.
I am to giue *Beggers* their due praiſe, yet / what
néede I doe that, ſcithence no man, I thinke, will
take any thing from them that is their due.   To
be a *Begger* is to be a *Braueman,* becauſe tis now

in fafhion for very braue men to *Beg*. No but
what a *Rogue* am I to build vp your honours vpon
examples ? doe we not all come into the world like
arrant *Beggers*, without a rag vpon vs? doe we not
all goe out of the world like *Beggers*, fauing onely
an old fheete to couer vs? and fhall we not walke
vp & downe in the world like *Beggers*, with old
blankets pind about vs? yes, yes, wee will, roard
all the *Kẽnell*, as though it had bin the dogs of
Parifh garden : Peace cries the *Penileſſe Orator*,
and with a *Hem* proceedes.

What though there be Statutes to *Burne* vs
i'th eares for *Rogues*? to Syndge vs i'th hand
for pilferers? to whippe vs at pofts for being
Beggers ; and to fhackle our heeles i'th ftockes
for being idle vagabondes? what of this? Are
there not other Statutes more fharpe then thefe
to punifh the reft of the Subiects, that fcorne
to be our companions? What though a prating
Cõftable, or a red nofd beadle fay to one of vs,
Sirra *Goodmã Rogue*, if I ferued you well, I fhould
fee you whipped through the towne ? Alas ! Alas !
Silly Animals ! if all men fhould haue that which
they deferue, we fhould doe nothing but play the
Executioners and tormenters one of another.

A number of taylors would be dambd for kéeping a *Hell* vnder their fhop bord : all the brokers
would make their *Wils* at *Tiborne*, if the fearching

D. III.   1 2

for ftolne goods which they haue *Receiued*, fhould like a *Plague* but once come amongft them, yea if all were ferued in their right kinde, *Two parts* of the land fhould be whipped at *Bridewell* for lechery, and *Three parts* (at leaft) be fet i'th ftocks for *Drunkennes*. The life of a *Begger* is the life of a fouldier : he fuffers hunger, & cold in winter, and heate and thirft in Sommer : he goes lowfie, hee goes lame, hees not regarded, hees not re-warded : here onely fhines his glorie ; The whole *Kingdome* is but his *Walke*, a whole Cittie is but his parifh, In euery mans kitchin is his meate dreft, in euery mans feller lyes his beare, and the beft mens purffes keepe a penny for him to fpend.

Since then the profeffion is ancient (as hauing beene from the beginning) and fo generall, that all forts of people make it their laft Refuge : Since a number of Artificers maintaine their houfes / by it. Since we and many a thoufand more liue merrily with it ; let vs my braue *Tawny-faces*, not giue vp our patched cloakes, nor change our cop-pies, but as we came beggers out of our mothers bellies, fo refolue and fet vp your ftaues vpon this, to returne like beggers into the bowels of the earth. *Dixi*.

Scarce was the word *Dixi* belch'd out of his rotten Aly lunges, but all the Bench-whiftlers from one end to the other, gaue a ringing *Plaudite* to

the *Epilogue* of his fpeech, in figne of approbation :
whereupon they rofe vp as confufedly as they fate
downe, and hauing payd fo farre as their purfes
would ftretch for what they had deuoured, making
Oes in chalke for the reft when they met there
next, And euery man with his *Mort* beeing affigned
to their quarter, which order giuen, at what
following *Fayres* to fhake hands, and what Ale-
bufh to tipple, with *Items* likewife giuen where to
ftrike downe *Geefe*, where to fteale hennes, and
from what hedges to fetch fheetes, that may ferue
as pawnes, away they departed,

Turba Grauis Paci, plaudæq, inimica Quieti.

No fooner were their backes turned, but I that all
this while had ftood in a corner (like a watching
candle) to fee all their villanies, appeared in my
likenes; and finding the *Coaft* to be perfectly
cléere ; none remayning in the houfe but the
Hofteffe to thefe *Guefts*, her did I fommon to a
fecond parlee. The fpirit of her owne malt walkt
in her brayne-pan, fo that what with the fwéetneffe
of gaynes which fhe had gotten by her merchant
ventures, and what with the fumes of drinke,
which (like a lufty gale to a wind mill,) fet her
tongue in going, I found her apt for talke, and
taking holde of this opportunitie, after fome intreaty to difcouer to me what thefe *Vpright-men,*

Ruflers and the reft were, with their feuerall
qualities, and manners of life, Thus fhe began.

YOu fhall vnderftand then (quoth fhe) that the
chiefeft of thofe that were my *Tablemen* to
day, are called *Vpright-men*, whofe picture I will
draw to the life before you.   An *Vpright-man* is
a fturdy *big bonde knaue*, that neuer / walkes but
(like a *Commander*) with a fhort troncheon in his
hand, which hee cals his *Filchman*.   At Markets, *Fayres* & other meetings his voice amōgft
Beggers is of the fame found that a Conftables is
of, it is not to be controld.   He is frée of all the
fhiers in England, but neuer ftayes in any place
long ; the reafon is, his profeffion is to be idle,
which being looked into, he knowes is punifhable,
and therfore to auoid the whip, he wanders.   If
hee come to a *Farmers* doore, the almes hee begs
is neither meate nor drinke, but onely money : if
any thing elfe be offered to him, he takes it with
difdaine & laies it vnder a hedge for any that come
next, but in reuenge of this, if hee fpy any geefe,
hennes, ducks, or fuch like walking fpirits haunting
the houfe ; with them he coniures about midnight;
vfing them the next morning like traytors, either
behedding them or quartering them in pieces : for
which purpofe, this band of *Vpright-men* feldome

march without fiue or fix in a company, fo that
country people rather giue them mony for feare
then out of any deuotion. After this bloudy mas-
facre of the poore innocent pullen, the Actors in
their bloudy tragedy repaire to their *Stalling kennes*,
and thofe are tipling houfes, which will lend money
vpon any ftolne goods, and vnto which none but
fuch guefts as thefe refort : there the fpits go
round, and the cannes walke vp and downe,
there haue they their *Morts* and their *Dopyes*, with
whome (after they haue *Bowfed* profoundly) they
lye (in ftead of fetherbeds) vppon litters of cleane
ftrawe, to increafe the *Generation* of *Rogues* and
Beggers : For thefe *Vpright-men* ftand fo much
vppon their reputation, that they fcorne any *Mort*
or *Dopye* fhould be féene to walke with them ;
and indeede what néede they care for them, when
he may commaund any *Dopye* to leaue another
man and to lye with him ; the other not daring
to murmure againft it. An *Vpright-man* will
feldome complaine of want, for whatfoeuer any
one of his profeffion doth fteale, he may challenge
a fhare of it, yea and may command any inferiour
Roague to fetch in booty to ferue his tourne.
Thefe cary the fhapes of foldiers, and can talke
of the *Low countries*, though they neuer were
beyond *Douer.* /

A Ruffler.

THe next in degrée to him is cald a *Ruffler* : the *Ruffler* and ẏ *Vpright man* are ſo like in conditions, that you would ſweare thē brothers : they walke with cudgels alike ; they profeſſe Armes alike, though they be both out at elbows, and will ſweare they loſt their limmes in their Countries quarell, when either they are lame by diſeaſes, or haue bin mangled in ſome drunken quarrell : Theſe commonly are fellowes that haue ſtood aloofe in the warres and whilſt others fought, they tooke their héeles & ran away from their Captaine, or elſe they haue bin *Seruingmen*, whome for their behauiour, no man would truſt with a liuery ; if they cannot ſpend their daies to their mindes by their owne begging or robbing of country people that come late from *Markets* (for vpon thoſe they moſt vſually exerciſe their trade) then doe they compell the inferiour ſubiects of their *Cōmon wealth*, (as *Rogues*, *Palliards*, *Morts*, *Dopies* &c.) to pay tribute vnto them. A *Ruffler* after a yeere or two, takes ſtate vppon, and becomes an *Vpright-man*, (but not an *honeſt man*.)

An Angler.

AN Angler is a lymb of an *Vpright-man*, as béeing deriued from him : their apparell in which they walke is cōmonly frieze Ierkins and

gaily flops: in the day time, they *Beg* from houfe
to houfe, not fo much for reliefe, as to fpy what
lyes fit for their nets, which in the night following
they fifh for.   The *Rod* they angle with is a ftaffe
of fiue or fix foote in length, in which within
one inch of the top is a little hole boared quite
thorough, into which hole they put an yron hooke,
and with the fame doe they angle at windowes
about midnight; the draught they pluck vp béeing
apparell, fhéetes, couerlets, or whatfoeuer their
yron hookes can lay hold of: which prize when
they haue gotten, they do not prefently make fale
of it, but after foure or fiue daies, or according
as they fufpect inquirie will be made after it, doe
they bring fuch goodes to a Broker, (traded vp for
the purpofe) who lends vpon them halfe / fo much
money as they be worth, which notwithftanding
ferues the *Angler* a while for fpending money, &
enriches him that buyes it for a long time after.

A Roague.

A *Rogue* is knowne to all men by his name,
but not to all men by his conditions; no
puritane can difcemble more than he, for he will
fpeake in a lamentable tune & crawle along the
ftréetes, (fupporting his body by a ftaffe) as if there
were not life enough in him to put ftrength into
his legs : his head fhall be bound about with

lynnen, loathſome to behold ; and as filthy in
colour, as the complexion of his face; his apparell
is all tattered, his boſome naked, and moſt commonly no ſhirt on : not that they are driuen to
this miſery by méere want, but that if they had
better clothes giuen them, they would rather ſell
them to ſome of their owne fraternity then weare
them, and wander vp and downe in that piteous
manner, onely to moue people to compaſſion, and
to be relieued with money, which being gotten, at
night is ſpent as merrily and as lewdly, as in the
day it was won by counterfeit villany.   Another
ſect there be of theſe, & they are called *Sturdy
Rogues* : theſe walke from country to country
vnder cullor of trauelling to their friends or to
finde out ſome kinſeman, or elſe to deliuer a letter
to one gentleman or other, whoſe name he will
haue fairely endorſed on paper folded vp for that
purpoſe, and hanſomely ſeald : others vſe this ſhift
to carry a Certificate or paſport about them, with
the hand and ſeale of ſome Iuſtice to it, giuing
notice how he hath béene whipped for a vacabond,
according to the lawes of the *Realme*, & that he is
now to returne to ſuch a place where he was borne,
or dwelt laſt, by a certaine day limitted, which is
ſure to be ſet downe long enough ; for all theſe
writings are but counterfet, they hauing amongſt
them (of their owne *Ranck*,) that can write and

read, who are their fecretaries in this bufineffe. Thefe fellowes haue fingers as nymble as the *Vpright-man*, and haue their wenches, and meeting places; where whatfoeuer they get, they fpend, and whatfoeuer they fpend is to fatisfie their luft; fome of this broode are called *Curtals*, becaufe they / weare fhort cloakes: their company is dangerous, their liues deteftable, and their ends miferable.

A wilde Rogue.

THe *Tame Rogue* begets a *Wilde-Rogue*; and this is a fpirit that cares not in what circle he rifes, nor into the company of what Diuels hee falles: In his fwadling clouts is he marked to be a villaine, and in his breeding is inftructed to be fo: the mother of him (who was deliuered of her burden vnder a hedge) either trauelling with him at her back, or elfe leading him in her hand, and will rather endure to fee his braynes beaten out, than to haue him taken frō her, to be put to an honeft courfe of life. So enuious they are & fo much doe they fcorne any profeffion but their owne: they haue bin *Rogues* themfelues, and difdaine that their children fhold be otherwife. Thefe *Wilde Rogues* (like wilde géefe) kéepe in flocks, and all the day loyter in the fields, if the weather bee warme, and at *Brick-kils*, or elfe difperfe them-

felues in cold weather, to rich mens doores, & at
night haue their meetings in Barnes or other out
places, where (twenty or more in a cōpany) they
ingender male and female, euery one catching her
whom he doth beſt fancy : the ſtronger and more
ſturdy, kéeping the weaker in ſubiecttion : their
language is bawdy talke, damned oathes, and
plots where to filch the next morning, which they
performe betimes : riſing as earely as the Sun, &
inioyning their punckes to looke out for cheates,
to make their méeting at night the merrier.

A Prigger of Prancers.

A *Prigger* of *Prancers* is a horſe-ſtealer, for
to *Prig*, ſignifies in the *Canting language* to
ſteale, and *Prancer* ſignifies a horſe. Theſe walke
(in frieze or lether Ierkins) with a wand in their
hands, watching in what paſture any horſes fit for
their turne, and thoſe within thrée or foure nights
after are cōueyd away at the leaſt 60 miles from
the place : if they méete the *Owners* in their ground,
they haue ſhifts to auoide his ſuſpition by feigning
they haue loſt their way to ſuch a towne. Theſe /
Hackney men that let out horſes will requeſt
ſeruice at gentlemens houſes, their ſkill being to
kéepe a Gelding well, and if they get entertain-
ment, they ſtand to their word, for they kéepe the
Gelding ſo well, that his Maiſter ſhall neuer finde

fault with any difeafe he hath, vnleffe it be that
he had the dizzynes in his head, which made him
réele out of his ftable to bée fold forty miles
off at a fayre.   Thefe haue their female fpyes that
Suruey medowes and Clofes, and long onely for
horfe-flefh.

A Palliard.

A *Palliard* comes next into my minde, & he
likewife is cal'd a *Clapperdugeon* : his vpper
garmēt is an olde cloake made of as many pieces
patch'd together, as there be villanies in him : this
Palliard neuer goes without a Mort at his heeles
whom he calles his wife : Being either in the ftréete
of a citty or in a country village, they diuide
themfelues, and beg almes at feuerall doores, but
whatfoeuer is gotten (be it bread, chéefe, malt, or
wooll) they fell it to fome *Rogue* or other, and
with ỹ money are merry at a *Bowſing Ken.*   A
Palliard carryes about him (for feare of the
worft) a *Certificate* (vnder a minifters hand with
the parifhes name, which fhall be fure to ftand
farre enough) where this Mort and he were marryed, when all is but forged : many Irifhmen are
of this lowfie *Regiment*, and fome *Welchmen* : And
the better either to draw pitty from men, as alfo
to giue cullor to their lame wandring ; with *Spere-
wort* or *Arfenick* will they in one night poyfon

their leg be it neuer fo found, and raife a blifter, which at their pleafure they can take off againe.

A Frater.

A *Frater* is a brother of as damnd a broode as the reft : his office is to trauell with a long wallet at his backe, and a blacke box at his girdle, wherein is a pattent to beg for fome Hospitall or Spittle houfe ; Many of which pattēts (efpecially if they be in paper or parchment without the *Great Seale*) are counterfeit. And thofe that are not fo, ferue the *Bearers* of them but / as inftruments to play the *Knaues* by : for though they get neuer fo much, the poore creatures for whome they beg receiue little of it : they lye foaking with a *Dopye* in a typling houfe, whilft the fpittle wretches are ready to ftarue for fuftenance at home : let country women returning from Markets if they be alone, & in a dāgerous place, take héede of thefe *Proƈors*, for they haue the Art to vnhorfe them, and a confcience to fend them packing without any peny in their purfes.

A Quire-Byrd.

YOur *Quire-Birdes* are fuch as haue fung in fuch cages as *Newgate* or a country *Gaole*, and hauing their bells giuen them to fly, they féeke prefently to build their nefts vnder fome honeft mans roofe, not with intent to bring him

in any profit, but onely to put themfelues into
money or apparell (though it be by filching) and
then they take their flight.

An Abraham-man.

OF all the mad rafcalls (that are of this wing)
the *Abraham-man* is the moft phantaftick :
The fellow (quoth this old lady of the *Lake* vnto
me) that fat halfe naked (at table to day) from
the girdle vpward, is the beft *Abraham-man* that
euer came to my houfe & the notableft villaine :
he fweares he hath bin in bedlam, and will talke
frantickly of purpofe ; you fee pinnes ftuck in
fundry places of his naked flefh, efpecially in his
armes, which paine hee gladly puts himfelfe to
(beeing indeede no torment at all, his fkin is either
fo dead, with fome fowle difeafe, or fo hardned
with weather,) onely to make you beleeue he is
out of his wits: he calls himfelfe by the name of
Poore Tom, and comming neere any body, *cryes* out,
Poore Tom is a cold.   Of thefe *Abraham-men*, fome
be exceeding mery, and doe nothing but fing *fongs*,
fafhioned out of their owne braines, fome will dance,
others will doe nothing but either laugh or wéepe,
others are dogged and fo fullen both in looke and
fpéech, that fpying but fmall company in a houfe,
they boldly and bluntly enter, compelling the
feruants through feare to giue them what they

demaund, which is / commonly bacon, or fome
thing that will yéelde ready mony. The *Vpright-
man*, and the *Rogue* are not terribler enemies to
poultry ware, than *Poore Tom* is ; neither does any
man fhift cleane lynnen oftener than he does his
wenches.

A Whipiacke.

THen is there another fort of nymble-fingred
knaues, and they are called *Whipiacks* :
who talke of nothing but fights at Sea, piracies,
drownings and fhipwracks, trauelling both in the
fhape and names of Mariners, with a counterfeit
Licence to beg from towne to towne, which licence
they call a *Gybe*, and the Seales to it, *Iarkes*. Their
cullor of wandring from Shire to fhire, (efpecially
along the Sea-coafts) is to harken after their fhip
that was ouerthrowne, or for the merchandize
ftolne out of her, but the end of their land-voiages
is to rob Boothes at fayres, which they call *Heauing
of the Booth*. Thefe *Whip iacks* will talke of the
Indies, and of all countries that lye vnder heauen,
but are indeede no more than frefh water Soldiers.

A counterfet Cranke.

BAfer in habit, and more vile in condition than
the *Whipiack*, is the *Counterfet cranke* : who
in all kind of weather, going halfe naked, ftaring
wildly with his eyes, and appearing diftracted by

his lookes, complayning onely that he is troubled
with the falling ficknes : Albeit you giue them
cloathes they wil weare none, but rather with thofe
rags which they haue hanging about them fhould
bee made lothfome by myre, or their naked
bofome and Armes to appeare full of brufes, and
to be bloudy with falling, therby to kyndle in men
the greater compaffion : to caufe that foaming in
their mouthes, which is fearefull to behold by
the ftanders by, they haue this trick, priuily to
conuey a peece of white foape into one corner of
their Iawes, which caufeth that froth to come
boyling forth. Thefe *Crankes* haue likewife there
meetings, and there wenches at command.

A | Dummerar.

EQuall to the *Cranck* in diffembling is the
Dummerar, for as the other takes vpon
him to haue the falling fickneffe, fo this counterfets
Dumbnes ; but let him be whipped well and his
tongue (which he doubles in his mouth, and fo
makes a horrid and ftrange noife in ftead of fpéech)
will walke as faft, as his handes doe when hee
comes where any booty is.

A Iack-man and a Patrico.

ANd becaufe no common wealth can ftand
without fome *Learning* in it, Therefore
are there fome in this *Schoole* of *Beggers*, that

practife writing and *Reading*, and thofe are called *Iackmen* : yea the *Iackman* is fo cunning fometimes that he can fpeake Latine : which learning of his, lifts him vp to aduancement, for by that means he becomes *Clarke* of their *Hall*, and his office is to make counterfet licences, which are called *Gybes*, to which hee puts feales, and thofe are termed *Iarkes*. This *Iackman* (for his knowledge) is hayle fellow well met w a *Patrico*, who amongft *Beggers* is their prieft ; euery hedge beeing his parifh, euery wandring harlot and *Rogue* his parifhioners, the feruice he fayes, is onely the marrying of couples, which he does in a wood vnder a tree, or in the open field, and the folemnity of it, is thus. The parties to be wedded, find out a dead horfe, or any other beaft, and ftanding one on the one fide and the other on the other, the *Patrico* bids them to liue together till death them part, & fo fhaking hands, the wedding dinner is kept at the next Ale-houfe they ftumble into, where the mufick is nothing but knocking with kannes, and their dances none but drunken *Brawles*.

An Irifh Toyle.

IN this *Forreft* of *Wilde-men*, the fafeft *Toyles* to pitch is the Irifh *Toyle*, which is a net fo ftrongly and cunningly wouen together, that

they who goe a hunting with it catch the *Common* /
wealth, and connycatch the fubiects : For an *Irifh*
Toyle is a fturdy vagabond, who fcorning to take
paines that may make him fweat, ftalkes onely vp
and downe the country with a wallet at his backe,
in which he caries laces, pinnes, points, and fuch
like, and vnder cullor of felling fuch wares, both
paffeth too and fro quietly, and fo commits many
villanies as it were by warrant.

A Swigman.

L Ike vnto him in conditions is a *Swig-man* or
 Pedler, carying a pack behinde him in ftead
of a wallet : their trades are all one, fauing that
the *Swigman* is fomewhat better in behauiour,
though little differing in honefty. They both
ftand in feare of the *Vpright-man* and are forced
oftentimes to pay him toale out of their packes.

A Kinchyn Co.

T He laft *Ranke* of thefe *Runnagates* is fild vp
 with *Kinchyn Coes* ; and they are little boyes
whofe parents (hauing beene beggers) are dead,
or elfe fuch as haue run away from their maifters,
and in ftead of a trade to liue by, follow this kinde
of life to be lowfie by. Thefe *Kinchins*, the firft
thing they doe is to learne how to *Cant*, and the

onely thing they practife is to créepe in at windowes, or Celler doores.

Thus haue I opened vnto you halfe the neft of this generation of *Vipers*, now will I difcouer the other halfe, wherein fits a broode of Serpents as daungerous and as lothfome as thefe. Of which A Kinchē the *Yong-ones* and the *Leaft*, are called Mort. *Kinching Morts*, and thofe are girles of a yeare or two old, which the *Morts* (their mothers) carry at their backes in their *Slates* (which in the *Canting Tongue* are Shéetes) : if they haue no children of their owne, they will fteale them from others, and by fome meane disfigure them, that by their parents they fhall neuer be knowne. The fecond bird of this fether is a A Déll. *Dell*, and that is a yong wench, ripe for the Act of generation, but as yet not fpoyled of her maidenhead : thefe *Dells* are referued as difhes for the *Vpright-men*, for none but they muft haue the firft taft of / them ; & after the *Vpright-men* haue deflowred them, (which commonly is when they are very yong) then are they free for any of the brother-hood, and are called *Dells* no more but *Dopers*. Of thefe *Dells*, fome are termed *Wilde Dells*, and thofe are fuch as are borne and begotten vnder a hedge : the other are yong wenches that either by death of parents, the villanie of Executors, or the crueltie of maifters and miftreffes fall into this infamous and damnable courfe of life. When they haue gotten the title of *Dopies*, then are they common A Dopye. for any, and walke for the moft part with their betters (who are a degree aboue them) called *Morts*, but wherfoeuer an *Vpright-man* is in pre-fence, the *Doxye* is onely at his command : Thefe *Doxyes* will for good victuals or a fmall peice of money, proftitute there bodies to feruingmen if they can get into any conuenient corner about their maifters houfes, & to ploughmē in barnes, haylofts or ftables : they are common pick-pockets, familiars (with the bafer forts of cut-purfes,) and oftentimes fecret murtherers of thofe infants which are begotten of their bodies. Thefe *Dopyes* haue one efpecial badge to be knowne by, for moft of them goe working of laces, and fhirt ftringes, or fuch like ftuffe, only to giue colour to their idle wandring.

Of *Morts* there be two kindes, that is to fay, *A walking Mort* and an *Autem-mort* : the A walkeing *Walking-Mort* is of more antiquitie than Mort. a *Dopye*, and therefore of more knauerie : they both are vnmarried, but the *Doxy* profeffes herfelfe to bee a maide, (if it come to examination) and the *Walking Mort* fayes fhee is a widow, whofe huf-band dyed either in the *Portugall voyage*, was flaine in *Ireland*, or the *Low Countries*, or came

to his end by fome other misfortune, leauing her
fo many fmall infants on her hand in debt, whome
not being able by her honeft labour to maintaine
fhe is compelled to begge. Thefe *Walking Morts*
trauell from Country to Countrie, making laces
(vpon ftaues) and fmall purfes, and now and then
white vallance for beds : Subtile queanes they are,
hard-harted, light-fingerd, cunning in diffembling,
and dangerous to be met if any *Rufler* or *Roague*
bée in their company. They feare neither God
nor good lawes, but onely are kept in aw by
the *Vpright-men*, who often times fpoyle them of
all they haue, which to preuent, the *Walking Morts*
vfe this pollicy, they leaue their money (fometime
fiue fhillings, / fometimes ten fhillings) in feuerall
fhires, with fome honeft farmers wife or others
whom they know they may truft, and when they
trauell that way againe, at halfe yeares end, or a
quarters, fetch it to ferue their turnes : but dare
neuer goe in good clothes, leaft the *Vpright-men*
either ftrip them into rags, or elfe ftarke naked,
as they vfe to doe.

 An *Autem Mort*, is a woman married, (for
An Autem *Autem* in the *Beggers* language is a
Mort. Church:) thefe *Morts* feldome kéepe
with their hufbands, but are from them fometimes a moneth or two, yet neuer walke they
without a man in their company, and boyes and

girles at their heeles of ten or twelue yeares
old, whome they imploy at windowes of houſes in
ẙ night time, or earely in the mornings, to pilfer
away any thing that is worth ẙ carying away,
(which in their tõgue) they call *Nilling of the
Ken*. Theſe *Autem Morts* walke with wallets on
their ſhoulders, & *Slates* (or ſhéetes) at their
backes, in which they vſe to lie. Their hus-
bands commonly are *Rufflers*, *Vpright-men*, or
Wilde Rogues, and their companions of the ſame
breede.

There is another Parrot, (in this *Bird-cage*)
whoſe feathers are more ſléeke, and   A Baudy
tongue more ſmooth than the reſt; and   Basket.
ſhe is called *A Bawdy baſket*: Theſe *Bawdy baſkets*
are women that walke with baſkets or capcaſes
on their armes, wherein they haue laces, pinnes,
needles, white inckle, tape, round white ſilke
gerdels, and ſuch like : theſe will buy Conny-
Skinnes, and in the meane time ſteale linnen or
pewter : they are faire-ſpoken, and will ſeldome
ſweare whilſt they are ſelling their waires ; but
will lye with any man that hath a mind to their
commodities. The *Vpright-men* and *Theſe* hold
ſuch league together, that whatſoeuer they haue
is common to them both, and oftentimes will they
with money relieue one another.

The ſelfe ſame *Truce* is taken betwéene the

Vpright-men and the *Demaunders* of *Glymmer*, Demaunders that is to fay, thofe who trauell vp of Glymer. and downe with licenfes to begge, becaufe their houfes haue beene confumed with fire, for *Glymmer* (in canting) fignifies fire. Thefe *Glymmering Morts* are fo tender hearted, that they fhed teares if they make but mention of their loffes, and tel a lamentable ftory how the fire deftroyed their barnes, ftables, &c., all that they fpeake being méere lyes : they likewife carrie wallets at their backes, and are onely attended vpon and defended / by the *Vpright-men*, who neuer walke along with them through any towne, but keepe aloofe.

And thefe (quoth the *Hoſteſſe* of the *Beggers*) are all or the chéefeft (both *Hee-Diuels*, and *Shee-Diuels*) that daunce in this large circle. I haue brought you acquainted with their names, their natures, their tradings, and their trafficke : if you haue a defire to know more of them, you fhall find whole congregations of them at *Saint Quintens*, *The three-Cranes* in the *Vintry*, *Saint Tybs*, and at *Knapſburie*, which foure places are foure feuerall barnes within one mile compaffe néere London, being but Nick-names giuen to them by the *Vpright-men* : In thofe Innes doe they lodge euery night; In thofe dœ *Vpright-men* lie with *Morts*, and turne *Dels* into *Doxyes*

(that is to fay, rauifh young wenches) whilft the
Rogue is glad to ftand at *Reuerfion* and to take
the others leauings. In Middlefex likewife ftand
foure other *Harbours* for them, namely, *Draw the
pudding out of the fire*, (which is in the parifh of
Harrow on the Hill.) *The Croffe Keyes*, (which
is in *Cranford* parifh,) *Saint Iulians*, (which is in
Thiftleworth parifh.) And the houfe of *Pitty* in
Northall Parifh. The *Kinges Barne* néere Dar-
ford, and *Ketbrooke* néere *Blackheath*, are likewife
houfes of good receite for them : In all Shires haue
they fuch Innes as thefe ; and in all of them and
thefe recited, fhall you find fometimes 40. *Vpright-
men* together ingēdring beggers with their *Morts*.
No finne but is here committed without fhame.
Adultery is common amongft them, Inceft but
laughed at, *Sodomy* made a ieft : At thefe *Hauens*
do they caft anchor boldly, becaufe none are by
to barre their entrance ; yea thofe that are owners
of thefe *Barnes* and *Back-houfes*, dare not but giue
welcome to thefe *Vnruly Guefts* ; for if they fhould
not they would at one time or other fet fire of
their houfes, or by blody and treacherous practifes
take away their liues. For this caufe fir, (quoth
fhee) am I glad to looke fmilingly vpon them, and
to play the *Hoftes*, becaufe my abiding ftands fo
farre from company, yet I proteft (quoth fhee)
I hate the fight of them, as knowing them to be

hell-hounds, and haue made difcouery of their
diuelifh conditions, becaufe you may teach others
how to auoide them : And howfoeuer you may
be drawen peraduenture to publifh thefe abufes
to the world (fayd fhee) yet I pray conceale my
name, the publifhing of which may coft me my
life.

By / this tyme, the fumes of Ale which had dis-
tempered her braines, and fet her tongue a going
were difperfed ; fo that both her lookes and fpéech
fhewing that fhe did not now defemble : but
vttered thefe things vnfainedly, I gaue her many
thankes for her *Difcouery*, coũcelled her to change
her difcomfortable *Lodging*, and to dwell in a place
more inhabited, (which fhee promifed to doe) and
away I went.   A thoufand cogitations kept mée
company as I traueled alone by my felfe : Sorry
I was to heare that in thofe places where *Innocence*
and *Simplicity* fhould be borne, fo much, & fuch
vgly *Vilany* fhould be nourifhed, yet was I glad
that I came to the knowledge of their euils, becaufe the drefling of fuch wounds in a Common-
wealth, is the curing of them.

Looking therefore with more pearcing eyes into
the *Country-life*, I began to hate it worfe than
(before) I loued it, I fell to difpraife it fafter than
euer I did commend it.   For I found it full of
care, and full of craft ; full of labour, and yet full

of penury ; I faw the poore hufbandman made a
flaue to the rich farmour ; the farmour racked by
his landlord : I faw that couetoufneffe made déere
yeares when fhe had fulleft barnes ; and to curffe
plentie for being liberal of her bleffings.   I had
heard of no finne in the Cittie, but I met it in the
village ; nor any *Vice* in the tradefman, which was
not in the ploughman.   All places therefore being
haunted with euill Spirits, I forfooke the fieldes
and the Mountaines, and took my iourney backe
againe to the Citie, whofe cuftomes (both good
and bad) I defired to be acquainted with.   It was
my fortune to trauell fo late, that the Moone had
clymed vp to the very top of Midnight, before I
had enterance into the gates of the Cittie, which
made me make the more haft to my lodging.
But in my paffage, I firft heard (in fome good
diftance before me) the found of a bell, and then
of a mans voice, both whofe tunes féemed at that
dead houre of the night verie doleful.   On I
haftened to know what noyfe it fhould be, and in
the end found it to be *The Bell-man of London.*
The found of his *Voice* at the firft put me in mind
of the day of *Iudgement* ; Men (me thought)
ftarting out of their fleepes, at the *Ringing* of
his bell, as then they are to rife from their
graues at the call of a trumpet : But when I
approached neare vnto him, and beheld a man with

D. III.   15

a lanthorne and candle in his hand, a long ftaffe
on his / necke, and a dog at his tayle, I fuppofed
verily, becaufe the Moone fhon fomewhat dimly,
that the *Man* in the *Mɔone* had lept downe from
heauen & (for haft) had left his bufh of thornes
behind him. But thefe Imaginations vanifhing,
as faft as they were begotten : I began to talke
to my *Bell-man*, and to afke him, why with fuch
a Iangling, and balling, and beating at Mens
doores hee went about to waken either poore
men that were ouer-wearyed with labour, or fick
men that had moft neede of reft ? hee made anfwere
vnto me, that the *Ringing* of his *Bell*, was not
(like an Allarum in a towne of garrifon,) to fright
the inhabitants, but rather it was mufick to charme
them fafter with fléepe : the *Beating* at their
doores affured thofe within that no théeues were
entred, nor that falfe feruants had wilfully or
negligently fuffered the doores to ftand open, to
haue their maifters robd ; & that his crying out
fo loud, was but like the fhrill *Good Morrow* of
a *Cock* to put men (that had wealth enough) in
minde of the time how it flydeth away, and to
bid thofe that were full of bufineffe to be watch-
full for their due houres when they were to rife.
He cald himfelfe therefore the *Centinell* of the
Citty, the watchman for euerie ward, the honeft
Spy that difcouered the prentizes of the night, and

that as a lanthorne in the poope of a Ship, was
a guide or comfort to fea-men in moft pitchy
darkneffe, fo was his walking vp and downe in
the night time, a preuention to the Citty oftentimes of much and many daungerous fires. I
lik'd well that thus he praifed himfelfe, becaufe
in thofe praifes lay the commendation of an
honourable, ciuill, and pollitick gouernment. And
fo farre delt I with him that in the end he brought
me acquainted with his office, afwell as hee knew
it himfelfe, and difcouered vnto me the properties
of his *walkes*, as how farre his boundes reached;
what mad hobgoblins hee oftentimes encountred
with, what mifchiefes he now and then preuented,
what knaueries he was now and then an eye witneffe to, and to what fecret villanies (brought to
bed in darkneffe) he was compeld to be (though
not the midwife) yet a goffip, prefent at the labour
and deliuerie. Of all which I hauing a longing
defire to get the true pictures, and perfwading him
that he was bound by his place, by his confcience,
and by the lawes of common humanity to lay open
fuch plots as were fo / dangerous to the common
wealth whereof he was a member, he yeelded at
the length to difcouer all that he knew : And
for that purpofe not only caryed me home to his
lodging where he gaue me the notes and names
of fundry abufes begotten in the dead of night,

But alfo went vp and downe the Citty with me
all the next day, fhewing me the very doores
and fignes at which they dwelt, and the very
faces of thofe that were ȳ diuells *Factors* in thofe
lowe countrie cōmodities of hell.   I learnt much
by the *Bell-mans* intelligence but more afterwards
by my owne obferuation and experience : what merchandize I ftored my felfe with by both ȳ *Voiages*
here doe I vnlade, & what profit fo euer arifes by
the trafficke of them, fhall if you pleafe be wholy
yours.   And for that the *Lading* was of fundry
commodities, I will deliuer them forth in their
feuerall parcells, as I receiued them.

Of cheating Lawe.

ALL *Vices* mafke themfelues with the vizards
of *Vertue* : they borrowe their names, the
better and more currantly to paffe without fus-
pition : for murder will be called *Manhood*,
Dronkenneffe is now held to be *Phifick*, *Impudence*
is *Audacitie*, *Ryot*, good fellowfhip &c.   So are
thefe *Villanies* (whofe faces I meane to difcouer)
paynted ouer with frefh orient cullers, becaufe
their lookes may be more pleafing, and leffe fus-
pected to haue craft vnderneath them.   And for
that purpofe haue their *Knaueries* gotten the
names of Arts or Lawes, as the Act of fuch a
Thing or fuch a law, not that they are inftitutions

fet downe by law for the good of men, or of a common-wealth ; but as the Law is grounded vpon *Reafon*, and hath *Maximes* of *Iuftice*, vpon which fhe buildeth all her *Pollicies* whereby fhée gouerns kingdomes. So thefe new-found *Lawes* of the Diuels inuention, are grounded vpon *Mifchiefe*, and are nothing elfe but certaine Acts and Rules, drawne into heads (in an affembly of damned *Wretches*) for the vtter vndoing of *Men*, and confufion of a *Weale Publicke*.

Of all which *Lawes*, the *Higheft* in place, and the *Higheft* in perdition is the *Cheating* Law or the Art of winning money by falfe dyce : Thofe that practife this ftudie call themfelues *Cheators*, / the dyce *Cheaters*, and the money which they purchafe *Cheates* : borrowing the tearme from our common Lawyers, with whome all fuch cafuals as fall to the Lord at the holding of his *Leetes*, as *Waifes*, *Strayes*, & fuch like, are fayd to be *Efcheated to the Lords vfe* and are called *Cheates*. This fort of *Gamefters*, were at firft a few in number, (the Art being odious) they were poore, (as being hated and driuen from all good mens company.) But now, there are fo many profeft *Cheators* and fo many that giue countenance to their occupation, that they might make an armie fufficient to giue the *Turke* a battaile : now are they not hungry thread bare knaues, but

gallants that ruffle in filkes, & are whorryed
through the ftreetes in Coaches, their purfes being
full of crownes, and their fingers being held vp
able to command the prowdeft Curtizan.   Yea to
fuch a ranckenes hath cuftome brought this *Vice*,
and to fuch a boldneffe, that in the moft noble
affemblies, at the *Beft Ordinaries* where your onely
Gallants fpend afternoones, & in your moft ciuill
meetings of Merchants, your welthieft Cittizens,
if they fall to play with dyce for any round
fummes of money.   It is now growne to a
fafhion to haue fome one or other to take vp
the *Cheators* weapons, and (without all refpect
of honefty, friendfhip, or focietie) to beate all
commers.

A *Cheator* playes his Maifters prize at 14.
feuerall weapons, and thofe weapons are thefe.

The Names of falfe Dyce.

A Bale of bard fincke Dewces.
A Bale of Flat fincke Dewces.
A Bale of Flat fice Aces.
A Bale of bard fice Aces.
A Bale of bard Cater-Treas.
A Bale of Flat Cater-Treas.
A Bale of Fullams.
A Bale of light Graniers.
A Bale of Langrets, contrary to the vantage.

*A Bale of Gordes, with as many High men as Low
men for Passage.*
A Bale of Demies.
A Bale of Long Dyce for euen and od.
A Bale of Bristles.
A Bale of Direct Contraries.

Thefe are the 14. diuelifh hookes, by which the
Cheator angles for other mens money; hee cares
not in what riuer, hee makes no confcience with
what baite, fo hee may haue good draughts to
maintaine himfelfe in riots, and his whore in rich
apparell, that's the white he fhootes at. Neither
doth he let all thefe arrowes flie at one marke, nor
in all weathers. But fome he fhootes in one game,
fome in another, and as he findes what fooles are
in his company, fo does he beftow his bolts. To
fet downe all the *Legierdemayne* of this *Handy-
craft*, would peraduenture inftruct fome ill-minded
perfons in that villany, which is publifhed onely
to haue others fhun it; I will therefore fhew you
a few of their iugling trickes (that are *Graduates*
in the Art) and by the fhape of them, iudge the
reft, for all are alike.

A *Langret* is a *Dye*, which fimple men haue
feldome heard of, and happily neuer feene (but
to their coft.) It is (to the eye of him that is
but a *Nouice*) a *Good* and *Square Die*, yet it is cut
longer vpon the *Cater* and *Trea*, then vpon any

other point, and is for that caufe called a *Langaret* : thefe *Langrets* are alfo called *Bard Cater Traes*, becaufe in the rũning, the longer end wil commonly (of his owne fway) draw downewards, and turne eyther *Sice*, *Sincke*, *Dewce*, or *Ace* vpwardes on the board ; the principall vfe of them is at *Nouum*. For fo long as a paire of *Bard Cater Treas*, be walking, fo long can you caft neither 5. nor 9. vnles it be by great *Chance*, that the rooghnes of the table, or fome other ftoppe force them to ftay, and to runne againft their kind ; for without *Cater*, *Trea*, 5. or 9. you know can neuer come.

Here fome may imagine, that by this meanes hee that hath the firft Dyce in his hand, may ftrip all that play at the table of their money ; but this muft be their helpe. An odde die called a *Flat Cater Trea*, (and no other number) is to be readie at hand, for granting the *Trea* & *Cater* to be alwayes vpon the one *Dye*, then is there no *Chance* vpon the other *Dye* but may ferue to make 5. or 9. and fo caft forth and loofe all.

The *Cheater* therefore marketh well the *Flat*, and bendeth a great part of his ftudie to learne when he is abroad, for fo long as that is ftirring, he will neuer *Caft* at *Much*. The fhift which a / *cheater* is driuen to, in conueying the *Flat* in and out, is a notable *cunning*, and in their *Trade* is cald *Foyfting* : which is nothing elfe but a *fleight*

to carry *Dice* eafily in the hand fo often as the
Foifter lifteth ; fo that whē either he or his partner cafteth the *Dyce,* the *Flat* comes not abroad
till he hath made a *Great Hand,* otherwife the *Flat*
is ftill fure to be *One,* vnleffe ẙ *Cheator* of purpofe
fuffers the filly *Nouices,* with whome hée playes,
to caft in a hand or two to giue them courage and
to liue in hope of winning.

The damnable *Oathes* and *Quarrels* that waite
at the table of *Gamefters,* are occafion that many
men forbeare to venture money in thofe fports,
who otherwife would play ; the *Cheator* therfore
(being a cunning obferuer of all fafhions) will
feldome fweare, (if he haue gotten a *Gull* into his
company, whom he is loath to anger for feare hee
loofe him,) and as feldome fwagger, but will rather
put vp an open wrong, then by a foolifh braule to
breake off the company, and fo hinder himfelfe
and his confort of purchafe : But if hee fweare
you would take him for a puritane, for his oathes
are, *Of Honefty, of Troth, by Saint Martin &c.* and
take this note, that when he fweares affirmatiuely,
he meanes alwaies the contrary. As for example,
if I fay vnto you when the Dyce come to your
handes, *Of Honefty caft at all,* my meaning is, you
fhall caft at the table, or elfe at very little : or if
when one being ftript out of all his money, offer
to pawne a *Ring* or a *Iewell,* and I fweare by

D. III.   16

Saint Martin I think it is fine gold, then doe I meane that it is pure copper, and fo of the reft : He that is drawn in to venture his money, is (amongft this curfed brotherhood of *Cheators*) tearmed a *Cozen*, and is handled fo kindly, as if he were a cozen indéede: if hee once fet in a foote, and that they fall to *Hunt* him, then all the craft is to make the *Conny* fweate, that is to fay, fo wifely to handle him, that he may haue a defire more and more to play and to keepe company ; yet fo warily to encreafe this appetite in him that hee *Smoake* not the *Cheator*, which is, that hee fmell not what knauery is bent againft him, and fo flip the coller like a *Hound*, and fhake off the company for euer.

At the *Taking vp* of a *Cozen*, the firft *Veny* that a *Cheator* giues him, is to learne before he play what ftore of *Bit* he hath in his *Bay*, that is, what money he hath in his purffe, and whether / it be in *Great cogges* or *Small*, that is, in gold or filuer, and at what game hee will fooneft ftoope ; for that being knowne his humor is fed, and he is choked with the meate he loues beft. For fome that will not play a groate at *Nouum*, will loofe a hundred pound at *Hazard*, and he that will not lofe a fhilling at *Dyce*, will play away his patri-mony at Cardes; for which caufe the *Cheator* furnifheth himfelfe for all voyages, but fpecially

prouides for *fine cheates*, and to atchiue which with
more eafe, hee acquaints himfelfe with Dyce-makers,
that worke in corners, (Varlets they are that are
Factors to the diuell, and for money will exchange
their foules in a bayle of Dyce.) Thefe *Dyce-
makers*, arme the *Cheator* with the forefaid 14.
weapons, and then is he a *Cheater compleate.*

One notable pollicy is (as a *Rule*) fet downe in
this *Schoole* of *cheating*, and that is, a *Cheator neuer
difcouereth the fecrets of his Art to any* : vnleffe
it be to fuch a one, who being left by his parents
rich in money and poffeffions, hath to the muficke
of fquare ratling bones danced fo long, that hee
hath danced him felfe into the company of beggers, and is brought to fuch want and miferie,
that hee would leaue no ftone vnturnd to finde a
pennie vnder it. Such a wretch is inftructed in
thofe *Villanies*, by which he himfelfe hath beene
wrought to infamie : the poyfon ẏ once he fwal-
lowed doth hee now caft vp to kill others with it.
Neither doth the *Cheator* beftow this learning vpon
his young Scholler, out of a commifferation of his
low eftate, but onely to make vfe of him, euen
in the heigth of his extremitie. His *Iornyman*
therefore doth he make him, and becaufe the
Cheator is happily a man fo noted in all companies, that few or none will venture money where
he playes, the *Nouice* is taught to play his Scollers

prize, whilſt the other ſtands by and lookes on, yet
ſo that the *Cheator* hath the ſweetnes of the gaines.
The *Nouices* imployments then are amongſt his
rich *Kinred*, *Countrimen* or acquaintance to find
out *Cozens*; whome hee muſt by one tricke or
other get to a Tauerne, or inuite them to a ſupper,
at the end of which, the *Cheator* layes about him
to draw them to play, and ſecretly lends his *Pupill*
money, to maintaine game, both their wits working
how to cheate thoſe that are in the cõpany.   Wee
haue béene too long at *Dyce*, let vs now fall to
Cardes.

Of | Barnards Law.

D*Yce* and *Cardes* are *Twynnes*, *Idlenes* was
the father of them, *Deſire of Gaines* the
mother, *Honeſt Recreatiõ* ſaies ſhe, was their nurſie
and ought to haue the bringing of them vp, but
(howſoeuer) the Diuell makes them now his adopted
children, and no wonder, for they are alike in conditions, as being both (like him) full of deceipt :
if there be cozenage in tripping of a dye, there is
the like craft in ſhuffling and ſorting of a paire
of Cardes, inſomuch that what game ſoeuer is on
foote, *He* that is marked out to be the *Looſer* (by
the *Synodicall* aſſembly and *Fathers* of the *Bernards
Law*) is ſure neuer to depart a *Wynner*.

To ſpeake of all the ſlights vſed by Card-players,
in al ſorts of *Games*, would but weary you that are

to read, and bee but a thank[l]es and vnpleafing labour for me to fet them downe. Omitting therefore the deceipts practifed (euen in the faireft & moft ciuill companies) at *Primero, Saunt, Maw, Tromp,* and fuch like games, I will onely lay open the villanies of a bafe kind of people, that trauell vp and downe the whole land, fometimes in the habit of Gentlemen, fometimes of Seruingmen, fometimes of Grafiers, Farmers, and plaine fellowes, maintaining themfelues onely by the cozenage they vfe in Carde-playing : which kind of *Play* of theirs, they call *The Barnards Law.*

To Act which knauifh Comedy of *Wily-Beguily,* 5. *Perfons* are required, and thofe are,

1   *The Taker.*
2   *The Cozen.*
3   *The Verfer.*
4   *The Barnard.*
5   *The Rutter.*

Thefe are the *Players* : and now fhall you heare their parts.

1   *The Taker,* is he that by fome fine inuention fetcheth in the Man, whome they defire to draw into *Gaming.*

2   *The Cozen,* is the partie that is *Taken.*

3   *The Verfer,* is a fellow more *Graue* in fpéech and habit, and féemes / to be a *Landed man* ; his

part is to fecond what the *Taker* begins, and to giue countenance to the Act.

4 The *Bernard* is the chiefe *Player*, for hee counterfets many parts in one, and is now a drunken man, anon in another humour, and fhifts himfelfe into fo many fhapes, onely to blind the *Cozen*, and to féede him with more delight, the more eafily to beguile him.

5 The *Rutter* is as arrant a knaue as the reft ; his part is difcharged, when hee hath begun a fray with his owne fhadow, whilft the reft that haue made a younger brother of the poore Cozen, fteale out of fight. Now to the Comedy it felfe. The prologue of which if it goe off well, there is good hope all fhall end well : All the cunning thereof is how to *Begin*, and to doe that, the *Taker* ftudies his part at his fingers ends. The Stage on which he playes the Prologue, is either in *Fleeteftreete*, the *Strond*, or in *Poules*, and moft commonly in the afternoone, when Coũtry Clyents are at moft leyfure to walke in thofe places, or for difpatching of their bufineffe, trauell from *Lawyer* to *Lawyer*, through *Chancery* lane, *Holburne*, and fuch like places. In this heate of running to and fro, if a plaine fellow well and cleanly apparrelled, either in home-fpunne ruffet, or fréeze, (as the *Seafon* requires) with a fide pouch at his girdle happen to appeare in his rufticall likeneffe. *There is a*

Cozen *sayes one.* At which word out flies the
Taker, and thus giues the onset vpon my old
Penny-father. Sir, God saue you, you are welcome to London, how doe all our good friends
in the Countrie? I hope they be wel : the *Russet-
ting* amazed at these salutations of a stranger,
replies : Sir, all our friendes in the Contrie are
in health, but pray pardon me, I know you not
beleeue it : No (answeres the *Taker*) are you not
a *Lancashire* man, or of such a Country? if he
say, yes, then the *Fish* nibbles and he giues him
more line to play with, if hee say, no, then the
Taker hath about with another weapon and sweares
soberly, In good sooth sir, I know your face, and
am sure we haue béene merry together, I pray (if
I may beg it without offence) bestow your name
vpon me, and your dwelling place. The innocent
Man, suspecting no poison in this gilded cup, tels
him presently his name and abiding, by what
gentlemen hee dwels &c. which being / done, the
Taker (for thus interrupting him in his way, and
for the wrong in mistaking him for another) offers
a quart of wine : if the *Cozen* be such an Asse to
goe into a tauerne, then he is sure to be vnckled,
but if hee smacke my *Taker* and smell gun-powder
traines, yet will not be blowne vp ; they part
fairely ; and then to the *Verser* goes the *Taker*,
discouering what he hath done, and deliuers the

mans name, country, and dwelling to the *Verſer* :
who boldly ſtepping to him, or croſſing the way
to méete him full in the face, takes acquaintance
preſently of him, ſalutes him by his name, inquires
how ſuch, and ſuch gentlemen doe, that dwell in
the ſame towne by him, and albeit the honeſt
Hob-nayle-wearer, can by no meanes be brought
to remēber this newe friend, yet, will hee nill hee,
to the tauerne hee ſweares to haue him, and to
beſtow vpon him the beſt wine in London.

Diuerſe other pullies (if theſe two faile) haue
they to drawe ſimple men into their company, as
by dropping a ſhilling in the open way, which
being taken vp in the Country mans ſight, muſt
be ſpent in wine, becauſe hee ſhall haue his *Halfe-
part* : or by intreating him to ſtep into a tauerne,
til the *Verſer* haue writ a word or two into the
Countrie, which hee muſt carry to his friends,
offering the *Cozen* a ſhilling for his paines.   But
the concluſion of all is, that if they thinke his bag
is well lyned with ſiluer, to the tauerne by one
ſubtle hooke or other, they will pull him, where
being ſet with the *Verſer* and the *Taker*, and wine
called for : In comes the *Barnard* ſtumbling into
the *Roome* as it were by chance, ſéeming to be
halfe drunke : and crying the company mercy for
being ſo bold with them, they modeſtly anſwere,
no hurt is done, and aſke him if he will drinke

with them : he takes their offer, and fweares to
pay for a pynte of wine, which they by no meanes
will fuffer.   But the *Barnerd* telling them hée has
money for what hee cals, and vfing phrazes fit for a
drunken man, out flies fome twentie or fortie Angels
on the board which hee puts vp prefently againe, and
fayes, feing they will not fuffer him to pay for a
pint, he will play at cards for it with any one of
them, at a new game which hee learnt but now,
with the loffe onely of a pot of Ale.   The reft of
his confort, making as though what they do is to
be rid / of him, are content to play for a pynte
and no more.   The *Taker* or the *Verfer* is the
man muft play with him, the Cards are fetcht,
Mumchance or *Decoy* is the game : the firft wager
is wine, the fecond two pence in money, from two
pence they rife to a fhilling, from that to a pound,
and hauing drawne fome good ftore of gold from
the *Barnard*, the *Cozen* (allured with the fwéetnes
of gaine, and hope of wynning, feeing the other
halfe drunke, as he imagines) is offered to be halfe
in whatfoeuer is won : he ftoopes to this lure, but
the bufh is fo well beaten by thefe fubtle fowlers,
that in the end, all the birds are flowne out of the
Cozens hand, and he hath not one peny left him
in his purfe : if then he fmell the knauerie, and fall
to calling for a Conftable, fwearing the dronken
rafcall hath cozened him, (for the *Bernard* you

D. III.   17

muſt know carries away all the money) then enters
the *Rutter*, who picking ſome ydle quarell either
in the roome, or at the ſtréete doore, the couy of
cheators take their flight in the meane time, and
that (with the ſharing of the purchaſe in another
Tauerne) is the *Epilogue* to their comedy, but the
firſt *Entrance* to the poore countrymans *Tragedy*.

    Theſe commedians *Strowle* likewiſe vp and
downe ẙ country in the habites of *Seruingmen*,
and ſilly fellowes, haunting *Brainford*, *Kingſton*,
Croydon, *Rumford* and ſuch other places néereſt
London vpon the market dayes onely, and at the end
of market, when Butchers, Graſiers & others whom
they thinke to be ſtored with money are on their
way home, then will one of this crew ouertake
them in ryding, and light at ſome towne of purpoſe
to mend his girt, to remoue a ſhooe of his horſe,
or vpon any other excuſe, intreating the company
(with whom he is newly acquainted) to ſtay and
drinke a pot with him in the meane time.   And
in theſe country voyages doe they Saile by other
points of the compaſſe ; ẙ windes are not ſo boy-
ſtrous, nor the Seas ſo rough as the former, for
here is there neither one ẙ playes the drunkard
nor any that ſwaggers, but theſe diueliſh Maſquers
paſſe vnder theſe names at ſuch meetings, viz.

    1 The party that fetcheth in the *Gull* (whoſe
feathers they meane to pluck) is not called the

Taker, but the *Setter*. 2 He that feconds him, keepes his firft Tytle & is called the *Verfer*. 3 He that loofeth his money, not a *Cozen* but a *Cony*. 4 He that comes / in and before counterfetted the dronken *Bernard* is now fober and called the *Barnacle*.

Sometimes likewife this *Card-cheating*, goes not vnder the name of *Bernards lawe*, but is called *Batt fowling*, and then ỹ *Setter* is the *Beater*, the foole that is caught in the net, the bird, the *Tauerne* to which they repaire to worke the *Feate*, is the *Bufh*; the wine the *Strap*, and the cardes the *Limetwigs*.

Thus haue I difcouered a ftrange Art, by which *Conyes* are caught after a new maner of hunting, and *Cozens* found out that were neuer of the kindred before. Thus the honeft farmer, fimply going about his bufineffe, is ftripped of that money, which fhould further his law-fuites, and fo perhaps is ouerthrowne: Thus the *Seruingman* being fent with his lords treafure, is cheated and tourned out of feruice: Thus the prentice hauing his Maifters wealth in his hand, is robd (by tame théeues) and in the end driuen to run away or to dye in prifon. Thus the *Gentleman* comming new to his land is made a begger. Thus the Merchant is vndone. Thus all men are abufed. Thus the common wealth is difhonored by féeding fuch vipers in her wombe, that cannot liue but by gnawing out her bowels.

Vincents Law.

THe *Dycing cheator*, and the cozening *Card-player*, walke in the habites of Gentlemen, and cary the faces of honeſt men, So likewiſe doe thoſe that are *Students* in the *Vincents Lawe*: whoſe Inne is a Bowling Alley, whoſe bookes are bowles, and whoſe law caſes are lurches and rubbers. The paſtime of bowles is now growne to a common exerciſe, or rather a trade of which ſome of all companies are frée ; the ſport is not ſo common as the cozenage vſed in it, which to haue it liue with credyt and in a good name is called the *Vincents Law.*

In this Law they which play booty are the *Banckers*.

He that *Betteth* is the *Gripe*.

He that is cozened is the *Vincent*.

The *Gaines* gotten is called *Termage*.

The *Bankers* are commonly men apparelled like honeſt and ſub / ſtanciall Citizens, who come into the Bowling Allies, for a rubbers or ſo, as though it were rather for ſport, then for any gaines, pro-teſting they care not whether they win or looſe : which careleſnes of theirs is but a ſhadowe to their pretended knauerie : whilſt they are crying *Rub*,

Rub, *Rub*, & a *Great one*, In come the fpectators dropping one by one, and ftand leaning ouer a Rayle to behold them ; of which oftentimes fome fimple men that neuer faw common Bowling Ally before may perhaps be of the number, and is brought in of purpofe by one of their owne *Brotherhood* to be rid of his money : if fuch a yong bird happen amongft them, and doe once but chirp, thats to fay either take or offer any lay, they all harken to his note, efpecially if he fing fhrilly, thats to fay be deepe : if there be good ftore of *Lookers* on, then are there certaine olde foakers, whofe office is to doe nothing but liften for bets, either euen or od, & thefe are called *Gripes* ; which *Gripes* will refufe no *Lay*, if the ods may grow to their aduantage, for the *Gripes* & the *Banckers* are fworne brothers to the Diuell (their father in law) and ẙ bowles haue fuch vertue in them that their byaffes will directly ron, as the *Gripes* haue placed their *Bets*. The *Bankers* (albeit they fo play as if they minded nothing but their owne game) yet haue ftill an eare how the layes are made, and according to that leuell doe they throw their bowles, fo that be fure the bowlers play booty : for fuppofe 7 be vp for the game, and that the one fide hath 3. the other none, then the *Vincent* (who is the *Nouice* that ftandeth by, and is not acquainted with the tallents of thefe *Gripes*,

nor féeles not when they draw bloud of him, no
nor doth not fo much as carry an euil! thought of
the bowlers that they fhould play booty, looking
fo grauely and fo like to honeft men,) hée poore
colt, feeing three to none, begins to grow lufty, and
to offer oddes on that fide which is faireft for the
game ; what ods faies the *Gripe*? 3. to one cryes
the *Vincent* : no fayes the *Gripe* it is more, and
with that the *Bankers* are come to foure for none :
then the *Vincent* offers to lay foure to one : I take
fix to one faies the *Gripe*, I lay it cryes the *Vincent*,
and fo they make a bet of fix crownes, fhillings, or
pence, as the *Vincent* is of ability to lay, and thus
will fondry take their oddes of him.   On then goe
the *Bankers* with the game and win another caft
which is fiue for none ; at this / fooles fortune of
his, the *Vincent* gryns for Ioy, fcratches his elbow,
and is fo proud that no ground about the Ally can
hold him, thinking verily both by the ods and
goodneffe of the play, it is impoffible for his fide
to loofe, and therefore (beeing now foole-hardy)
hee takes and layes bets freely : all eyes then
greedely marking the euent of this ftorme ; At
the length on a fuddaine, the Sun begins to fhine
on the other fide that were none, and they win
perhaps fo long till they come to three for fiue,
and ftill as their luck alters, diuerfitie of bets are
layd ; till at laft they are fiue for fiue : and then

the *Gripe* comes vpon the *Vincent*, and offers him ods, which if the *Vincent* faften vpon, he loofeth all, for vppon what fide foeuer the *Gripe* layes, that fide euer wins, how great foeuer the oddes be at firft in the contrary part, fo that the cozenage growes in playing booty. This fowre banquet to the *Vincent* is feafoned with fweete meates to the *Bankers* & the *Gripes* ; who at night meete in fome Tauerne, and fhare the money gotten by this bafe meanes, which money they call *Termage*.

Now to fhadow the villany the more, the *Banker* that wins and is aforehand with the game, wil lay franckly that he fhall wyn, and will bet hard, and lay great ods : but with whome? either with them who play with him that are as crafty knaues as himfelfe, or elfe with the *Gripe*, and this makes the *Vincēt* to ftoope to the blowe the fooner. Befides if any honeft men that hold themfelues fkilfull in bowling, offer to play any fet-match againft thefe common bowlers, if thefe *Bankers* feare to haue the worft, and fufpect the others play to bee better than theires, then haue they a trick (in watring of the Alley) to giue fuch a moifture to the banck, that he who offers to Strike a bowle with a fhore, fhall neuer hit it whilft he liues becaufe the moyfture of the banck hinders the proportion ot his Ayming. Many other prac- tifes there are in bowling tending to cozenage, but

ẙ greateſt and groſeſt is *Booty* : in which ẙ deceipt
is ſo open & palpable, ẙ I haue ſeene men ſtone-
blind offer to lay *Betts* franckely, although they
could ſee a bowle no more then a poſt, onely by
hearing who played, and how the old *Grypes* had
made their layes.

Thus ſports that were inuented for honeſt re-
creation, are by the wicked abuſing of them, turned
to mens confuſion : And not / onely in theſe games
before rehearſed, but alſo in thoſe that are both
more laudable, and more lawfull. For in the *Tennis-
court*, *Cheating* hath a hand ; yea and in *Shooting*
(which is the nobleſt exerciſe of our Engliſh
Nation,) arrowes do now and then fly with falſe
feathers. Since then that all kinds of gaming
ſerues but as gulphes to deuoure the ſubſtances
of men, and to ſwallow them vp in beggery, my
councell is vtterly eyther to refraine ſuch paſtimes,
or if men are of ſuch Spirits that they muſt néedes
venture their money, then to bee very prouident
how they play, and to be choiſe of their company.
Now let vs turne ouer the volumes of other *Lawes*,
enaſted in the Parliament of theſe Diuels.

The Blacke Art.

HAuing waded thus farre in theſe puddles
of damn'd impiety, it ſhall not be amiſſe
to go on, and ſearch euen to the bottome and

fartheſt ſhore of them : to effect which the ſooner,
we muſt now deale in the *Blacke Art*. It is not
that *Blacke Art*, by which men coniure vp Spirits,
and raiſe Diuels in Circles, to tell where money is
hid, or whether goods that are ſtolen are conuaied;
But this *Blacke Art*, is to fetch away money where
it lyes, and to raiſe vp a fiend in a rich Mercers
or Gold-ſmiths ſhop at midnight without the gibriſh of a ſtaring Coniurer. This *Blacke Art* workes
in darkneſſe as well as the other ; it deales with
the Diuell as the other doth, and is as vnlawfull as
the other is : if you will néeds (in a word) know
the miſticall meaning of *This Blacke Art*, it is
called in Engliſh *Picking of Lockes*, And this
Engine of miſchiefe turnes vpon theſe 5. wheeles.
Viz.

The *Picklocke* is called a *Charme*.
He that watcheth if any body come, is the *Stand*.
The tooles that doe the buſineſſe are called
Wreſters.
Picking of the locke is called *Farſing*.
The gaines gotten is *Pelfrey*.

Now albeit that two perſons only are imployed
in this Vndermining of a doore (viz. the *Charme*
and the *Stand*) yet ẏ burgulary is committed by
other hands, which are in a readineſſe to receiue
the goods (when the houſe is entred) and to

conuey / them in parcels away. The *Charme*, (who is ỹ mafter of this black Art, goes like a coniurer, with a number of keyes & wrefts like fo many *Pentacles*) about him, which he calles picklocks, and for euery fundry fafhion they haue a fundry terme ; but being ignorant of their wordes of Art, I omit them; only affuring you thus much, that the *Charme* hath fuch cunning & fuch dexteritie in opening a lock (and that without any great noife) that no ward whatfoeuer (be it neuer fo doubled) but flies back at his Iugling with it. Some haue their inftruměts from *Italy*, made of Steele, fome are made here in *England* by Smithes that are partners and partakers in their villanous occupations. But howfoeuer, the *Trade* of *Lockpicking* may well be called the *Black-Art*, for none ftudy it, but thofe that for other mens goods haue fold their verie foules to the Diuell.

The Curbing Law.

The *Black Art* and the *Curbing Law*, are grounded both vpon the felfe fame pofitions : for the *Black Art* teaches how to breake open a lock, the *Curbing Law* how to hooke goodes out of a windowe; they both are workers in Iron, both are begotten in Idlenes, both liue by villanie, and both die with infamy. A fmith is the maker and fetter up of thefe two trades, and the hangman is

the vtter vndoer of them. This *Curbing Law*
ſpreds it ſelfe into foure maine branches :

He that hookes is called the *Curber*.
He that playes the ſpy is the *Warpe*.
The *Hooke* is the *Courb*.
The goodes are called *Snappings*.
The *Gin* to open the windowe is a *Tricker*.

The office of the *Curber* is for the moſt parte
betimes in the mornings (at the diſcharging of a
watch) to be vp more earely than a noiſe of
ſhrugging fidlers ; and the huſbandry which hee
followes, is in the day time to watch what ſhops
or windowes ſtand fitteſt for his trade, which if he
finde eaſily to bee opened, then the cony is in the
purſute without much feretting : But if he muſt
take paines for his liuing, out come his *Trickers*,
and then (as if hee were a brother of the *Black
Art*) doth hee with thoſe / Iron engines, cut a
barre of Iron in ſunder, in ſuch ſorte that ſcarce the
ſtanders by ſhall heare him.   The windowe being
thus open, and that hee hath good hope to meete
with fatte Snappings (or rich purchaſe) the *Warp*
buſtles to play his part, and watches with cats-eies
in the darke, looking (like one a ſquint, or as if he
ſtoode to catch hares) two waies, one to ſpie who
comes, the other to note what comes out at the
window : to carry which away he is furniſhed with

a long cloake. But firſt muſt the *Curber* play his
prize, and that is with an Iron about nine foote
in length, at whoſe end (being crooked) are thrée
Tynes turned contrary, ſo that they catch euery
way, if any ſnappings be within their reach. This
hook (or *Curb*) is made with ioynts like an Angling rod, and in the day time is conueyed into the
forme of a truncheon, and worne like a walking
ſtaffe, till night, when it is put to doe other ſeruice.
Whatſoeuer the *Curber* with this angle fiſhes for
and takes, the *Warp* beares it away, and he deliuers
it either to a Broker or ſome Bawd (for they all
are of one feather,) of which *Receiuers* they haue
as preſent money for it, as if they traded with
Merchants. Then is there (belonging to this
faculty) a *Diuer*, and he is iuſt in the nature of
a *Curber*, for as the one practiſes his villany with
a hooke, ſo the *Diuer* workes his Iugling feates by
ẙ help of a boy, (called a *Figger*) whom hee thruſts
in at a caſement, being ſo well ſtudied that he hath
the principles of the *Black-Art*, & can pick a lock
if it be not too much croſſe warded ; this *Figger*
deliuers to the *Diuer* what ſnappings he findes in
the ſhop or chamber.

The Prigging Law.

BEing weary with going thus farre on foote, let vs now (fithence we haue ouertaken a horfeman) get vp and ride along with him. Yet now I looke vpon him well, it is more fafety and better policie to let him ride by himfelfe, for he rides circuite with the Diuell, and *Derick* muft bee his hoft, and *Tiburne* the Inne at which he will light. This ranck-rider is of the *Family* of Knights-errant, or of thofe wandring *Rogues* that march in the firft files of my booke, his name is a *Prigger*, deriuing his title from his practize, which is called the *Prig / ging Law*, whofe grounds are the *Cleanly and cunning ftealing of horfes*.

This *Prigging* Arte runnes into fix riuers, all of them falling into one ftreame, and all of them flowing from one head.

He that fteales the horfe is called the *Prigger*.

The horfe is called a *Prancer*.

The feller away of the ftolne horfe is a *Martar*.

The *Tolling-houfe* is called *Alhallowes*.

The tiller is the *Rifler*.

The fureties at the toll-booke are called *Querries*.

A Prigger on foote is called a *Trayler*.

The *Prigger* if hee bee a lance-man (that is to fay, one that is already horft) then rides he in ftate, attended by followers, who are either like his fer-

uants in liueries, or in the habite of Gentlemen, or
moſt commonly in the ſhapes of *Drouers* : in this
equipage doe they walke vp and downe medowes
and paſtures or other incloſed grounds, as if their
purpoſe were to buy cattell, whereas their eyes are
onely buſied in noting horſes, that are worth the
ſtealing, and whether their héeles are fettred ẘ
horſe locks or no.　This firſt cirkle being drawne
in ẙ day time, the next night following our *Priggers* fall to coniuring, and by the ſpelles of the
Black Art, pick open the *Tramelles* or locks, &
then like Battes or Owles away they fly ouer hedge
and ditch out of thoſe quarters.　The owners in
the morning may ſmell out their footeſteps & ſee
which way they are rid poſt, but vnleſſe the Diuell
himſelfe either went with a candle & lanthorne
before them, the *Priggers* would neuer be found,
or elſe carried them on his back, and bid them to
hold faſt by his hornes whilſt he gallopped, it were
not poſſible to ouertake them.　For this policie
they vſe, if the *Prigger* ſteale a horſe in *Yorke-ſhire*,
he ſelles him in *Surrey*, *Kent* or *Suſſex* ; and their
Martars (ſo called of hunting *Marts* or *Faires*)
who receiue thē at ẙ *Priggers* handes, chop them
away in ſome blinde faires or other after they haue
kept them a moneth or two, till the breath of the
Hue and *Crie* be blowne ouer.

　　If the horſe be of any value, and much inquired

after, or cary fuch brands or eare-markes about
him, that they cãnot put him off without danger,
then doe thefe *Priggers* brand him with a croffe- /
brand on the former, or take away his eare-marke,
and fo keepe him at hard meate till he be perfectly
recouered or elfe will they fell him in *Cornewall*,
or *Wales* if he be fetched out of *Cumberland*,
Lincolne-fhire, *Norfolke* or *Suffolke*. But if the horfe
be onely coloured and without Brandes, then haue
they fhifts to fpot them fo ftrangely, that a man
fhall hardly know his owne horfe if he meete him ;
as to marke a black horfe with faddle-fpots, or to
ftar him in the forhead, and change his taile : the
fecrets of which are not fit in print to be difcouered,
left laying open the abufe, I fhould teach fome how
to practife it.

   This is the life of the *Prigger*, who trauailes vp
and downe the whole kingdome vpon his geldings
of 20 and 40 pound price, and is taken for a man
of good worth, by his outward fhew, being (amongft
his owne fraternity of horfe-ftealers) called a *Prigging lance-man.* But he that borrowes a nag out
of another mans pafture, and cares not fo he may
get money for him, how he puts him away, onely
to fupply his wants, is called a *Trayler* ; thefe
Trailers trot vpon the hoofe, and are footemen,
meane in apparell, though not meane in their
theeuing trade : you fhall haue them attired like

plaine country grans, walking (like our thredbare
gallants in Poules) in bootes ẁout ſpurres, &
ſometimes without bootes, long ſtaues on their
neckes, and black buckram bags at their backs,
as if they were Lawyers clients and carried letters
vp and downe : But thoſe buckram bags are the
horſes wardrobe. In thoſe bags doe theſe ſneaking
Traylers put ſaddle, bridle, ſpurres, ſtirrops, and
ſtirrop leathers ; all this hackney houſhold ſtuffe
beeing made ſo quaintly, that the deepe ſlop of a
hoſe is able to hide it : for the ſaddle is faſhioned
without any tree, (yet hath it cantle & bolſters) but
artificially quilted together with cloth and bumbaſt,
and with ſuch foldes that it may eaſily be wrapt vp
in a littlē roome : the ſtirrops goe with vices and
ginnes, that one may put them into a paire of
gloues, ſo likewiſe doe the ſpurres, and then
a little white leather head ſtall and reynes, with
a ſmall ſcottiſh brake or ſnaffle, all of them ſo
neatly framed, that a ſmall bag will containe them.
And looke how the *Lance-man* rides poſt when
hee ſits vpon his prey, ſo when the *Trayler* is in
the ſaddle, away hee gallops as if euerie Iade of
ſeuen / nobles price were a winged *Pegaſus*, ſelling
him as farre off from the place where hee ſtole
him, as poſſibly hee can.

Now becauſe theſe *Priggers* though they breake
the Lawe in one point, yet they make it whole in

another ; and very orderly come to the Toll booke, bringing 2 (of their owne religion) ciuilly attired (fitting the place) who not only affirm but offer to depofe that they know the horfe to be his owne that fels it; yet are thefe caitifs no better then olde knights of the poft, ẙ will periure thẽfelues for pots of Ale, & neuer faw perhaps either ẙ *Prigger* or the *Prancer* before thefe wicked Elders, hauing for villanies béene banifhed out of Weft-minfter Hall, or for their periuries ftood and loft their eares on the pillorie, retire themfelues into the Countrie, and profeffe this kind of life, being by the horfe-ftealers called (though they are farre vnworthy of fo good a name) *Querries* : leauing whom (with the horfemen their good Lords and mafters) either to an amendment of manners, or to the mercy of the Hangman, who muft teach them to ride this wodden curtall; let vs, becaufe wee are now lifting them out of the faddle, turne ouer a new leafe, and read a lecture in the *Lifting* Law.

The Lifting Law.

THe *Lifting* Law is not the Law of *Porters*, who liue by *Lifting*, and cry to one another, lend mee your hand when honeftly they are to carry a burthen for a penny, and fafely to deliuer it to the owner backe againe : but this law teacheth a kind of lifting of goods cleane away. In fuch

Liftings are three forts of *Leauers* vfed to get vp the baggage, *viz.*

He that firft ftealeth the parcell is called *The Lift*.

He that receiues it is the *Marker*.

He that ftands without and carries it away, is the *Santar*.

The goods thus purchafed, is called *Garbage* : which *Garbage* is fometime plate, or Iewels, fometimes pieces of veluet, fometimes cloakes or lawyers gownes, fometimes one thing, fometimes another.

The *Practitioners* of this *Lifting* Law, take feuerall degrees, for fome of them (and they are the *Punies*) are but *Bafe Rogues*, that / liue by *Lifting* quart pots, platters, and fuch trafh out of tipling houfes, vnder colour of fpending two or three pottes of Ale. Thefe are the *Rafcallitie* of this *Heard.* But the Gentleman *Lifter* walkes with his *Marker* at his heeles, as if he were a Country Gentleman of 500. a yeare, & comming into a Mercers or Gold-fmiths fhop, prefetly cafts by his cloake, (to colour his intents) the *Marker* ftanding bare-headed not farre from him, his worfhip then cals for a bolt of Satten, Veluet, cloth of gold, or filuer, or any other of the richeft commodities, and not liking the pile, colour, or bracke, his eye muft haue the choice of more ; the *Marker* in the meane time whileft the Mercer

is bufie and turnes his backe, hath the *Garbage*
thruft towardes him by the *Lifter*, and conueies
it vnder his cloake : the *Sentar* who walkes in the
ftreete, paffing then in great hafte by the doore,
is called backe by the *Marker*, as if he were fuch a
Gentlemans, Knights, or Noble-mans feruant : but
the *Senter* fweares he cannot ftay, the *Marker* tels
him hee muft needes haue one word with him, and
fo ftepping along with him fome part of the way,
fecretly conueies the *Garbage* to the *Sentar*.

Other *Lifts* there are, that haunt *Noble-mens*
houfes, at Marriages, or folemne *Reuelings*, in
Chriftmas, and the *Hals* of companies when they
make feafts, at which times they lift away goblets,
or other pieces of plate, Napery, or any thing
worth the ventring for.

Others ply Counfellours chambers, that are
well cliented, and fit downe in the outer roomes
like Country men, hauing blacke boxes by their
fides, and papers in their handes : but their atten-
dance is not for counfell, nor to pay any fées, but
to *Lift* away gownes, or cloakes, by the *Rules* of
their owne *Law*. The like pare of Indentures
doe they draw in fhops, betwéene *Scriueners* and
themfelues.

Another more cunning then all thefe *Liftings*,
is when in an euening, a *Batfowler* walkes vp and
downe the ftréetes, and counterfets that hee hath

let fall a ring, a Iewell, or a peece of gold, requeſt-
ing ſome Prentice, (when there is but one in the
ſhop) to lend him his candle a while to find his
loſſes, who ſimply doth ſo, but the *Lifter* poring
a good while and not meeting with his ring, lets
the candle in the end ſlip out of his fingers, and
whileſt the prentice ſteps in to light it againe, the
Sentar or he / himſelfe ſteales what garbage they
can finger, and are gone in the meane time.

You haue another kind of *Lifter*, or more
properly a cunning night ſhifter, and it is thus :
You ſhall haue a fellow, that in an euening or
night time, or ſome time at noone dayes, as hee
likes the company, and ſorts his opportunity, that
will wilfully drop ſometime a ſpoone, other while
a ring, or elſe ſome péece of coyned money, as the
likenes of gold, and ſiluer, and ſo ſpurning it afore
them in the view of others, to the end they ſhould
cry halfe part ; which he taking hold of, ſayth,
nay by my troth, what will you giue me & take
it all? and ſo ſome gréedy fooles offer thus much,
thinking it gold, which the *Lifter* takes, as knowing
it counterfeit, and ſo are they cunny-caught.

Then is there a kind of *Lift*, who like a Iugler
doth all his feates of himſelfe, not caring for the
helpe of others ; he goes attired like a Seruingman,
booted and ſpurd and dirtie as if hee had new
ridden ; his haunts are the beſt townes in the

countrie vpon market dayes, but moſt commonly *Faires* : the birdes he watches for are Knights, Eſquires, or Gentlemē, that light at ẙ greateſt Innes, whither moſt reſort is ; who ſhall no ſooner come from horſe, but this *Lifter* is readie to hold his ſtirrop, or to walk his horſe, as officiouſly as if he wore his cloth : So that to the *Gueſt* he ſeemes to be one belonging to the houſe, and to the ſeruants of the houſe hee appeares to bee a follower of the Gentleman newly alighted. But the *Gueſt* being departed from his Inne, to the towne or into the faire, backe comes this counterfeit *Blew-coate*, running in all haſte for his maſters cloake-bag or portmantua, & cals to the oſtler or chamberlaine by his name to deliuer it, becauſe ſome things muſt bee taken out for his *Knight*, or the Gentleman his maiſter, that are in it. The prey is put (hereupon) into the Vultures tallants, and away flies he preſently to his neſt, to féede and fat his rauenous gorge with the garbage which he hath gotten.

But what *Neſts* thinke you they flie to ? Marry to the houſe either of ſome notorious trebble-chind baude (in whoſe beddes commonly theſe Serpentes lie lurking) who keepes a tipling houſe, and brings vp yong *Trugs* (vnder the colour of filling *Kannes*) that are harlots to the *Lifts* ; or elſe to the ſhops of certaine *Brokers*, who traffick onely in this kind

of Merchandize, and / by bils of fale, (made in the
name of *Robin-Goodfellow* and his crue,) get the
goods of honeft Citizens into their hands, either
detaining them fo long in their chefts till they be
no more fought after, or elfe fo altering them that
ẙ *Owners* fhall hardly know them. Thus the *Lift*
and his mates prepare the lime-twigs and catch the
bird, but the *Bawde* and *Broker*, eate the flefhe
and giue the other onely the feathers.

The High Law.

ALL this while haue I read vnto you the
beggarly law, and bafe common *Lawes* of
Villany, by which the *Out-Lawes* of a kingdome,
and *Out-cafts* of a well-gouerned *Common-wealth*,
maintaine their damnable courfes. Now muft
you caft vp your eyes and looke aloft, if
you haue a defire to behold the picture of *The
High Law* : which taketh that name from the
high exploits that are acted by it : the Schollers
that learne it are called *High Lawyers* ; yet they
neuer walke to Weftminfter to pleade, though
oftentimes they are called to the *Barre*, but then
it is to haue them *Hold vp their hands*, that the
Hangman may tell them their fortune. All the
former Lawes are attained by wit, but the *High
Law* ftands both vpon *Wit* and *Manhood*. For
the *High Law* is nothing elfe but taking a purfe

by the *High-way fide*, fo that to bee a good prac-
titioner in this *Law*, a man néeds no more but a
bold fterne looke, a good heart, and a good fword;
the cafes that he is to plead vpon, is onely *Stand*
and *Deliuer*. All trauellers are fo beaten to the
trials of this *Law*, that if they haue but rode
ouer *Shooters Hill*, or *Salifbury Plaine*, they are as
perfect in the principles of it, as if they had beene
7. years in the company of *High-Lawyers*. The
Counfell a *High-Lawyer* giues, is common, but his
fees are vnreafonable, for he ftrips his Clients of
all. The motions which hee makes are both in
Terme and out of *Terme* ; I fhall not néed therefore to open any of his *Cafes*. But onely will tell
you thus much, that this high-law is comprehended
in fiue *Volumes, viz.*

The théefe that commits the *Robbery*, and is cheife
clerke to Saint *Nicholas*, is called the *High Lawyer*.

He that fetteth the watch is a *Scripper*.

He that ftandes *Centinell* and does watch, is an
Oke.

Hee that is robd, is the *Martin*.

When he yeildeth, it is called *Stooping*.

All the fhires in England haue feene thefe *High-
lawe* matters tryed, and therefore if any would
know them or the profeffors of them to a haire,
let him but ftep into the *Old Baily* at any Seffions,
and he fhall heare more.

The facking Law.

THe companion of a théefe is commonly a
Whore; it is not amiffe therefore, to
pinneon them together: for what the theefe gets
the ftrumpet fpends. The trade of thefe *Tale-
bearers* goes vnder the name of the *Sacking-law*;
and rightly may it be called facking, for as in the
facking of a City, all the villanies in the world are
fet abroach, fo when a Harlot comes to the facking
of a mans wealth and reputation (for fhe befiegeth
both together) fhe leaues no ftratagem vnpractifed
to bring him to confufion. *Weftminfter* and *Hol-
born* haue chambers full of thefe ftudents of the
Sacking-law. In Clerken-well, they had wont &
are ftill well cliented: White Friers is famous for
their meeting: The Spittle flourifhes with the yong
fry, that are put to it to learne it. Sacks come
to thefe milles euery houre, but the *Sacking-lawe*
empties them fafter then a Miller grindes his
bufhels of corne. He that hath a luft to practife
this law, muft bee furnifhed with thefe fiue bookes,
viz.

The *Baud*, who if fhe be a woman is called a
Pandareffe.

The *Apple-fquire*, who is to fetch in wine.

The *Whore*, who is called the *Commodity*.

The *Whore-houfe*, which is called a *Trugging-
place.*

Thefe fiue Authors are fo well knowne, and
haue bin fo turned ouer leafe by leafe, that euery
man (almoft) that liues in fight of the fmoake
of the Citie, hath them at his fingers ends ; or if
he cannot, it is an eafie matter to finde them by
a Table.   I will onely refer you to the fuburbs.
But there is a fecond part of this *Sacking-law,* and
that inftructs *Punckes* to attire themfelues neatly
in fummer euenings, and about ten or eleuen of
the clock at night to walke vp and downe the
moft peopled ftréetes of the citie, very foberly and
gingerly, til ẙ wine (by / one *Gull* or other) be
offered, which with a little intreaty fhe takes; but
being in the midft of their bowles, or perhaps the
filly cony being trayned home to a lodging, where
he falles to *Nibling* ; in comes a Ruffian with a
drawne rapier, calles the *Punck* (as fhe is) damned
whore, afkes what Rogue that is, and what he
does with his wife.   The conclufion of all this
counterfeit fwaggering being a plot betwixt this
panderly ruffian and the whore to geld the filly
foole of all the money hee hath in his purfe, and
fometimes to make him (rather than his credit
fhould be called into queftion) to feale a bill or
bond for other fums of money at fuch and fuch
daies, and fo fend him packing, when he hath
paide too deare for a bad difh of meate which he
neuer tafted : the bafe Applefquire and his yong

miftreffe, laughing to fee what a woodcocke they
puld, and fharing the feathers betweene them.
But when fuch comedies (of the *Sacking-Law*)
as thefe, are playd, then the Actors haue other
names than are fet downe before, and thefe
they be :

The whore is then called the *Traffick*.

The man that is brought in, is the *Simpler*.

The Ruffian that takes him napping, is the
Crofbiter.

The Figging Law.

THe Parliament of thefe hell-hounds, it feemes
wil foone breake vp, for they ftand now
onely vpon the laft lawe ; which they call *Figging-
Lawe* : in making of which law, two perfons haue
the chiefe voices, that is to fay, ẙ *Cut-purfe* & the
Pick-pocket, and all the branches of this law reach
to none but them and fuch as are made free
denizens of their incorporation. This *Figging-
Lawe* (like the body of fome monftrous and
terrible beaft) ftands vpon ten feete, or rather lifts
vp proudly ten Dragon-like heads, the names of
which heads are thefe. *viz.*

He that cuts the purfe is called the *Nip*.

He that is halte with him is the *Snap*, or the
Cloyer.

The knife is called a *Cuttle-bung*.

He that picks the pocket is called a *Foiſt*.

He that faceth the man, is the *Stale*.

The taking of the purſe is called *Drawing*.

The ſpying of this villanie is called *Smoaking* or *Boiling*.

The purſe is the *Bung*.

The money the *Shelles*.

The act doing, is called ſtriking.

This *Figging Lawe* hath more quirkes and quiddities in it than any of the former; it is as dangerous to meddle with as the *High-law*, in pleading of whoſe caſes men are at Daggers drawing : the ſchollers of this Art are cunning Sophiſters, and had neede to haue more eies then two in one head, becauſe the Arguments they hold, and their bold villanies which they practiſe are argued vpon and iuſtified to his teeth with whom they contend. The *Foiſt* and the *Nip*, (that is to ſay, the Pocket diuer and the cut purſe) are pewfellowes together and of one religion, but differ in ſome points. A purſe well lined is the wet Eele they both bob for, but they ſtriue to catch it by the taile after ſeuerall faſhions. For the *Nip* workes with his knife, the *Foiſt* with his hand : the *Nip* cuts the purſe, the *Foiſt* drawes the pocket : both their occupations are taught them by the Diuell, yet they both brag of the excellencie of them, and are ready ſomtimes to ſtab one another, about defending which is beſt, for the *Foiſt* counts himſelfe the better man, and therefore is called (by the liuery of his company) a gentleman *Foiſt*, and ſo much ſcornes the title of a cut purſe, ẙ he weares not a knife about him to cut his owne meate, left hee be held in ſuſpition to be a *Nip*, which he eſtéemes the baſeſt office in the whole Army of *Cheaters*.

Theſe ſchollers of the *Figging lawe*, are infinite in number, their *Colledge* is great, their orders many, and their degrees (which are giuen to them by the *Seniors* of the houſe) very ancient, but very abominable.

The language which they ſpeak is none of thoſe which came in at the confuſion of *Tongues*, for neither infidell nor Chriſtian (that is honeſt) vnder-ſtandes it, but the *Dialeʒt* is ſuch and ſo crabbed, that ſeuen yeeres ſtudy is little enough to reach to the bottome of it, and to make it run off glib from the tongue : by meanes of this *Gibriſh*, they know their owne nation when they meete, albeit they neuer ſawe one another before ; and ſo conforme-able are they to the ordinances of the *Brotherhoode*, that whatſoeuer ẙ *wicked Elders* amongſt them ſhall preſcribe, *Aʒtum / eſt*, tis a lawe, and they will not breake it: yea not the proudeſt of them dare be ſo bold as to exerciſe his Art in any other place but in thoſe that are appointed to him, nor once prefume to fet his foote into anothers walke, but by licence of the *figniory*.

For that purpofe therefore, (as if a whole king-dome were theirs) they allot fuch countries to this Band of *Foifts*, fuch townes to thofe, and fuch a City to fo many *Nips* : whereupon fome of thefe *Boote-halers* are called *Termers*, and they ply Weftminfter hall. Michaelmas terme is their harueft and they fweat in it harder then reapers or hay-makers doe at their workes in the heate of fommer : no Counfellor, Attourney, Petifogger nor Sollicitor is vp earelier then they : nor at the hall fooner than they : when clients begin to come crowding in, *Watermen* ply not their fares more nimbly then the *Nips* and *Foifts* beftir themfelues to pick vp their fhelles : the hall and ỹ old palace are their *Hiues*, and they worke in them like bees : ỹ *Exchequer chamber, Star-chamber, Kings-bench* & *Common pleas, &* *Chancery* are ỹ beds of flowers, to which they fly humming to & fro continually to fuck the honey of gold & filuer. If a poore client doe but ftand by his Lawyer, whilft he is pleading, and drawes out his purfe to pay fees for counfell, or to the Court for difpatch of his bufi-neffe, thefe Furies are fure to bée at his elbowe watching (with hawkes eyes,) on which fide he puts vp his purfe ; to that fide they fly, and if their tallents cã but touch it, it is their owne. Others of them haue all the flefh and fifh markets allowed them for their walkes, as *Cheapfide*, *Eaft-cheape*, the *Shambles*, both *Fifhftreetes*, the *Stockes*, and ẙ *Borough* in Southwarke ; in which places thefe faithfull Stewards of *Lucifers* houfhold, cheapen all commodities, only to note, what money, wiues or feruants that come to buy, haue in their purfes, and where they put it vp, which beeing well obferued, the *Stall* plies his market, and followes him or her (whofe filuer is condemned) till they come to a preffe of people, then does the *Stall* keepe a thrufting and a Iuftling, whilft in the meane time the *Foift* is either in their pocket or the *Nip* hath the purfe faft by the ftrings.

Others haunt Playhoufes only & the Beare-garden : fome haue their precinct lying in the walkes of Poules, their houres of / meeting there being betwéen 10 and 11, ẙ ftrokes they ftrike being fometimes in the middle *Ile* if it be in *Terme* time, when ẙ walkes are full, but moft cōmonly, at the doores of the Church, which they will choake, and ftriue for paffage, whilft another does the feate.   A running at *Tilt*; the Lord Maiors day, any great fhooting, any fray, any folemne arraignement, or execution, is better to thefe *Hell hounds* than a quarter day is to a Landlord or than 5 feffions are to the hangman.   Yea fo feareles are thefe Diuells to be throwne headlong, & quick into the pit of damnation, that euen in Gods owne houſe & the ſacred *Temple*, doe they deſperately commit their villanies, ſtanding moſt deuoutly with eies eleuated vp to heauen, before the preacher, where the preſſe of people is thickeſt, whilſt their hãds are nibling in honeſt mens pockets for their purſes, who are careles of ſuch worldly matters there, as not miſtruſting that any ſo bad-minded dare enter into ſo holy a place. Theſe *Nips* and *Foiſts* goe oftentimes cleanly away with the ſhelles which they get, but oftentimes are they dogged by certaine followers (called *Cloyers*) who hang vppon them like Burres, and are more troubleſome than waſpes : for no ſooner is a *Bung* drawne, but the *Cloyer* ſteps in for his *Tenth*, which hee calles *Snappage*; if the *Nip* denie *Snappage* the *Cloyer* forthwith *Boyles* him, that is, bewraies him or ſeaſeth on his cloake.

You muſt vnderſtand likewiſe, that both of *Nips* and *Foiſts* there are two ſortes, for there be City *Nips* and country *Nips*, whoſe office is to haunt nothing but *Faires* : theſe country *Nips* neuer come into London to doe any peece of ſeruice, but at *Bartholmewtide* onely. Betweene theſe two ſects, is mortall enmity ; for if the City *Foiſt* ſpy one of the country *Foiſts* in London he forthwith labours and layes waite to ſmoake or Boyle him, the like does the country *Nip* or *Foiſt*

by him of the City.   There are alſo weomen *Foiſts*
and *Nips* aſwell as men, but farre more dangerous
then the men : All the troopes of both *ſexes* beeing
ſubiect to the diſcipline of the *Grand Nips* & *Foiſts*,
and from whom, the better to receiue directions
both what to doe, and what quarters to keepe (for
they ſhift their walkes according to the pleaſure
of the cheefe *Rangers*) they haue a certaine houſe,
ſometimes at one end of the towne ſometimes at
another, which is their hall ; at this Hall the
whole company do meete / very orderly, by which
meanes whenſoeuer any notable or workmanlike
Stroke is ſtricken, though it were as farre as the
North-borders, yet can the reſt of the *Fig-boies*
here reſident in London, tell by whom this worthy
Act was plaid.

At this ſolemne meeting in their *Hall,* they
chooſe *Wardens* & a *Steward* : the *Wardens* office
is to eſtabliſh wholeſom lawes to keepe life in their
rotten common wealth, and to aſſigne out to euery
man his *Stations.*   The Treaſurers office is very
truly (though he be an arrant théefe) to render
an account of ſuch moneies as are put into his
hands vppon truſt : for of euery purſe (that is
cleanly conueied and hath good ſtore of *Shelles*
in it) a ratable proportion is deliuerd (in *Banck*
as it were) to the Treaſurer, to the intent that
when any of them is taken and caſt into priſon,

a *Flag* of truce may prefently be hung out, and compofition offered to the wronged party, thereby to faue a brother of the fociety from riding *Weft-ward*. This had wont to be an order amongft them : But now the Vnder keepers of *Newgate*, (if complaint bee made to them for the loffe of any purfe) haue a trick to get a warrant, into which warrant they put the names of 9 or ten of the moft notorious *Foifts* and *Nips* that are free of their Gaole (which they call *Whittington Colledge,*) and thofe *Nips* or *Foifts* doe the Iaylors nip, till the money (perhaps double) be reftored, albeit not one of them ÿ are fpecified in the warrant were guilty of the fadt : This trick doth greatly im-pouerifh the tradefmen of this myftery, and may in time vtterly ouerthrow the ftudents of the *Figging Law.*

The Fiue Iumps at Leap-frog.

THe whole volume of thefe deteftable *Lawes* is now read ouer ; to catch a heate there-fore after fo long fitting, let vs exercife our felues a while at a new play, called *The fiue Iumps at Leap-frog.* The property of the game at *Leap-frog,* is (as euery prentice and Carter knowes) for one man to ftoope, and to let another man come ouer him ; fo in thefe *Iumpes* the running cheaters fweate only to make a man ftoope fo lowe, that

D. III.   21

they may breake his backe, and then they ride ouer his miferie with laughter.

The firſt *Iump* is called *Horſe-courſing*, and that is done thus : A fellow in good clothes and with an honeſt face to the eie, hires of a carier a Nag to ride along ẅ him to *Cambridge, Oxford, Norwich*, or any great towne of trade : but let the iourney be neuer ſo long, this *Rider* will end it in a fornoone at moſt ; for whilſt the Carier is buſie about his teeme on the way and looking to his charge, my horſecourſer ſteps aſide into ſome by-lane, and lights at ſome paltry towne neere the citty where he will lie, till he haue in capons and wine eaten vp the Carriers beaſt aliue ; and then departs on foote, ſending the poore man word where his prancer ſtands at rack and Manger, who if he will haue him muſt diſburſe forty ſhillings or three pound for his Iades diet. The *Hackney-men* of *Rocheſter* haue been oftentimes come ouer with this *Iump* at *Leap-frog*, and know the game well, for a man cannot name it but they are ready to giue it a curſe.

The ſecond *Iump* is called *carying* of *ſtones*, and that is performed in this maner : A crue of *Sharking companions* (of which there be ſundry conſorts lurking about the ſuburbs of this City) being driuen out of meanes, by leading baſe and idle liues, or elſe by their riotous expences amongſt whores, practife to liue vpon the fee fimple of their wits; & hauing amongft them all fome little money left (which they call their *Shooing-horne*) they feeke out fome blind victualling houfe, or Cookes houfe, without the barres, whofe Hoft (if it be poffible) is either an affe eafie to be ridden, or elfe a common drunkard. In this Colts houfe will they fit carowfing halfe-cannes day and night, and pay royally at firft for what they call, that *fhooing-horne* of theirs drawing the Hoft and Hofteffe on to beleeue they fhall be made for euer by thefe guefts; who to gull the poore *Goofe-cap* the better, draw all their acquaintance they can to ẏ houfe, neuer either drinking or feeding, but mine Hoft muft fit at the bords end like a *Magnifico* in pomp, with his ale-dropt greafie doublet fhining by candle light, as if it were an old rufty Armor fcuruily fcowred. But whē thefe *Horfe-leeches* haue fuckt their guts full, or rather the pitifully-complaining Hofts guts empty, that he findes by his fcores he can truft no more: then do they at one time or other talke of ftate matters, or of Religion, when the Goodman of the houfe can fcarce ftand on his legs vnder / his owne roofe, and trip him in fome words; which the next day (beeing told of it, and the words iuftified to his face) he knowes he dares not anfwere; with which hooke holding his nofe to the grindftone, they

write their mind in great round *Oes* of chalke,
behinde a doore, which *Oes* they call ftones : the
waight of them beeing fuch that looke how many
fhillings they make, fo many times the wretched
Hofteffe cries *O*, as groning vnder the burden.
Now Sir of thefe *Oes*, twenty fhillings make a
loade, and ten pound make a Barge full : which
when they haue well freighted, thefe *Dunkirkes*
hoyft Saile and to Sea againe they goe in another
veffell; to finde another *Brafeman*, that is to fay,
into another tipling houfe to finde another *Iade*
whom they may all faddle and get vp vpon : if
their laft Hoft follow them with a Bailefe or a
Sergeant, they only hold vp a finger, naming a
Purfeuant and cry *Mum*, no more mine Hoft, you
wot what : which wordes are of more power to
blow him away, then if they firde him thence with
traines of gunpowder.   By meanes of this *Iump*,
fome *Victuallers* haue leaped cleane out of doores
and with the fall haue beene ready to lie in the
ftreetes.

The third *Iump* is called *Fawning* : thofe that
leape at it are *Fawneguefts* ; and that is done in
the edge of an euening, when a *Cheater* meeting
a ftranger in the darke and taking him for another,
gets the ftranger by fome flight to a Tauerne,
where calling for two pintes of fundry wines, the
drawer fetting the wines downe with two cups, as

the cuſtome is, the *Iumper* taſtes of one pinte (no matter which) and findes fault with the wine, ſaying tis too hard, but roſe-water and ſugar would ſend it downe merrily ; and for that purpoſe takes vp one of the cuppes, telling the ſtranger he is well acquainted with the Boy at the barre, and can haue two peny worth of roſewater for a peny of him, and ſo ſteps from his ſeate ; the ſtranger ſus· pecting no harme becauſe the *Fawne-gueſt* leaues his cloake at the end of the table behinde him. But this *Iump* comming to be meaſured, it is found that he that went to take his riſing at the barre, hath ſtolne ground and out-leaped the other more féete than he can recouer in haſte, for the cup is leaped away with him, for which the woodcock that is taken in the ſprindge, muſt pay fifty ſhillings or three pound, and hath nothing but an / old thredbare cloake not worth 10 groates to make amends for his loſſes.

The fourth *Iump* is called *Foletaking* ; and that is done feuerall waies, ſometimes by ſetting a couple of ſuttle rogues to ſing ballads on a ſtall, till a number of people preſſe about them to buy their traſh, and then their purſes being diſcouered, are quickly in the *Nips* fingers.   Others are *Foole-taken* by letting chambers to fellowes like ſeruing-men, in the name of ſuch an Eſquire, or ſuch a Knight, or ſuch a Captaine new come frō the low countries, bringing in a trunck exceeding heauy, and crambd full of brick-bats, which is left in the hired chamber, & fiue times the value of it lifted away in ftead of it. With this *Iump*, many maid-feruants, and their wealthy Maifters haue beene ouer-reached by counterfeit kinfemen that haue brought a cheefe or a gammon of Bacon to the poore wench, claiming kinred of her whether fhe will or no, and afterwards beeing (for his cheefe and bacon) inuited to the Citizens table, haue in the night time taken away plate, or other com-modities in exchange of his white-meates.

The fift *Iump*, is called *Spoone-meate*, and that is a meffe of knauerie ferued in about Supper time in the edge of an euening likewife : It is done thus : A filly fellow in fhew, attired like a clowne, fpurnes (being nere fome candle that ftāds on a ftall) a paper before him, in which is wrapt vp a fpoone : taking vp which and looking on it by the light, and making it knowne (by his loud talking & wondring what he hath found) that he tooke it vp by chance, people flock about him, and imagine it is a filuer and guilt fpoone, for it lookes very faire, but he feeming to be an innocent coxcomb, knowes not, hee faies what hee fhould doe with fuch a gew-gawe ; whereupon euery one is catching at it, and offers him money for it : he wifhes he had rather found money than fuch a

bable, for he eates not his pottage in plate ; in the
end fome Fox amongft all the Cubbes that ftand
about him, whifpers in his eare, to haue it from
all the reft and thrufts a crowne priuily into his
hand. The *Iumper* takes it, and fneakes away,
the other gets home as faft as he can, longing till
he call his wife, all his houfhold and neighbors
about him, to fhewe what a penyworth / hee met
with ; but the gilt fpoone comming to be tried of
what mettall hee is made, the poore mans money
prooues copper, and hee himfelfe is laughed at for
a *Coxcomb.*

How long fhall I faile vpon thefe godleffe
waters?   Is it not time to get to fhore?   Is it
not fit that I fhould now found a retreate and
not weary my pen in the execution of fuch bafe
and barbarous minded Caitiefs?   What a battaile
haue I vndertaken? and with what an ignoble
enemie ? to contend with whom is an act in-
glorious, and to conquer whom, (but that they
are open and profeffed foes to the *Republick,* to
honefty, to ciuility, and to all humanity) were
afmuch difhonor, as by them to be ouercome?
Who would imagine that in a Kingdom fo fertile
in all forts of wholefome difcipline, there fhould
grow vp fuch ranck and fuch peftilent beds of
hemlock : that in the very hart of a ftate fo rarely
gouerned & dieted by good lawes, there fhould

breede fuch loathfome and fuch vlcerous impos-
tumes? that in a City fo politick, fo ciuill, and fo
feuere, fuch vgly, bafe, and bold impieties dare
fhew their faces? What an Army of infufferable
Abufes, deteftable *Vices*, moft damnable *Villanies*,
abominable *Pollutions*, inexplicable *Mifchiefes*, *for-
did Inquinations, horrible* and *Hel-hound-like-
perpetrated* flagitious enormities haue beene here
miniftred together? vnder what diuellifh commanders are they conducted? what colors of
damnation doe they fight vnder? what difmal
Enfignes doe they fpred? what forces doe they
bring into the field? how full of courage they
are? how full of cunning? how politick are the
Ringleaders of thefe *Faries*? how refolute are all
ẙ troopes? what ftrange Armor haue they (of
fubtiltie, & defperate boldnes) to encounter and
fet vpon their oppofites? what Artillery haue
they to batter downe Order, Law, cuftome, plaine
dealing, and all the goode guards and defences of
Gouernement? What remaineth therefore, (in an
affault fo dangerous to a Common wealth, and fo
hotly and daily profecuted,) but that Iuftice her felfe
muft come into the field, leading with her all her
forces? That the *Triple Body* of the ftate may
knit all their *Nerues* together and fit in Counfell,
fetting downe ftratagems and lawes how to race
for euer (out of fo noble a Kingdome) fuch / rebels

to the peace and honour of it : That the Reuerend
Iudges may (out of a deteftation of the liues of
thefe monfters) lock vp their eies and eares from
pitty, when any of thefe *Sauages* are caught and
brought before them : That all inferior minifters
of Iuftice, may be vigilant, faithfull and feuere in
hunting them into Gaoles, that are the fitteft
toyles for them to fall into, and that the hang-
man may not lie lazing & complaine for want
of worke, fo many infected bodies being to bee
found in euery corner of the Land, whom no
medicine can cure, but the phyfick which hee
beftowes vpon him at the *Gallowes?* Where
I leaue them, as to the hauen in which they
muft all caft anchor, if *Dericks* Cables doe
but hold, (and vnleffe they amend.) Giue
thankes to *The Bel-man* of *London,*
if either profit or pleafure
bee gained by the
Difcouerie.

FINIS. /

XI.

LANTHORNE
AND CANDLE-LIGHT.

1609.

NOTE.

See note before the preceding ' Bel-man ' book ; and our Memorial-Introduction.—G.

LANTHORNE
and Candle-light.

OR,
The Bell-Mans ſecond Nights-walke.

In which
He brings to light, a Brood of more ſtrange Villanies
then euer were till this yeare diſcouered.

Decet nouiſſe malum, feciſſe, nefandum.

The ſecond edition, newly correɛted and amended.

LONDON
Printed for Iohn Buſby, *and are to be ſolde at his ſhop in* Fleete-
ſtreete, in Saint Dunſtanes Church-yard. 1609.

To the verry worthy Gentleman Maifter
Francis Muftian *of Peckam*.

Sir.

IT may (happily) feeme ftrange vnto you, that fuch an army of *Idle-words* fhould march into the open field of the world vnder the *Enfigne* of your *Name*: (you beeing not therewith made acquainted till now) you may iudge it in me an *Error*, I my felfe con-feffe it a boldneffe. But fuch an ancient & ftrong *Charter* hath Cuftome confirmed to *This Printing age of ours*, (by giuing men authoritie to make choice of what *Patrons* they like,) that fome *Writers* do almoft nothing contrary to ỹ cuftome, and fome by vertue of that Priuiledge, dare doe any thing. I am neither of *that firft order*, nor of *this laft*. The one is too fondly-ceremonious, the other too impudently audacious. I walk in the midft (fo well as I can) betweene both : with fome fruites that haue growne out of my *Braine*, haue I bin fo farre from being in loue, that I thought them not worthy to be tafted by any

particular friend, & therefore haue they bin ex
pofed only to thofe that would entertain them :
neither did I thinke the *Faireſt* that euer was
Mine, fo worthy, that it was to be lookd vpon
with the *Eye* of *vniuerfal cenfure.* Two forts
of *mad-men* trouble the *ſtationers* fhops in *Paules
Church-yard* : they that out of a *Meere* and *Idle
vaine-glory* will euer be *Pamphleting* (tho their
bookes beeing printed are fcarfe worth fo much
Browne paper), and this is a very poore, and foolifh
ambition : Of the other fort are they that beeing
free of *Wits Merchant-venturers*, do euery new
moon (for gaine onely) make 5. or 6. voiages to
the *Preſſe*, and euery *Term-time* (vpon *Bookfellers
ſtalles*) lay whole litters of blinde inuention : fellowes ẙ (if they do but walke in the middle Ile)
fpit nothing but ynck, and fpeake nothing but
Poeme. I would keepe company with neither of
thefe two *mad-men*, if I could auoid them, yet I
take the laſt to be the wifeſt and leſſe dangerous :
for fithence al the arrowes that men fhoote in the
world, flye to two marks only (either pleafure or
profit) he is not much to be cōdemned that hauing
no more *Acres* to liue vppon then thofe that lie in
his head, is euery houre hammering out one peice
or other out of this ruſty *Iron age*, fithence the
golden and filuer *Globes* of the world are fo locked
vp, that a Scholler can hardly be fuffred to behold

them. Some perhaps wil fay, that this lancing of the peftilent fores of a Kingdome fo openly, may infect thofe in it that are found, and that in this our fchoole, (where clofe abufes / & grofe villanies are but difcouered and not punifhed) others that neuer before knew fuch euils, wil be now inftructed (by the booke) to practife them. If fo, then let not a traitor, or a Murderer be publikely arraigned, left the one laying open to the world, how his plots were wouen to contriue a treafon, or the other, what pollicies he was armed with, for the *fhedding of blood*, the ftanders-by (that are honeft) be drawn (by their rules) to run head-long into the fame mifchiefe : no, Our ftrong phificke works otherwife. What more makes a man to loath that *Mongrell Madneſſe* (that halfe Englifh, halfe Dutch finne) *Drunken-neſſe*, then to fee a common *Drunkard* acting his *Scænes* in the open ftreete? Is any *Gameſter* fo foolifh to play with falfe *Dice*, when he is affured that al who are about him know him to be a *Sworne Cheator*? The letting therfore of *Vice* blood in thefe feuerall *Veines*, which the *Bel-man* hath opend, cannot by any Iudicial rules of phificke, endanger the Bodie of the Common-wealth, or make it feeble, but rather reftore thofe parts to perfect ftrength, which by diforder haue ben difeafed.

Giue mee leaue to lead you by the hand into
a *Wilderneſſe* (where are none but *Monſters*, whoſe
crueltie you need not feare, becauſe I teach the
way to tame them : vgly they are in ſhape and
diueliſh in conditions : yet to behold them a far
off, may delight you, and to know their quallities
(if euer you ſhould come neere them) may ſaue
you from much danger.)   Our Country breedes no
Wolues nor Serpents, yet *Theiſe* ingender here, and
are either *Serpents* or *Wolues*, or worſe then both :
what ſoeuer they are, I ſend vnto you not the Heard
of the one, or the Bed of the other, but only a
Picture of either.   View them I pray, and where
the cullours are not well layde on, ſhadow them
with your finger : if you ſpy any diſproportion,
thus excuſe it, ſuch *Painting is fit for Monſters* :
How rudely ſoeuer the Peece is drawne, call it a
Picture.   And when *one* more worthe your viewe
lies vnder the workemans pencil, this *Bad-one*
ſhall bring you home a *Better* : In the meane
time, I ceaſe, and begin to be (if you pleaſe)

All yours,

THOMAS DEKKER.

To my owne Nation.

Readers,

*A*Fter it was proclaimed abroad, that (vnder the conduct of the Bel-man of London,) *new forces were (once more) to bee leauied againſt certaine Wilde and Barbarous Rebells, that were vp in open armes againſt the Tranquilitie of the* Weale publique: *It cannot bee tolde, what numbers of voluntaries offred themſelues dayly to fight againſt ſo common, ſo bolde, ſo ſtrange, and ſo dangerous an enemy.* Light Horſe-men *came in hourely, with diſcouerie where theſe* Mutineeres *lay intrenched: deliuering (in briefe notes of intelligence) who were their* Leaders, *how they went* Armed, *and that they ſerued both on Horſe & Foot; only their* Strengthes *could not bee diſcryed, becauſe their* Numbers *were held infinite. Yet inſtructions were written and ſent euerie minute by thoſe that were Fauourers of Goodneſſe ſhewing what Militarie Diſciplines the foe vſed in his* Battailes, *and what* Forts *(if hee were put at any time to flight) he wold retire to;*

*vvhat ſtratagems hee would praĉtize and where he
did determine to lye in* Ambuſcado. *They that could
not ſerue in perſon in* This Noble quarrell *ſent their*
Auxiliary *Forces, well armed with Counſell. So that
the* Bel-man *(contrarie to his owne hopes,) ſeeing
himſelfe ſo ſtrongly and ſtrangely ſeconded by
friends, doth now brauely aduance forward in maine
battalion. The day of encounter is appointed to be
in this* Michaelmas Tearme. *The place,* Paules
Chur[c]h-yard, Fleeteſtreet, *and other parts of
the Cittie. But before they ioyne, let me giue you
note of one thing, and that is this.*

There is an Vſurper, *that of late hath taken
vppon him the name of the* Bel-man, *but being not
able to maintaine / that Title, hee doth now call
himſelfe the* Bel-mans *brother: his ambition is
(rather out of vaine glorie then the true courage
of an Experienced Soldier) to haue the leading of
the* Van, *but it ſhall be honor good enough for him
(if not too good) to come vp with the* Rere. *You
ſhall know him by his Habiliments, for (by the
furniture he weares) hee will bee taken for a Beadle
of* Bridewell. *It is thought he is rather a Newter
than a friend to the cauſe: and therefore the* Bel-
man *dooth heere openly proteſt that he comes into the
field as no fellowe in armes with* Him.

*Howſoeuer it be ſtrucke, or whoſoeuer giues the
firſt blow, the viĉtorie depends vpon the vallor of you*

that are the Winges to the Bel-mans army; *for which conqueſt he is in hope you will valiantly fight, ſithence the quarrel is againſt the head of monſtrous abuſes, and the blowes which you muſt giue are in defence of* Law, Iuſtice, Order, Ceremony, Religion, Peace, *and that honorable title of* Goodneſſe.

Saint George! *I ſee the two* Armies *mooue forward: and beholde, the* Bel-man *himſelfe firſt chargeth vppon the face of the Enemy. Thus:*

To the Author.

HOw e're thou maift by blazing all *Abuſe*,
  Incurre fuſpect, thou ſpeak'ſt what thou
    haſt prou'd,
    (Tho then to keepe it cloſe it thee
    behou'd,
So, *Reaſon* makes for thee a iuſt excuſe)
Yet of thy paines the *Beſt* may make good vſe;
Then of the *Beſt*, thy paines ſhould be approu'd,
And for the fame of them ſhouldſt be belou'd.
Sith thou of *Falſehoods Floud* do'ſt ope the *Sluce*,
That they at waſte continually may runne,
By ſhewing men the *Reaches* that they haue,
That honeſt men may ſo or'e-reach a *Knaue*,
Or found their ſwallowing *Deepes*, the ſame to
  ſhunne :
But if from hence, a *Knaue* more cunning growes,
That *Spider* ſucks but poiſon from thy *Roſe*.

                    Thy friend if thine owne,
                        Io : Da :

To his Friend.

F *Vice*, whofe *Counter-mine* a ftate con-
       founds,
    Worfe then *Sedition* : of thofe Mortall
       Woundes
Which (throughly fearch'd) doe *Kingdomes* hearts
    endanger :
Of *Plagues* that o're run Citties : of thofe ftranger
Big-fwolne Impoftumes, poifning the ftrong health
Of the moft *Sound*, beft *Dieted Common-wealth*,
Thou tell'ft the *Caufes*, and doeft teach the *Cure*,
By *Mea'cine* well-compounded, cheape, and fure :
And (as *One* read in deepe *Chirurgery*,)
Draw'ft of thefe *Eu'lls*, the true Anatomy.
Then, on thy *Plainneffe* let none lay reproofe,
Thou tak'ft *Sinne's* heigth (as men doe ftarres)
    aloofe.

                          M: R:

To my induſtrious friend.

IN an ill *Time* thou writ'ſt, when Tongues had rather
Spit venome on thy lines, then from thy labours
(As *Druggiſts* doe from poiſon) medicine gather ;
This is no *Age* to crowne *Deſert* with *Fauors*.
But be thou *Conſtant* to thy ſelfe, and care not
What Arrowes Mallice ſhootes : the *Wiſe* will neuer
Blame thy Lowd ſinging, and the Fooliſh dare not :
None elſe but *Wolues* will barke at thine *Endeuor*.
When thou (in thy dead Sleepe) lieſt in thy *Graue*,
Theſe *Charmes* to after-Ages vp ſhall raiſe thee ;
What heere thou leau'ſt, aliue thy *Name* ſhall ſaue,
And what thou now diſpraiſeſt, ſhall then *praiſe* thee.
Tho, *Not to know ill*, be wiſe *Ignorance*,
Yet thou (by *Reading Euill*) doeſt *Goodneſſe* teach,
And, of *abuſe* the *coullors* dooſt aduance
Onely vpon *abuſe* to force a *breach* ;
The honor that thy *pen* ſhall earne thereby,
Is this : *that tho Knaues Liue, their ſlights (Here) dye*.

E: G:

Lanthorne & Candle-light,
Or
The Bell-mans ſecond Nights walke.

Of Canting,

How long it hath beene a language: how it comes
to bee a language: how it is deriued, & by
whom it is ſpoken.

CHAP. I.

Hen all the *World* was but *one*
Kingdome, all the *People* One language
in that Kingdome ſpake through all
the world at
but one language. A the beginning.
man could trauell in thoſe dayes
neither by Sea nor land, but he mett his Country-
men & none others.

Two could not then ſtand gabling with ſtrange
tongues, and conſpire together (to his owne face)
how to cut a third mans throat, but he might

vnderftand them.   There was no *Spaniard* (in that
Age) to Braue his enemy in the Rich and Lofty
Caftilian: no *Romaine* Orator to plead in the
Rethoricall and *Fluent Latine*: no *Italian* to court
his Miftris in the fwéete and Amorous *Thufcane*:
no *French-man* to parley in the full and ftately
phrafe of *Orleans*: no *Germaine* to thunder out
the high and ratling *Dutch*: the vnfruitfull
crabbed *Irifh*, and the Voluble fignificant *Welch*,
were not then fo much as fpoken of: the quick
Scottifh Dialect (fifter to the *Englifh*) had not then
a tongue, neither were the ftringes of the *Englifh*
fpéech (in thofe times) vntyed.   When / fhe firft
learn'd to fpeake, it was but a broken language:
the fingleft and the fimpleft *Words* flowed from
her vtteráce: for fhe dealt in nothing but in *Mono-
fillables*, (as if to haue fpoken words of greater
length would haue crackt her Voice) by which
meanes her *Eloquence* was pooreft, yet hardeft to
learne, and fo (but for neceffity) not regarded
amõgft *Strangers*.   Yet afterwards thofe

English toung
comparable to
the best.

Nobleft Languages lent her *Words* and
phrazes, and turning thofe *Borrowings*
into *Good hufbandry*, fhée is now as rich in
Elocution, and as *aboundant* as her prowdeft &
Beft-ftored Neighbors.

Whilft thus (as I faid before) there was but
one *Alphabet of Letters*, for all the world to *Read*

by, all the people that then liued, might haue
wrought vpon one péece of worke in countries
farre diftant a funder, without miftaking one
another, and not néeding an *interpreter* to runne
betwéene them. Which thing *Nymrod* (the firft
Idolater,) perceiuing, and not knowing better how
to imploy fo many thoufand Milliōs of *Subiēcts* as
bowed before him, a fire of *Ambition* burn'd
within him, to climbe vp fo high that hee might
fée what was done in heauen : And for that
purpofe, workmen were fummoned from all the
corners of the *Earth*, who prefētly were fet to
Build the Tower of Babell. But the *Maifter
workemā* of this *Great Vniuerfe*, (to
check the *Infolēnce* of fuch a *Sawcie*
builder) that durft raize vp *Pynnacles*, equall to
his owne (aboue), commanded the felfe-fame *Spirit*
that was both bred in the *Chaos* and had mainteind
it in diforder, to bee both *Surueyor* of thofe workes
and *Comptroller* of the *Labourers.* This *Meffenger*
was called *Confufion.* It was a *Spirit* fwift of fight,
& faithfull of feruice. Her lookes wilde,
terrible and inconftant. Her attire, care-
lefly loofe, and of a thoufand feuerall coulors. In
one hand fhée grip'd a heape of ftormes with
which (at her pleafure) fhe could trouble ỹ waters:
In the other fhe held a whip, to make thrée
Spirits that drew her, to gallop fafter before her :

*Building of
Babell.*

Confusion
described.

the *Spirits* names were / *Treafon, Sedition,* & *War,* who at euery time when they went abroad, were ready to fet *Kingdomes* in an vproare. She roade vpon a Chariot of Clowdes, which was alwayes furnifhed with *Thunder, Lightning, Winds, Raine, Haile-ftones, Snow,* & all the other Artillery belonging to the feruice of *Diuine Vengeance,* & when fhe fpake, her *Voyce* founded like the roaring of many *Torrents,* boyftroufly ftrugling together, for betweene her Iawes did fhe carry 1000000. *Tongues.*

This ftrange *Linguift,* ftepping to euery Artificer that was there at worke, whifpred in his eare; whofe lookes were there-vpon (prefently) fild with a ftrange diftraction : and on a fuddaine whilft euery man was fpeaking to his fellow, his language altred, and no man could vnderftand what his fellow fpake. They all ftared one vpon another, yet none of them all could tell wherefore fo they ftared. Their *Tongues* went, and their hands gaue action to their *Tongues* : yet neither words nor action were vnderftood. It was a Noife of a thoufand founds, and yet the found of the noife was nothing. Hée that fpake, knew hée fpake well : and he that heard, was madde that the other could fpeake no better. In the end they grew angry one with another, as thinking they had mocked one another of purpofe. So

Beginning of languages.

that the *Mafon* was ready to ftrike the *Bricklayer*,
the *Bricklayer* to beate out the braines of his
Labourer : the *Carpenter* tooke vp his Axe to
throw at the *Caruer*, whilft the *Caruer* was ftab-
bing at the *Smith*, becaufe hee brought him a
Hāmer when he fhould haue made him a *Chizzell*.
He that called for *Timber*, had *Stones* laide before
him, & when one was fent for *Nailes*, he fetcht a
Tray of Mortar.

Thus *Babell* fhould haue béene raized, and by
this meanes *Babell fell*. The Frame could not
goe forward, the ftuffe was throwne by, the
workemen made hollyday. Euery one packd vp
his tooles to be gone, yet not to goe the fame
way that he came : but glad was he, that could
méete another, whofe fpéech hee vnderftood : for
to what / place foeuer he went, others (that ran
madding vp and downe) hearing a man fpeake
like themfelues, followed onely him : fo that they
who when the worke began were all countrimen,
before a quarter of it was finifhed, fled from one
another, as from enemies & ftrãgers : And in this
maner did Men at the firft make vp natiõs : thus
were words coynd into *Languages*, & out of thofe
Languages haue others béene molded fince, onely
by the mixture of nations, after kingdomes haue
béen fubdued. But I am now to fpeake of a
People & a *Language*, of both which (many

thoufands of yeares fince that *Wonder* wrought at *Babell*) the world till now neuer made mention: yet confufion neuer dwelt more amongft any *Creatures.* The *Bell-mā* (in his firft *Voyage* which he made for *Difcoueries*) found them to bée *fauages*, yet liuing in an Iland very tēperate, fruitfull, full of a Noble Nation, and rarely gouerned. The Lawes, Māners and habits of thefe *Wild-men*, are plainly fet downe, as it were in a former painted *Table.* Yet leaft happily a *ftranger* may looke vpon this fecond *Picture* of them, who neuer beheld *The firft*, it fhal not bée amiffe (in this place) to repeate ouer againe the *Names* of all the *Tribes* into which they *Diuide* themfelues, both when they *Serue* abroad in the open fields, and when they lye in garrifon within *Townes* & walled *Citties.*

The *Bellmans* first booke.

And thefe are their Rankes as they ftand in order. *viz.*

Rufflers.
Vpright-men.
Hookers, *alias* Anglers.
Roagues.
Wilde Roagues.
Priggers of Prancers.
Paillards.
Fraters.

Prigges.
Swadders.
Curtalls.
Irifh Toyles.
Swigmen.
Iarkmen.
Patricoes.
Kinchin-Coes.

Abra / ham-men.	Glymmerers.
Mad Tom *alias of* Bed-	Bawdy-Baſkets.
lam.	Autem Morts.
Whip-Iackes.	Doxies.
Counterfet Crankes.	Dells.
Dommerats.	Kinchin-Morts.

Into thus many *Regiments* are they now deuided: but in former times (aboue foure hundred yeares now paſt) they did conſiſt of fiue Squadrons onely.

viz.
1. Curſitors, alias Vagabondes.
2. Faytors.
3. Robardſemen.
4. Draw-latches.
5. Sturdy Beggars.

And as theſe people are ſtrange both in names and in their conditions, ſo doe they ſpeake a Language (proper only to theſelues) called *canting*, _{Of canting.} which is more ſtrange. By none but _{How long.} the ſouldiers of *Theſe tottred bandes* is it familiarly or vſually ſpoken, yet within leſſe than foureſcore yeares (now paſt) not a word of this Lãguage was knowen. The firſt Inuentor of it, was _{Canting hath} hang'd; yet left he apt ſchollers behind _{bin vſed.} _{The first can-} him, who haue reduced that into *Methode*, _{ter hanged.} which he on his death-bed (which was a paire of gal-lowes) could not ſo abſolutely perfe&ct as he deſired.

It was neceffary, that a people (fo faft increafing, & fo daily practifing new & ftrange *Villanies*), fhould borrow to themfelues a fpéech, w̃ (fo neere as they could) none but themfelues fhould vnderftand : & for that caufe was this Language, (which fome call *Pedlers Frēch,*) In-

How canting grevv to be a language.

uēted, to th'intent that (albeit any Spies fhould fecretly fteale into their cōpanies to difcouer thē) they might fréely vtter their mindes one to another, yet auoide ẙ dãger. The Language therefore of *canting*, they ftudy euen from their Infancy, that is to fay, from the very firft houre, that they take vpon them the names of *Kinchin Coes*, till they are grown *Rufflers*, or *Vpright men*, which are the higheft in degrée amongft them.

This / word *canting* féemes to bee deriued from the latine *verbe (canto)* which fignifies in Englifh, to fing, or to make a found with words, thats to fay to fpeake. And very aptly may *canting* take his deriuatiō *a cantando*, from finging, becaufe amongft thefe beggerly conforts that can play vpon no better inftruments, the language of *canting* is a kinde of muficke, and he that in fuch affemblies can *cant* beft, is counted the beft Mufitian.

Now as touching the Dialect or phrafe it felfe, I fée not that it is grounded vpon any certaine rules; And no meruaile if it haue none, for fithence both the *Father* of this new kinde of Learning, and the *children* that ftudy to fpeake it after him, haue beene from the beginning and ftil are, the *Breeders* and *Norifhers* of a bafe diforder, in their liuing and in their *Manners*: how is it poffible, they fhould obferue any *Method* in their fpeech, and efpecially in fuch a Language, as ferues but onely to vtter difcourfes of villanies?

And yet (euen out of all that *Irregularity* vnhanfomneffe, & Fountaine of *Barbarifme*) do they draw a kinde of forme : and in fome wordes, (afwell fimple as compounds) retaine a certaine falte, tafting of fome wit and fome Learning. As for example, they call a cloake (in the *canting* tongue) a *Togeman*, and in Latin, *Toga* fignifies a gowne, or an vpper garment. *Pannam* is bread : & *Panis* in Lattin is likewife bread, *caffan* is cheefe, and is a worde barbaroufly coynd out of the fubftātiue *cafeus* which alfo fignifies a chéefe. And fo of others.

Then by ioyning of two fimples, doe they make almoft all their compounds. As for example : *Nab* (in the *canting* tongue) The Dialect of canting. is a head, & *Nab-cheate*, is a hat or a cap, Which word *cheate* beeing coupled to other wordes, ftands in verry good ftead, and does excellent feruice : For a *Smelling cheate*, fignifies a Nofe : a *Prat-*

ling chete, is a tongue.   *Crashing chetes,* are teeth:
Hearing chetes are Eares : *Fambles* are Hands :
and therevpon a ring is called a *Fabling chete.*
A *Muffling chete,* signifies / a Napkin.   A *Belly
chete,* an Apron : A *Grunting chete,* a Pig : A
Cackling Chete, a Cocke or a Capon : A *Quacking
chete,* a duck : A *Lowghing chete,* a *Cow* : A
Bleating chete, a Calfe, or a Sheepe : and so may
that word be marryed to many others besides.

The word *Coue,* or *Cofe,* or *Cuffin,* signifies a
Man, a Fellow, &c.   But differs something in
his propertie, according as it meetes with other
wordes : For a Gentleman is called a *Gentry Coue,*
or *Cofe* : A good fellow is a *Bene Cofe* : a Churle
is called, a *Quier Cuffin* ; *Quier* signifies naught,
and *Cuffin* (as I said before) a man : and in
Canting they terme a Iustice of peace, (becaufe
he punisheth them belike) by no other name
then by *Quier cuffin,* that is to say a Churle, or
a naughty man.   And so, *Ken* signifiing a house,
they call a prison, a *Quier ken,* thats to say, an
ill house.

Many peeces of this strange coyne could I shew
you, but by these small stampes, you may iudge
of the greater.

Now becaufe, a Language is nothing els, then
heapes of wordes, orderly wouen and compofed
together : and that (within so narrow a circle as

I haue drawne to my felfe) it is impoffible to imprint a *Dictionarie* of all the Canting phrafes : I wil at this time not make you furfet on too much, but as if you were walking in a Garden, you fhall openly pluck here a flower, and there another, which (as I take it) will be more delightfull then if you gathered them by handfulls.

But before I lead you into that walke, ftay and heare a *Canter* in his owne language, making Rithmes, albeit (I thinke) thofe charmes of *Poefie* which (at the firft) made the barbarous tame, and brought them to ciuillity, can (vppon thefe fauage Monfters) worke no fuch wonder. Yet thus he finges (vppon demaund whether any of his owne crue did come that way) to which he anfwers, yes (quoth he)

Canting / rithmes.

E *Nough—with bowfy Coue maund Nace,*
Tour the Patring Coue in the Darkeman Cafe,
Docked the Dell, for a Coper meke,
His wach fhall feng a Prounces Nab-chete,
Cyarum, by Salmon, and thou fhalt pek my Iere
In thy Gan, for my watch it is nace gere,
For the bene bowfe my watch hath a win &c.

This fhort Leffon I leaue to be conftrued by him that is defirous to try his fkill in the language, which he may do by helpe of the following *Dic-*

tionary ; into which way that he may more redily come, I will tranflate into Englifh, this broken French that followes in Profe. Two *Canters* hauing wrangled a while about fome idle quarrell, at length growing friends, thus one of them fpeakes to the other, *viz.*

A Canter in profe.

S *Towe you beene Cofe : and cut benar whiddes and bing we to Rome vile, to nip a boung : fo fhall wee haue lowre for the bowfing ken, & when we beng back to the Dewefe a vile, we will filch fome Duddes off the Ruffmans, or mill the Ken for a lagge of Dudes.*

Thus in Englifh

Stowe you, beene cofe : hold your peace good fellow.
And cut benar whiddes : and fpeake better words.
And bing we to Rome vile : and goe we to London.
To nip a boung : to cut a purfe.
So fhall we haue lowre : fo fhall we haue mony.
For the bowfing Ken : for the Ale-houfe.
And when we bing backe : and when we come backe.
To the Dewfe-a-vile : into the Country.
We will filch fome duddes : we will filch fome clothes.
Off the Ruffmans : from the hedges.
Or mill the Ken : or rob the houfe.
For a lagge of Duddes : for a bucke of clothes.

Now | turne to your dictionary.

ANd becaufe you fhall not haue one difh twice fet before you, none of thofe *Canting* wordes that are englifhed before fhall here be found : for our intent is to feaft you with varietie.

The Canters Dictionarie.

A Vtem, a church.
 Autem-mort, a married woman.
 Boung, a purfe.
 Borde, a fhilling.
 Half a Borde, fix pence.
 Bowfe, drinke.
 Bowfing Ken, an ale-houfe.
 Bene, good.
 Benefhip, very good.
 Bufe, a Dogge.
 Bing a waft, get you hence.
 Cafter, a Cloake.
 A Commiffion, a fhirt.
 Chates, the Gallowes.
 To cly the Ierke, to be whipped.
 To cutt, to fpeake.
 To cutt bene, to fpeake gently.
 To cutt bene whiddes, to fpeake good wordes.
 To cutt quier whiddes, to giue euill language.
 To Cant, to fpeake.

To couch a Hogſhead, to lye downe a ſleepe.

Drawers, Hoſen.

Dudes, clothes.

Darkemans, the night.

Dewſe-a-vile, the country.

Dup the Giger, open the dore.

Fambles, hands.

Fambling Chete, a Ring.

Flag, a Goat.

Glaſiers, eyes.

Gan, a mouth.

Gage, / a Quart pott.

Grannam, Corne.

Gybe, a writing.

Glymmer, fire.

Gigger, a doore.

Gentry Mort, a Gentlewoman.

Gentry cofes Ken, a Noble mans houſe.

Harman bek, a Conſtable.

Harmans, the Stockes.

Heaue a bough, rob a Boothe.

Iarke, a Seale.

Ken, a houſe.

Lage of Dudes, a Bucke of clothes.

Libbege, a bed.

Lowre, money.

Lap, Butter, Milke, or Whaye.

Libken, a houſe to lye in.

Lage, Water.
Light-mans, the day.
Mynt, Golde.
A Make, a halfe-penny.
Margery prater, a Henne.
Mawnding, afking.
To Mill, to fteale.
Mill a Ken, rob a houfe.
Nofegent, a Nunne.
Niggling, companying with a woman.
Pratt, a Buttock.
Peck, meate.
Poplars, Pottage.
Prancer, a Horfe.
Prigging, Riding.
Patrico, a Prieft.
Pad, a Way.
Quaromes, a body.
Ruffpeck, Bacon.
Roger, or Tib of the Buttry, a Goofe.
Rome / -vile, London.
Rome-bowfe, Wine.
Rome-mort, a Quéene.
Ruffmans, the woodes, or bufhes.
Ruffian, the Diuell.
Stampes : legges.
Stampers : fhooes.
Slate : a fhéete.

Skew : a cup.

Salomon : the maſſe.

Stuling ken : a houſe to receiue ſtolne goods.

Skipper : a barne.

Strommel, ſtraw.

Smelling chete, an Orchard or Garden.

To ſcowre the Cramp-ring : to weare boults.

Stalling : making or ordeyning.

Tryning : hanging.

To twore : to ſée.

Wyn : a penny.

Yarum : milke.

And thus haue I builded vp a little *Mint,* where you may coyne wordes for your pleaſure. The payment of this was a debt : for the *Belman* at his farewell (in his firſt Round which hée walk'd) promiſed ſo much. If hée kéepe not touch, by tendring the due *Summe,* hée deſires forbearance, and if any that is more rich in this *Canting* commodity will lend him any more, or any better, hée will pay his loue double : In the meane time, receiue this, and to giue it a little more weight, you ſhall haue a *Cāting ſong,* wherein you may learne, how *This curſed Generation* pray, or (to ſpeake truth) curſe ſuch Officers as puniſh them.

A Can / ting ſong.

T He Ruffin cly the nab of the Harmanbeck,
*   If we mawnd Pannam, lap or Ruff-peck,*
Or poplars of yarum : he cuts, bing to the Ruffmans,
Or els he ſweares by the light-mans,
To put our ſtamps in the Harmans.
The ruffian cly the ghoſt of the Harmanbeck,
If we heaue a booth we cly the Ierke.

If we niggle, or mill a bowſing Ken,
Or nip a boung that has but a win,
Or dup the giger of a Gentry cofes ken,
To the quier cuffing we bing,
And then to the quier Ken, to ſcowre the Cramp-ring,
And then to the Trin'de on the chates, in the light-
*   mans*
The Bube & Ruffian cly the Harman beck & har-
*   mans.*

Thus Engliſhed.

T He Diuell take the Conſtables head,
    If we beg Bacon, Butter-milke or bread,
Or Pottage, to the hedge he bids vs hie,
Or ſweares (by this light) ith ſtocks we ſhall lie.
The Deuill haunt the Conſtables ghoaſt ;
If we rob but a Booth, we are whipd at a poaſt.

If an ale-houfe we rob, or be tane with a whore,
Or cut a purfe that has iuft a penny and no more,
Or come but ftealing in at a Gentlemans dore;
To the Iuftice ftraight we goe,
And then to the Iayle to be fhackled : And fo
To be hangd on the gallowes ith day time: the
      pox
And the Deuill take the Conftable and his ftocks.

   We haue *Canted* (I feare) too much, let vs now
giue eare to the *Bel-man,* and heare what he fpeaks
in englifh.

THE /
BEL-MANS SECOND
Nights walke.

CHAP. 2

T was Terme time in hel (for you muſt vnderſtand, a Lawyer liues there aſwell as heere:) by which meanes *don Lucifer* (being the iuſtice for that Countie, where the Brimſtone *Qui fixit leges pretio atq; refixit.* mines are) had better dooings and more rapping at his gates, then all the Doctors & Empericall Quack-ſaluers of ten citties haue at theirs in a great plague-time. The hal where theſe Termers were to try their cauſes, was very large and ſtrongly built, but it had *A description of the Hall where matters are tryed in Hell.* one fault: it was ſo hot that people could not indure to walk there: Yet to walke there they were compelled, by reaſon they were drawne thither vppon occaſions; and ſuch iuſtling there was of one another, that it

would haue grieued any man to be in the
thronges amongft em. Nothing could bee heard
Hinc exaudire but noife, and nothing of that noife
gemitus, &c. be vnderftood, but that it was a found
as of men in a kingdome, when on a fuddaine
it is in an vprore. Euery one brabled with him
that he walked with, or if he did but tell his tale
to his Councell, he was fo eager in the verry
deliuery of that tale, that you would haue fworne
he did brabble : and fuch gnafhing of
The iudge of
the court. teeth there was when aduerfaries met
Hæc Rhada-
manthus habet together, that the fyling of ten thoufand
durissima
regna; Casti- Sawes cannot yeeld a found more hor-
gatq; ditq,
dolos, subigitq ; rible. The Iudge of the Court had
sateri, &c.
a diuelifh countenance, and as cruell
hee was in punifhing thofe that were condemned
by Lawe, as hee was crabbed in his lookes,
whilft he fat to heare their tryals. But / albeit
there was no pittie to be expeted at his hands,
yet was he fo vpright in iuftice, that none could
euer faften bribe vppon him, for he was ready
and willing to heare the *cries* of all commers.
Neither durft any Pleader (at the infernall Barre)
or any officer of the Court, exat any Fee of
Plaintiffes, and fuch as complained of
Impios vinclis
perpetuis wrongs and were oppreft : but onely
domant.
they paide that were the wrong dooers ;
thofe would they fee dambd ere they fhould gette

out of their fingers, fuch fellowes they were ap·
pointed to vexe at the very foule.

The matters that here were put in fute, were
more then could bee bred in twentie
Vacations, yet fhould a man be *dis-* The customes and condition
patched out of hand. In one Terme of the court.
he had his Iudgement, for heare they neuer ftand
vppon *Returnes,* but prefently come to Triall.
The caufes decided here are many; the Clients
that complaine many; the Counfellors (that plead
till they be hoarfe,) many; the At- *Vnde nunquā*
tornies (that runne vp and downe,) *quum semel venit potuit*
infinite; the Clarkes of the Court, not *euerti.*
to be numbred. All thefe haue their hands full;
day and night are they fo plagued with the bawling
of Clients, that they neuer can reft.

The Inck where-with they write, is the blood
of Coniurers: they haue no Paper, but all thinges
are engroffed in Parchment, and that Parchment
is made of Scriueners fkinnes flead off, after they
haue beene punifhed for Forgerie: their Standifhes
are the Sculs of Ufurers: their Pennes, the bones
of vnconfcionable Brokers, and hard - hearted
Creditors, that haue made dice of other mens
bones, or elfe of periured Executors and blind
Ouer-féers, that haue eaten vp Widdowes and
Orphanes to the bare bones: and thofe Pennes
are made of purpofe without Nebs, becaufe they,

may caſt Inck but flowly, in mockery of thoſe, who in their life time were flowe in yeelding drops of pitty.

Would you know what actions are tried here?

What matters are tryed before the Diuell. I will but turne ouer the Recordes, and read them vnto you as they hang vppon the Fyle.

The / *Courtier* is fued heere, and condemned for *Ryots*.

The *Soldier* is fued heere and condemned for *murders*.

The *Scholler* is fued here & condemned for *Herezies*.

The *Citizen* is fued here and condemned for the *city-ſins*.

The *Farmer* is fued heere vpon Penal Statutes, and condemned for ſpoyling the *Mar-kets*.

Quiq; arma secuti impia. Epulæq; ante era paratæfuriarum maxima iuxta accubat, & manibus prohibet contingere mensas. Actions of batterie are brought againſt *Swaggerers*; and heere they are bound to the *peace*.

Actions of *Waſte* are brought againſt *drunkards* and Epicures; and heere they are condemned to begge at the Grate for one drop of colde water to coole their tongues, or one crum of breade to ſtay their hunger, yet are they denyed it.

Harlots haue proceſſe fued vpon them heere,

and are condemned to *Howling*, to *Rottenneſſe* and
to *Stench.*   No Actes of Parliament that haue
paſſed the * Vpper- houſe, can be broken,
but here the breach is puniſhed, and that

> * Heauen.

feuerely, and that ſuddenly : For here they ſtand
vppon no *demurres* ; no *Audita-Queræla* can heere
be gotten, no writs of *Errors* to *Reuerſe Iudgement* :
heere is no flying to a *court of Chancery* for releef,
yet euerie one that comes heather is
ferued with a *Sub-pœna.*   No, they deale
altogether in this Court vpon the *Habeas*
Corpus, vpon the *Capias*, vppon the *Ne*

> *Exercentur
> Pœnis, eter-
> nūq; malorum
> Supplicia ex-
> pendunt.*

exeat Regneum, vpon *Rebellion*, vppon heauie *Fines*
(but no *Recoueries*) vpon writers of *Out-lary*, to
attache the body for euer, & laſt of all vppon
Executions, after *Iudgement*, which being feru'd
vpon a man is his *euerlaſting vndooing.*

Such are the Cuſtomes and courſes of pro-
ceedings in the Offices belonging to the Prince
of Darkneſſe.   Theſe hot dooings hath he in
his *Terme-times.*   But vpon a day when a great
matter was to be tryed betweene an *Engliſhman*
and a *Dutchman*, which of the two were the
fowleſt Drinkers, and the caſe being a long time
in arguing, by reaſon that ſtrong euidence came
in reeling on both ſides, (yet it was thought that
the Engliſh-man would / carry it away, and caſt
the Dutchman) on a ſudden all was ſtaid by the

found of a horne that was heard at the lower end of the Hall. And euerie one looking back (as wondring at the ftrangeneffe) roome room was cride and made through the thickeft of the crowde, for a certaine fpirit in the likeneffe of a poft, who made a way on a little leane Nagge vp to the Bench where Iudge *Radamanth* with his two grim Brothers (*Minos* and *Æacus*) fat. This fpirit was an intelligencer fent by *Belzebub* of *Batharum* into fome Countries of Chriftēdome, to lye there as a fpie, & had brought with him a packet of letters from feuerall Leigiars, that lay in thofe Countries, for the feruice of the *Tartarian* their Lord and Maifter, which packet being opened, all the Letters, (becaufe they concernd *Subterranei* the generall good and ftate of thofe *Regni.* lowe Countries in Hell) were publikely reade. The contents of that Letter ftung moft, and put them all out of their law-cafes, were to this purpofe.

THat whereas the Lord of Fiery Lakes, had his Minifters in all kingdomes aboue the earth, whofe Offices were not onely to winne fubiects of other Princes to his obedi- *A letter* ence, but alfo to giue notice when any *against the* *Bel-man.* of his owne fworn houfhold, or any other that held league with him fhould reuolt or

flye from their duty & allegiance: as alſo dis-
couer from time to time all plots, conſpiracies,
machinations, or vnderminings, that ſhold be laid
(albeit they that durſt lay them ſhould dig deepe
enough) to blow vp his great Infernall cittie : ſo
that if his Horned Regiment were not ſuddenly
muſtred together, and did not luſtely beſtirre their
clouen ſtumps, his Territories wold be ſhaken, his
dominions left in time vnpeopl'd, his forces look'd
into, and his authoritie which hee held in the
world, contemned & laughed to ſcorne. The
reaſon was, ẏ a certaine fellow, The
Childe of Darkenes, a common Night- The Belman.
walker, a man that had no man to waite vppon him
but onely a Dog, one that was a diſordered perſon,
and | at midnight would beate at mens doores, bidding
them (in meere mockerie) to look to their candles
when they themſelues were in their dead ſleeps : and
albeit he was an Officer, yet he was but of Light-
carriage, being knowne by the name of the Bell-man
of London, had of late not only drawne a number
of the Deuils owne kindred into queſtion for
their liues, but had alſo (only by the help of the
lanthorn & candle) lookt into the ſecrets of the
beſt trades that are taught in hell, laying them
open to the broad eye of the world, making them
infamous, odious, and ridiculous : yea, and not
ſatisfied with dooing this wrong to his diuellſhip,

very fpitefullye hath hee fet them out in print,
drawing their pictures fo to the life, that now a
horfe-ftealer fhall not fhew his head, but a halter
with the Hang-mans noofe is ready to bee faftned
about it : A Foyft nor a Nip fhall not walke into
a Fayre or a Play-houfe, but euerie cracke will cry
looke to your purfes : nor a poore common Rogue
come to a mans doore, but he fhall be examined
if he can *cant* ? If this Baulling fellow therefore
haue not his mouth ftop'd, the light Angels that
are coynd below, will neuer bee able to paffe as
they haue done, but be naild vp for counterfeits.
Hell will haue no dooings, and the deuill be
no-body.

This was the lyning of the Letter, and this
Letter draue them al to a *Non-plus,* becaufe they
knew not how to anfwere it. But at laft aduice
was taken, the Court brake vp, the Tearme was
adiourn'd, (by reafon that the Hell-houndes were
thus Plagu'd) and a common counfell in hell was
prefetly called how to redres thefe abufes.

The *Sathanicall Sinagogue* beeing fet, vp ftartes
the *Father of Hell* and *damnation,* and looking
verrie terribly with a paire of eies that ftared as
wide as the mouth gapes at Bifhops-gate, fetching
foure or fiue deep fighes (which were nothing
elfe but the Smoke of fire & brimftone boyling
in his ftomacke, and fhewed as if hee were taking

tobacco, which he often times does) tolde his
children & feruãts (& the reft of the citizens
that dwelt within / the freedome of Hel, and
fat there before him vpon narow low formes)
that they neuer had more caufe to lay their
heads together, and to grow pollititians. Hee
and they all knew, that from the Corners of the
earth, fome did euerie houre in a day creepe
forth, to come and ferue him : yea, that *Huc omnis*
many thoufands were fo bewitched with *turba.*
his fauours, and his rare partes, that they would
come running quick to him ; his dominions (he
faid) were great and full of people : Emperors
and Kings, (in infinit numbers) were his flaues :
his court was ful of Princes : if the *Innumeræ*
world were deuided (as fome· report) *gentes populiq;*
but into three parts, two of thofe three were his :
or if (as others affirme) into foure parts, [in]
almoft three of that foure had hee firme footing.

But if fuch a fellow as a treble voic'd *Bel-man*,
fhould be fuffered to pry into the infernal Mis-
teries, & into thofe Black Arts which command
the fpirits of the Deep, & hauing fucked what
knowledge he can from them, to turne it al into
poifon, & to fpit it in the verie faces of the
profeffors, with a malicious intent to make them
appeare vgly and fo to grow hatefull and out
of fauor with ẙ world : if fuch a coniurer at

midnight fhould dance in their circles and not
be driuen out of them, hell in a few yeares would
not bee worth the dwelling in. The great Lord
of Limbo did therefore commaund all his Blacke
Guard that ftood about him, to beftirre them in
their places, and to defend the Court wherein
Graucolentis they liued : threatning (befides) that
Auerni. his curffe, & all the plagues of ftinking
hel fhold fall vpon his officers, feruants, and
fubiects, vnleffe they either aduiz'd him, *how*, or
take fome fpeedy order themfelues to punifh that
faucy intelligencer, the *Bel-man* of London. Thus
he fpake and then fat.

At laft, a foolifh Deuill rofe vp, and fhot the
bolt of his aduice, which flew thus farre, That the
Black-dogge of New-gate fhould againe bee let
loofe, and a farre off, follow the Balling *Bel-man*,
to watch into what places hee went, and what
deedes of darkeneffe (euerie night) / hee did.
Hinc rifus ! The whole Syniodicall affembly, fell
a laughing at this Wife-acre, fo that neither he
nor his blacke-Dogge durft barke any more.

Another, thinking to cleaue the verrie pinne
with his arrow, drew it home to the head of
Wifdome (as he imaginde) ; and yet that lighted
wide too. But thus fhot his Counfell, that the
Ghofts of all thofe theeues, Cheaters, and others
of the damned crew, (who by the *Bel-mans* dis-

couerie, had bene betraied, were taken and fent
weftward) fhould bee fetched from thofe fields
of Horror, where euerie night they walke,
difputing with Doctor *Story*, who keepes them
company there in his corner Cap: & that thofe
wry-neck'd fpirits fhould haue charge giuen them
to haunt the *Bel-man* in his walkes, and fo fright
him out of his wittes. This Deuill for all his
roaring, went away neither with a *Plaudite*, nor
with a hiffe : Others ftep'd vp, fome pronouncing
one verdict fome another : But at the laft, it beeing
put into their Diuelifh heads, that they had no
power ouer *him* farther then what fhold be giuen
vnto them, it was concluded and fet downe as a
rule in Court, that fome one ftrange *fpirit*, who
could tranfport himfelfe into all fhapes, fhould
bee fent vppe to London, and fcorning to take
reuenge vppon fo meane a perfon as a *Bel-ringer*,
fhould thruft himfelfe into fuch companyes, (as in
a warrant to bee figned for that purpofe) fhould
bee nominated : and beeing once growne familiar
with them, hee was to worke and winne them by
all poffible meanes to fight vnder the difmall and
blacke collours of the Grand Sophy, (his Lord
and Mafter) ; the fruite that was to grow vppon
this tree of euill, would bee greate, for it fhould
bee fit to bee ferued vp to *Don Lucifers* Table,
as a new banqueting Difh, fithence all his other

meates, (though they fatted him well) were grown
ftale.

Hereupon *Pamerſiell* the Meſſenger was called,
a paſport was drawne, ſigned and deliuered to him,
with certaine inſtruments how to carry himſelfe in
this trauell. / And thus much was openly ſpoken
to him by word of mouth.

Flye *Pamerſiel* with ſpeede to the great and
populous citie in the Weſt : winde thy ſelfe into
all ſhapes : bee a Dogge (to fawne) a Dragon (to
confound) bee a Doue (ſeeme innocent) bee a
Deuill (as thou art) and ſhew that thou art a
Iorniman to hel. Build rather thy neſt amõgſt
willowes that bend euerie way, then on tops of
Oakes, whoſe hearts are hard to be broken : Fly
with the *Swallow*, cloſe to ẙ earth, when ſtormes
are at hand, but keep company with *Birdes of
greater tallants*, when the weather is cleare, &
neuer leaue them till they looke like Rauens :
creepe into boſoms that are buttond vp in ſattin
and there ſpred the wings of thine infection :
make euerie head thy pillow to leane vpon, or
vſe it like a Mill, onely to grinde miſchiefe. If
thou meetſt a *Dutchman,* drinke with him : if a
Frenchman, ſtab : if a *Spaniard*, betray : if an
Italian poyſon : if an *Engliſhman* doe all this.

Haunt *Tauerns*, there thou ſhalt finde prodigalls:
pay thy two-pence to a *Player*, in his gallerie maiſt

thou fitte by a Harlot: at *Ordinaries* maiſt thou
dine with filken fooles: when the day ſteales out
of the world, thou ſhalt meete rich *drunkards*,
vnder welted gownes ſearch for threeſcore in the
hundred, hugge thoſe golden villaines, they ſhine
bright, and will make a good ſhew in hell, ſhriek
ẘ a cricket in the *brew-houſe*, & watch how they
coniure there: Ride vp and downe *Smith-field*,
and play the Iade there: Viſit priſons, and teach
Iaylors how to make nets of Iron there: binde
thy ſelfe Prentice to the beſt trades: but if thou
canſt grow extreame ritch in a very ſhort time,
(honeſtly) I baniſh thee my kingdome, come no
more into hell: I haue red thee a lecture, followe
it, farewell.

No ſooner was farwell ſpoken, but the ſpirit
to whom all theſe matters were giuen in charge
vaniſhed: the clouen footed Orator aroſe, and
the whole aſſembly went about their damnable
buſineſſe. ·

Gul-/Groping.

How Gentlemen are cheated at Ordinaries.

Chap. 3.

THe Diuels *foote-man* was very nimble of his
héeles (for no wilde-Iriſh man could out-
runne him), and therefore in a few houres, was

he come vp to London : the miles betweene *Hell*
and any place vpon earth being fhorter then thofe
betweene London and Saint Albones, to any man
that trauels from thence thither, or to any Lackey
that comes from hence hether on the Deuils er-
rands : but to any other poore foule, that dwells
in thofe low countries, they are neuer at an end,
and by him are not poffible to bee meafured.

No fooner was he entred into the Cittie, but hee
met with one of his Maifters daughters called
Pride, dreft like a Marchants wife, who taking
acquaintance of him, and vnderftanding for what
hee came, tolde him, that the firft thing hee was
to doe, hee muft put himfelfe in good cloathes,
fuch as were futable to the fafhion of the time,
for that here, men were look'd vppon onely for
their outfides : he that had not ten-pounds worth
of wares in his fhop, would carry twentie markes
Auferimur   on his back : that there were a number
cultu ; Gemmis of fumpter-horfes in the citty, who
aureq ; regnun
-tur omnia.   cared not how courfely they fed, fo
they might weare gay trappings : yea, that fome
pied fooles, to put on fatin and veluet but *foure*
daies in the yeare did often-times vndoe themfelues, wiues and Children euer after. The fpirit
of the *Deuils Buttry* hearing this, made a legge
to *Pride* for her counfell, and knowing by his
owne experience that euerie Taylor hath his hell

to himfelfe, under his Shop-board, (where he
dammes new Sattin) amongft them he thought
to finde beft welcome, and therefore into *Burchin-
lane* hee ftalkes verie mannerly, *Pride* going along
with him, and taking the vpper hand.

No / fooner was he entred into the rankes of
the *Linnen Armorers*, (whofe weapons
are Spanifh needles) but he was moft
terribly and fharpely fet vppon : euerie
prentice boy had a pull at him : he
feared they all had bin *Serieants*, becaufe they all had him by the back : neuer was
poore deuil fo tormented in hell, as he was
amongft them : he thought it had bene Saint
Thomas his day, & that he had bene called vpon
to be *Conftable* : there was fuch balling in his
eares : and no ftrength could fhake them off, but
that they muft fhewe him fome fuites of apparell,
becaufe they faw what Gentlewoman was in his
company (whom they all knew). Seeing no remedie, into a fhop he goes, was fitted brauely,
and beating the price, found the loweft to be
vnreafonable, yet paide it, and departed, none
of them (by reafon of their crowding about him
befor) perceiuing what cuftomer they had met
with ; but now the Taylor fpying the deuill, fuffered him to go, neuer praying that he wold
know the fhop another time, but looking round

Burchin lane
described.

Taylors at first
were called
*Linnen Ar-
morers*. ser-
ieants.

about his ware-houfe if nothing were miffing, at
length he found that he had loft his *côfcience* : yet
remembring himfelfe, that they who deale with
the diuel, can hardly keepe it, he ftood vpon it
the leffe.

The fafhions of an Ordinarie.

THe *Stigian traueller* beeing thus tranflated
into an accomplifh'd gallant, with all
acoutrements belonging (as a fether for his head,
gilt rapier for his fides, & new boots to hide his
polt foote) ; for in Bed-lam hee met with a fhoe-
maker, a mad flaue, that knew the length of his
laft ; it refted, onely that now he was to enter
vppon company futable to his cloathes : and
knowing that your moft felected Gallants are
the onelye table-men that are plaid with al at
Ordinaries, into an *Ordinary* did he moft gentleman like, conuay himfelfe in ftate.

It feemed that al who came thether, had clocks
in their bellies, for they all ftruck into the dyning
roome much about the very minute of feeding.
Our Caualier had all the / eyes (that came in)
throwne vpon him, (as beeing a ftranger : for
no Ambaffador from the diuell euer dined amongft
them before,) and he afmuch tooke efpeciall notes
of them.   In obferuing of whom and of the place,

he found, that an *Ordinary* was the only *Rendeuouz* for the moſt ingenious, moſt terſe, moſt
trauaild, and moſt phantaſtick gallant: the very
Exchange for newes out of al countries: the
only *Booke-ſellers* ſhop for conference of the beſt
Editions, that if a womã (to be a Lady) would
caſt away herſelf vpon a *knight, there* a man ſhould
heare a Catalogue of moſt of the richeſt London
widowes : & laſt, that it was a *ſchoole* where they
were all fellowes of one Forme, & that a country
gentleman was of as great comming as ẙ proudeſt
Iuſtice that ſat there on ẙ bench aboue him : for
he that had the *graine* of the table with his
trencher, payd no more then he that plac'd him-
ſelf beneath the ſalt.

The *diuels intelligencer* could not be contented
to fill his eye onely with theſe obieɕts, and to féed
his belly with delicate chéere : But hée drew a
larger piɕture of all that were there, and in theſe
collours.

The voider hauing cléered the table, *Cardes &*
Dice (for the laſt Meſſe) are ſerued vp to the
boord : they that are ful of coyne, *draw*: they
that haue little, ſtand by & giue *ayme*: they *ſhuffle*
and *cut* on one ſide: the bones *rattle* on the other:
long haue they not plaide, but othes fly vp &
down the roome like haile-ſhot: if the poore
dumb *dice* be but a little out of ſquare, the *pox*

& a thoufand plagues breake their neckes out at window : prefently after, the foure *knaues* are fent packing the fame way, or els (like heretikes are) condemned to be burnt.

In this battaile of *Cardes* and *Dice*, are feuerall Regiments & feuerall Officiers.

They that fit downe to play, are at firft cald *Leaders*.

They that loofe, are the *Forlorne Hope*.

He that winnes all, is the *Eagle*.

He that ftands by & Ventures, is the *Wod-pecker*.

The frefh Gallant that is fetcht in, is the *Gull*.

Hee that ftands by, and lends, is *the Gull-groper*.

The | Gull-groper.

THis *Gul-groper* is commonly an old Mony-mōger, who hauing trauaild through all the follyes of the world in his youth, knowes them well, and fhunnes them in his age ; his whole felicitie being to fill his bags with golde and filuer, hee comes to an Ordinary, to faue charges of houfe-keeping, and will eate for his two fhillings, more meate then will ferue thrée of the guard at a dinner, yet fweares hée comes thether onely for the company, and to conuerfe with trauailers. Its a Gold-Finch that fildome flies to thefe Ordinary Nefts, without a hundred or two hundred pound in twenty fhilling péeces about him. After the

tearing of fome feauen paire of Cardes, or the
damning of fome ten baile of Dice, fteps hée vpon
the Stage, and this part he playes. If any of the
Forlorne Hope bée a Gentleman of meanes, either
in *Eſſe*, or in *Poſſe*, (and that the olde Fox will
bée fure to know to halfe an Acre,) whofe money
runnes at a low ebbe, as may appeare by his
fcratching of the head, and walking vp and downe
the roome, as if he wanted an Oftler : The *Gull-
groper* takes him to a fide window and tels him,
hée's forry to fée his hard luck, but the Dice are
made of womens bones, and will cozen any man,
yet for his father's fake (whom he hath knowne
fo long) if it pleafe him, he fhal not leaue off play
for a hundred pound or two. If my yong Eftrich
gape to fwallow downe this mettall (& for the
moft part they are very gréedy, hauing fuch
prouander fet before them) then is the gold
powred on the board, a Bond is made for repaiment, at the next quarter day when *Exhibition*
is fent in : and becaufe it is all gold, and coft
fo much the changing, The Scriuener (who is a
whelpe of the old Maftiues owne bréeding) knows
what words will bite, which thus he faftens vpō
him, and in this Nette the Gull is fure to be taken
(howfoeuer :) for if he fall to play againe, & loofe,
the hoary Goat-bearded Satyre that ftands at his
elbow, laughes in / his fléeue : if his bags be fo

recouered of their Falling-ficknes, that they be
able prefently to repay the borrowed gold, then
Monfieur Gul-groper fteales away of purpofe to
auoide the receipt of it ; he hath fatter Chickens
in hatching : tis a fayrer marke he fhootes at.
For the day being come when the bond growes
due, the within named *Signior Auaro* will not
be within : or if he be at home, he hath wedges
enough in his pate, to caufe the bond to bée
broken, or elfe a little before the day, he féeds
my young Maifter with fuch fwéet words, that
furfetting vpon his proteftations, hée neglects his
paiment, as prefuming hée may do more.   But the
Law hauing a hand in the forfeiture of the bond,
laies prefently hold of our yong Gallant with the
helpe of a couple of Serieants, and iuft at fuch a
time when old *Erra Pater* (the Iew) that lent him
the money, knowes by his owne Prognoftication,
that the Moone with the filuer face is with him
in the waine.   Nothing then can free him out of
the phanges of thofe bloud-hounds, but he muft
prefently confeffe a iudgment, for fo much money,
or for fuch a Manor or Lordfhip (thrée times
worth the bond forfeited) to be paid or to be
entred vpon by him, by fuch a day, or within
fo many moneths after he comes to his land.   And
thus are young heires coozend out of their Acres,
before they well know where they lye.

The Wood-pecker.

THe *Wood-pecker* is a bird that fits by vpon a perch too ; but is nothing fo dangerous, as this Vulture fpoken of before. He deales altogether vpon Returnes, (as men do that take thrée for one, at their comming back from Ieru-falem, &c.) for hauing a Iewell, a Clock, a Ring with a Diamond, or any fuch like commoditie, he notes him well that commonly is beft acquainted with the Dice, and hath euer good luck : to him he offers his prize, rating it at ten or fiftéene pound, when happily tis not worth aboue fix, and for it he bargaines to receiue fiue fhillings or ten fhillings (according as it is in value) at euery / hand, fecond, third, or fourth hand he drawes : by which means he perhaps in a fhort time, makes that yéeld him forty or fifty pound, which coft not halfe twenty. Many of thefe Merchant ven-turers faile from Ordinary to Ordinary, being fure always to make fauing Voiages, when they that put in ten times more then they, are for the moft part loofers.

The Gull.

NOw if either *The Leaders*, or *The Forlorne Hope*, or any of the reft, chãce to heare of a yong *Frefh-water* foldier that neuer before followed thefe ftrange warres, and yet hath a

Charge newly giuen him (by the old fellow *Sol-
dado Vecchio* his father, when Death had ſhotte
him into the Graue) of ſome ten or twelue
thouſand in ready money, beſides ſo many
hundreds a yeare : firſt are Scoutes ſent out to
diſcouer his Lodging : that knowne, ſome lie in
ambuſh to note what Apothecaries ſhop hée reſorts
too euery morning, or in what Tobacco-ſhop in
Fléet-ſtréet he takes a pipe of Smoake in the
afternoone : that fort which the Puny holds, is
ſure to be beleaguerd by the whole troope of the
old weather beaten Gallants : amongſt whom ſome
one, whoſe wit is thought to be of a better block
for his head, than the reſt, is appointed to ſingle
out our *Nouice,* and after ſome foure or fiue dayes
ſpent in Complement, our heire to ſeauen hundred
a yeare is drawne to an Ordinary, into which he
no ſooner enters, but all the old-ones in that Neſt
flutter about him, embrace, proteſt, kiſſe the hand,
Conge to the very garter, and in the end (to ſhew
that hee is no ſmall foole, but that he knows his
father left him not ſo much monie for nothing,)
the yong Cub ſuffers himſelfe to be drawne to
the ſtake : to fleſh him, Fortune and the Dice
(or rather the Falſe-dice, that coozen Fortune, &
make a foole of him too) ſhall ſo fauor him, that
he marches away from a battaile or two, the onely
winner.   But afterwards, let him play how warily

foeuer he can, the damned Dice fhall croffe / him, & his filuer croffes fhall bleffe thofe that play againft him : for euen they that féeme déereft to his bofome, fhall firft be ready, and be the formoft to enter with the other Leaders into confpiracy, how to make fpoile of his golden bags. By fuch ranfacking of Cittizens fonnes wealth, the Leaders maintaine themfelues braue, the *Forlorne-hope*, that droop'd before, do'es now gallantly come on. The *Eagle* fethers his neft, the *Wood-pecker* pickes vp his crums, the *Gul-groper* growes fat with good féeding : and the *Gull* himfelfe, at whom euery one has a Pull, hath in the end fcarce fethers enough to kéepe his owne back warme.

The Poft-maifter of Hell, féeing fuch villanies to go vp and downe in cloakes lin'd cleane through with Veluet, was glad he had fuch newes to fend ouer, and therefore fealing vp a letter full of it, deliuered the fame to filthy-bearded *Charon* (their owne Water-man) to be conuaide firft to the Porter of Hell, & then (by him) to the Maifter Kéeper of the Diuels.

Portitoribus horrendus aquas & flumina seruat, Terribile squalore Charon, Cui plurima mente, Canities incultæ iacet.

Of Ferreting.

The Manner of vndooing Gentlemen by taking vp of commodities.

CHAP. IIII.

H Unting is a noble, a manly, & a healthfull exercife; it is a very true picture of warre, nay it is a war in it felfe; for engines are brought into the field, ftratagems are contriued, ambufhes are laide, onfets are giuen, allarums ftruck vp, braue incounters are made, fierce affailings are refifted by ftrength, by courage or by pollicy : the enemy is purfued, and the *Purfuers* neuer giue ouer till they haue him in execution : then is a Retreate founded, then are fpoiles diuided, then come they home wearied, but yet crowned with honor & victory. And as in battailes there be feuerall maners of fight : fo in the paftime of hunting, there are feuerall degrées of game. Some Hunting of the hunt the / *Lion*, and that fhewes as Lyon, &c. when fubiects rife in Armes againft their *King* : Some hunt the *Vnicorne* for the treafure on his head, and they are like couetous men, that care not whome they kill for riches : fome hunt the *Spotted Panther* and the freckled

Leopard, they are fuch as to inioy their pleafures, regard not how blacke an infamy ftickes vpon them : All thefe are barbarous & vnnaturall Huntfemen, for they range vp and downe the Deferts, the Wildernes, and inhabitable Mountaines.

Others purfue the long *liued Hart,* the couragious *Stag* or the nimble footed *Deere* : Hunting of the Bucke. thefe are the *Noblest hunters,* and they exercife the Nobleft game : thefe by following the Chace get ftrength of body, a frée and vndifquieted minde, magnanimity of fpirit, alacrity of heart and an vnwearifomneffe to breake through the hardeft labours : their pleafures are not infatiable but are contented to be kept within limits, for thefe hunt within Parkes inclofed, or within bounded Forrefts. The hunting of the Hunting of the Hare. *Hare* teaches *feare* to be bould, and puts *fimplicity* fo to her fhifts, that fhe growes cunning and prouident : the turnings and croffe windings that fhe makes, are embleames of this lifes vncertainty : when fhe thinkes fhe is furdeft from danger, it is at her héeles, and when it is nereft to her, the hand of fafety defends her. When fhe is wearied and has runne her race, fhe takes her death patiently, onely to teach man, that he fhould make himfelfe redy, when the graue gapes for him.

All thefe kinds of hunting are abroad in the open field, but there is a *clofe citty* *De magno prædæ petendæ* hunting onely within the walls, that *grege.* pulles downe Parkes, layes open forrefts, deftroies Chaces, woundes the Deere of the land, and make[s] fuch hauocke of the *goodlieft* Heards, that by their wills, (who are the rangers,) none fhould be left aliue but the Rafcalls : This kinde of hunting is bafe, and ignoble.   It is the meaneft, yet the moft mifchieuous, & it is called *Ferreting.* To behold a courfe or two at this, did the light *horfeman of Hell* one day leape into the faddle.

Citty | -Hunting.

THis *Ferret-Hunting* hath his Seafons as other games haue, and is onely followed at fuch a time of yeare, when the Gentry of What perfons our kingdome by riots, hauing chafed follovv the game of Ferret them-felues out of the faire reuenewes hunting. and large poffeffion left to them by their anceftors, are forced to hide their heads like Conies, in little caues and in vnfrequented places : or elfe being almoft windles, by running after fenfuall pleafures too feircely, they *Dolor ac voluptas inui-* are glad (for keeping them-felues in *cem cedunt.* breath fo long as they can) to fal to *Ferret-hunting,* ỹ is to fay, to take vp commodities.

No warrant can bée graunted for a Bucke in this *forreſt*, but it muſt paſſe vnder theſe fiue hands.

1 He that hunts vp and downe to find game, is called the *Tombler*.

2 The commodities that are taken vp are cald *Purſe-nets*.

The tragedy of Ferret-hunting diuided into 5 acts.

3 The Cittizen that ſelles them is the *Ferret*.

4 They that take vp are the *Rabbet-ſuckers*.

5 He vpon whoſe credit theſe *Rabbet-ſuckers* runne, is called the *Warren*.

How the Warren is made.

AFter a raine, Conies vſe to come out of their Holes and to ſit nibling on wéeds or any thing in the coole of the euening, and after a reueling when younger brothers haue ſpent al, or in gaming haue loſt al, they ſit plotting in their chambers with neceſſity how to be furniſhed preſently with a new ſupply of money.   They would take vp any *Num illaomnes artes perdocet, vbiquem attigit.* commodity whatſoeuer, but their names ſtand in too many texted letters allready in Mercers and Scriueners bookes : vpon a hundred poundes worth of *Roaſted* béefe they could finde in their hearts to venture, for that would away in turning of a hand : but where ſhall they find a Butcher or a Cooke that will let any man runne ſo much vpon the ſcore for fleſh onely ?

Sup / pofe therefore that Foure of fuch loofe fortun'd gallants were tied in one knot, and knew not how to faften themfelues vpon fome welthy cittizen. At the length it runnes into their heads that *fuch a young Nouice* (who daily ferues to fill vp their company) was neuer intangled in any *citty limebufh*: they know his prefent meanes to be good, and thos to come to be great: him therefore they lay vpon the Anuill of their wits, till they haue wrought him like wax, for him-felue *Dum spectant* afwell as for them : to doe any thing *oculi læsos,* in wax, or indéed till they haue won *leduntur &* *ipsi.* him to flide vpon this ice, (becaufe he knowes not the danger) is he eafily drawne: for he confiders within himfelfe that they are all gentlemen well defcended, they haue rich fathers, they weare good clothes, haue bin gallant fpenders, and do now and then (ftill) let it fly fréely : hee is to venture vppon no more rockes than all they, what then fhould hée feare? hée therefore refolues to do it, and the rather becaufe his owne exhibition runnes low, & that there lacke a great many wéekes to the quarter day; at which time, he fhalbe refurnifhed from his father.

The Match being thus agréed vpon, one of them that has béene an ould *Ferret-monger*, & knowes all the trickes of fuch Hüting, féekes out a *Tumbler*, that is to fay a fellow, who beates the

buſh for them till they catch the birds, he himſelfe
being contented (as he proteſts & ſweares) onely
with a few fethers.

The Tumblers Hunting dry-foote.

THis Tumbler being let looſe runnes Snuffing
vp and downe cloſe to the ground,
in the ſhoppes either of Mercers, Gould- The nature of a London Tumbler.
ſmithes, Drapers, Haberdaſhers, or of any
other trade, where hée thinckes hee may méete
with a Ferret : and tho vpon his very firſt courſe,
hee can find his game, yet to make his gallants
more hungry, and to thinke he wearies himſelfe
in hunting the more, hee comes to them ſweating
and ſwearing that the *Citty Ferrets* are ſo coaped
(thats to ſay haue / their lips ſtitched vp ſo cloſe)
that hee can hardly get them open to ſo great a
ſum as fiue hundred poundes which *Nil habet in-*
they deſire.   This hearbe beeing chewd *fælix paupertas*
durius in se,
downe by the *Rabbet-ſuckers* almoſt kils *Quam quod*
ridiculos
their hearts, and is worſe to them then *homines facit.*
nabbing on the neckes to Connies.   They bid him
if he cannot faſten his teeth vpon plate or Cloth,
or Silkes, to lay hold on browne paper or Tobacco,
Bartholmew babies, Lute ſtringes or Hobnailes,
or two hundred poundes in Saint *Thomas* Onions,
and the reſt in mony ; the Onions they coulde get
wenches enough to cry and ſell them by the Rope,

and what remaines fhould ferue them with mutton.
Vppon this, their *Tumbler* trottes vppe and downe
agen, and at laft lighting on a Cittizen that will
deale, the names are receiued, and deliuered to a
Scriuener, who enquiring whether they bee good
men and true, that are to paffe vppon the life and
death of fiue hundred poundes, findes that *foure*
of the *fiue*, are winde-fhaken, and ready to fall into
the Lordes handes.   Marry the fift man, is an
Oake, and theres hope that he cannot bee hewed
downe in hafte.   Vppon him therefore the Cittizen
buildes fo much as comes to fiue hundred poundes,
yet takes in the other foure to make them ferue
as fcaffolding, till the Farme bee furnifhed, and if
then it hold, he cares not greatly who takes them
downe.   In al haft, are the bondes feald, and the
commodities deliuered, And then does the *Tumbler*
fetch his fecond carreere, and thats this.

The Tumblers Hunting Counter.

THe wares which they fifhed for beeing in
the hand of the fiue fhauers, do now more
trouble their wits how to turne thofe Wares into
reddy mony, then beefore they were troubled to
turn their credits into wares.   The Tree being
once more to be fhaken, they knowe it muft loofe
fruite, and therefore their Factor muft barter away
their Marchandife, tho it be with loffe : Abroad

is in / to the Cittie: he Sailes for that purpofe, and
deales with *him* that *fold*, to buy his owne Commodities againe for ready mony. He will not
doe it vnder 30. l. loffe in the Hundred : Other
Archers bowes are tryed at the fame marke, but
al keepe much about one fcantling : back therfore
comes their *Carrier* with this newes, that no man
will difburfe fo much prefent money vppon any
wares whatfoeuer. Onely he met by good fortune
with *one friend* (and that friend is himfelfe) who
for 10. l. wil procure them a Chapman, marry
that chapman wil not buy vnleffe he may haue
them at 30. l. loffe in the Hundred : fuh, cry all
the Sharers, a pox on thefe Fox-furd Curmudgions,
giue that fellow your *friend* 10. l. for his paines,
& fetch the reft of his money : within an houre
after, it is brought, and powr'd downe in one
heape vppon a tauerne table ; where making a
goodly fhew as if it could neuer be fpent, al of
thē confult what fée the *Tumbler* is to haue for
Hunting fo wel, and conclude that leffe then 10. l.
they cannot giue him, which 10. l. is ỹ firft mony
told out. Now let vs caft vp this Account : In
euery 100. l. is loft 30. which being *Dedit hanc*
5. times 30. l. makes 150. l.: that Sum the *contagio labē,*
Ferret puts vp cléer befides his ouer- *plures.*
prifing the wares: vnto which 150. l. loft, ad 10. l.
more, which the *Tumbler* guls them off, & other

236 LANTHORNE AND CANDLE-LIGHT.

10. l. which he hath for his voyage, al which makes 170 l.; which deducted from 500. l. there remaineth onely 330. to be deuided amongſt 5. ſo that euery one of ẙ partners ſhall haue but 66. l. yet this they all put vp merily, waſhing down their loſſes ẘ Sack and Sugar, whereof they drinke that night profoundly.

How the Warren is ſpoyled.

VVHilſt this faire weather laſteth, and that there is any graſſe to nibble vpon, *Theſe Rabbet ſuckers* kéep to the *Warren* wherein they fatned : but the cold day of repaiment approaching, they retire deepe into their Caues ; ſo that when the *Ferret* makes account to haue *fiue* before him in chaſe, *foure* of the *fiue* ly hiddē, & / are ſtolne into other grounds. No maruell then if the *Ferret* growe fierce & teare open his own iawes, to ſuck blood from *him* that is left : no maruaile if he ſcratch what wool he can frō his back : the *Purſnets* ẙ were Set are all Taken vp and carried away. The *Warren* therfore muſt bée Searched ; *That* muſt pay for all : ouer *that* does hee range like a little Lord. Sargeants, Marſhals-men, and Baliffes are ſent forth, who lie ſcowting at euery corner, & with terrible pawes haunt euery walke. In concluſion the bird that theſe Hawkes flie after, is ſeazd vpon, then are his fethers

pluck'd, his *eſtate* look'd into : thē are his wings
broken, his lãds made ouer to a ſtrãger : then muſt
our yong ſon and heire pay 500 l. (for which he
neuer had but 66. l.) or elſe lie in priſon. To
kéep himſelfe from which, he ſeales to any bond,
enters into any ſtatut, morgageth any Lordſhip,
Does any thing, Saies any thing, yéelds
to pay any thing.   And theſe Citty *Infelix vitis excidit ipse suis.*
ſtormes (which will wet a man till he
haue neuer a dry threed about him, tho he be
kept neuer ſo warme) fall not vpon him once or
twiſe : But being a little way in, he cares not how
déepe he wades : ꝫ greater his poſſeſſions are, the
apter he is to take vp & to be truſted : *Grandia permultos tenuantur Flumina riuos.*
the more he is truſted, the more he
comes in debt, the farther in debt, the
neerer to danger.   Thus *Gentlemen* are wrought
vpõ, thus are they *Cheated*, thus are they *Ferreted*,
thus are they *Vndonne*.

Fawlconers.

Of a new kinde of Hawking, teaching how to catch birds by bookes.

H*Vnting* and *Hawking* are of kin, and therefore it is fit they ſhould kéepe
company together : Both of them are *Hawking.*
noble Games, and Recreations, honeſt and health⸗

ful, yet they may fo be abufed that nothing can
be more hurtfull. In *Hunting*, the *Game* is commonly ftill before you, or i'th hearing, and within
a little compaffe : In *Hawking* / the *game* flies farre
off, and oftentimes out of fight : A
Couple of *Rookes* therefore (that were
birds of the laft feather) confpired together to leaue their neft, in the Citty, and to
flutter abroad, into the countrie : Vpon two leane
hackneies were thefe two *Doctor doddipols* horft;
Ciuilly fuited, that they might carry about them
fome badge of a Scholler.

Facies non omnibus vna, nec diuersa tamen.

The diuels *Ranck-ryder*, that came from the
laft Citty-hûting, vnderftanding that two fuch
Light-horfemen, were gon a *Hawking*, pofts after
and ouer-takes them. After fome ordinary high-
way talk, he begins to queftion of what profeffion
they were? One of them fmyling fcornfully in
his face, as thinking him to be fome *Gull*, (and
indeed fuch fellowes take all men for
Gulles who they thinke to be beneath
them in quallitie) tolde him they were
Falconers. But the Foxe that followed them feeing
no properties, (belonging to a *Falconer*) about
them, fmelt knauery, took them for a paire of mad
rafcals, & therfore refolued to fée at what thefe
Falconers would let flie.

* Qui nisi quod ipsi faciunt, nihil rectum putant.

How to caſt vp the Lure.

A T laſt on a ſuddaine ſaies on[e] of them to him,
ſir, wee haue *Sprung* a *Partridge*, The first
and ſo fare you wel : which wordes Noate.
came ſtammering out with the haſte that they
made, for preſently the two *Forragers* of the
Countrie, were vppon the Spurre : *Plutoes Poſt*
ſeeing this, ſtood ſtill to watch them, and at length
ſaw them in maine gallop make toward a goodly
faire place, where either ſome Knight or ſome great
Gentleman kept : and this goodly houſe belike was
the *Partridge* which thoſe *falconers* had ſprung.
Hee beeing loath to looſe his ſhare in this *Hawking*, and. hauing power to transforme himſelfe as
hee liſted, came thither as ſoone as they, but beheld all (which they did) inuiſible. They both like
two Knights Errant alighted at the Gate, knocked
and were lette in : the one walkes the Hackneyes
in an outward Court, as if hee had bene but Squire
to Sir *Dagonet*, The other / (as boldly as Saint
George when he dar'd the dragon at his verrie
Den) marcheth vndauntedly vp to the Hall, where
looking ouer thoſe poore creatures of the houſe,
that weare but the bare Blew-coates (for *Aquila
non capit Muſcas*) wħat ſhould a Falconer meddle
with flies? hee onely ſalutes *him* that in his eye

ſéemes to bee a Gentlemanlike fellow : Of him
he aſkes for his *good Knight* or ſo, and
ſaies that he is a * Gentleman come from
London on a buſineſſe, which he muſt
deliuer to his owne Worſhipfull *Eare.* Vp the
ſtaires does braue *Mount Dragon* aſcend : the
Knight and he encounter, and with this ſtaffe
does he valiantly charge vpon him.

**Et quæ nō
fecimus ipsi,
vix ea nostra
voco.*

How the Bird is Caught.

S Ir I am a poore * Scholler, and the report
of your vertues hath drawne me hither,
venturouſly bolde to fixe your worthy
name as a patronage to a poore ſhort
diſcourſe which here I dedicate (out
of my loue) to your noble and eternall
Memory : this ſpeech he vtters barely.

** Senstos fuit
ille Caducus
Frange Puer.
Calamos et
inanes desere
Musas. Quid
nisi Monstra
legit?*

The *Hawking pamphleter* is then bid to *put
on,* whilſt his *Miſcellane Mæcenas,* opens a booke
fairely aparreld in vellom with gilt fillets & fore-
penny ſilke ribbon at leaſt, like little ſtreamers on
the top of a Marchpane Caſtle, hanging dandling
by at ẏ foure corners : the title being ſuperficially
ſuruaide, in the next leafe he ſees that the *Author
hee* hath made him one of his Goſſips : for the
booke carries his worſhips name, & vnder it ſtands
an Epiſtle iuſt the length of a Hench-mans grace

before dinner, which is long inough for any booke in confcience, vnleffe the writer be vnreafonable.

The knight being told before hand, that this little funbeame of *Phœbus* (fhining thus brifkly in print) hath his Mite or Atmy wayting vppon him in the outward court, thankes him for his loue and labour, and confidering with himfelfe, what coft he hath beene at, and how farre he hath ridden to come to him, he knowes that Patrons and Godfathers are to pay fcot and lot alike, and there / fore to cherifh his young and tender Mufe, he giues him foure or fixe Angells, inuiting him either to ftay breakefaft, or if the fundiall of the houfe points towards eleauen, then to tary dinner.

How the bird is dreft.

BUt the fifh being caught (for which our *Heliconian Angler* threw out his lines) with thankes, and legs, and kiffing his own hand, he parts. No fooner is he horft, but his *Hoftler* (who all this while walked the iades, and trauailes vp & down with him, like an vndeferuing plaier for halfe a fhare) afkes this queftion, *Strawes* or not? *Strawes* cries the *whole fharer and a halfe :* away then replies the firft, flie to our neft : *Stultus quoq ;* This neft is neuer in the fame towne *munere gaudet.* but commonly a mile or two off ; and it is nothing

els but the next Tauerne they come to.   But the
Village into which they rode being not able to
maintaine an Iuybuſh, an Ale-houſe was their
Inne : where aduancing themſelues into
the faireſt Chamber, and beeſpeaking
the beſt cheere in the towne for dinner,

How birds are drest after they be caught.

down they ſit, & *ſhare* before they ſpeake of
any thing els : That done, *he* that ventures vpon
all he meetes, and diſcharges the paper Bullets,
(for to tell truth, the other ſerues but as a *ſigne*,
and is méerely *nobody*) beginnes to diſcourſe, *how*
he caried himſelfe in the aćtion, *how* he was encountred : *how* he ſtood to his tackling, and *how*
well hee came off: he cals the Knight, a *Noble
fellow*, yet they both ſhrug, and laugh, and ſweares
they are glad they haue *Guld* him.

More arrowes muſt they ſhoote of the ſame
length that this firſt was off, and therfore there
is Trunckful of Trinckets, thats to ſay, their
budget of Bookes, is opend againe, to ſee what
leafe they are to turne ouer next ; which whilſt
they are dooing, the Ghoſt that al this ſpace
haunted them, and hard what they ſaid, hauing
excellent ſkill in the blacke-art, thats to ſay in
picking of lockes, maks the dore ſuddenly flye
open (which they had cloſely ſhut)./ At his
ſtrange entrance they being ſomwhat agaſt, began
to ſhuffle away their bookes, but he knowing what

cardes they plaide withal, offred to cut, and turnd
vp two Knaues by this trick : My maifters (quoth
he) I knowe where you haue bin, I know what
you haue don, I know what you meane to do. I
fée now you are Falconers indeed, but by the (and
then he fwore a damnable oth) vnleffe you teach
me to fhoote in this *Birding-peece*, I will raife the
Village, fend for the knight whome you boaft you
haue *guld*, and fo difgrace you : for your money
I care not.

The two Frée-booters feeing themfelues fmoakd,
told their third Brother, he feemd to be a gentleman and a boone companion : they prayed him
therefore to fit downe with filence, and fithence
dinner was not yet ready, hée fhould heare all.

This new kinde of *Hawking* (qd. one of them)
which you fée vs vfe, can afford no name vnles 5.
be at it, *viz.*

1. He that cafts vp the *Lure* is calld the
Falconer.

2. The *Lure* that is caft vp is an idle *Pamphlet*.

3. The *Tercel Gentle* that comes to the Lure, is
fome knight or fome gentleman of like qualitie.

4. The *Bird* that is preied vpon, is Money.

5. *Hee* that walkes the horfes, and hunts dry
foote, is cald a *Mongrell*.

The Falconer and his Spaniell.

THe Falconer hauing fcraped together certaine
fmall paringes of witte, he firft cuttes them
hanfomely in pretty peeces, and of thofe peeces
does he patch vppe a booke. This booke he
prints at his own charge, the *Mongrell* running
vppe and downe to look to the workemen, and
bearing likewife fome parte of the coft, (for which
he enters vpon his halfe fhare). When it is fully
finifhed, the *Falconer* and his *Mongrell*, (or it may
bée two *Falconers* ioyne in one,) but howfoeuer,
it is by them deuifed what Shire in *England* it is
beft to forrage next : that / beeing fet downe, the
Falconers deale either with a Herauld for a note
of all the Knights and Gentlemens names of worth
that dwell in *that circuit*, which they meane to
ride, or els by inquiry get the chiefeft of them,
printing of fo many Epiftles as they haue names ;
ỹ epiftles Dedicatory being all one, and vary in
nothing but in the titles of their patrons.

Hauing thus furnifhed themfelues and packed
Strange vp their wares, away they trudge like
havvking. tinckers, with a budget at one of their
backes, or it may be the *circle* they meane to
coniure in fhall not be out of *London*, efpecially
if it be Tearme-time, or when a Parliament is
holden (for then they haue choife of fweete-meats

to féed vppon.) If a gentleman feeing one of
thefe bookes Dedicated onely to his name, fufpect
it to be a baftard, that hath more fathers befides
himfelfe, and to try that, does deferre the Pre-
fenter for a day or two, fending in the meane
time (as fome haue done) into Paules Church-yard
amongft the ftationers, to inquire if any fuch worke
be come forth, & if *they* cannot tell, then to fteppe
to the Printers : Yet haue the *Falconers* a tricke to
goe beyond fuch Hawkes too, for all they flye fo
hie. And that is this : The bookes lye all at the
Printers, but not one line of an epiftle to any of
them (thofe bug-bears lurke in *Tenebris*) : if then
the *Spy* that is fent by his Maifter, afk why they
haue no dedications to them, *Mounfier* Printer tels
him, the author would not venture to adde any to
them all, (fauing onely to that which was giuen
to his Maifter,) vntill it was knowne whether he
could accept of it or no.

This fatisfies the Patron, this fetches money
from him : and this *Cozens* fiue hundred befides.
Nay there bee othere Bird catchers that vfe ftranger
Quaile-pipes : you fhal haue fellowes, foure or
fiue in a contry, that buying vp any old Booke
(efpecially a Sermon, or any other matter of
Diuinity) that lies for waft paper, and is clean
forgotten, ad a new-printed Epiftle to it, and with
an Alphabet of letters which they cary about them,

being able to / print any mans names (for a Dedication) on the fuddaine, trauaile vp and downe mofte
Shires in Englãd, and liue by this Hawking.

Are we not excellent Falconers now ? (quoth
three half fhares) : excellent villaines cryed the
deuils Deputy : by this the meate for dinner came
fmoaking in, vpon which they fell moft tirannically,
yet (for maners fake) offring firft, to the Balif of
Belzebub the vpper end of the table ; but he
fearing they would make a *Hauke* or a *Buzzard*
of him too, and report they had ridden him like
an Affe, as they had done others, out a doores
hee flung with a vengeance as he came.

O facred *Learning* ! why dooft thou fuffer thy
feauen leaued tree, to be plucked by barbarous and
moft vnhallowed handes ? Why is thy beatifull
Maiden-body, polluted like a ftrumpets,
*Cur ego si neq
ignoreq ; Potea* and proftituted to beaftly and flauifh
salutor.
Ignorance ? O thou *Bafe-broode*, that
make the *Mufes* harlots, yet fay they are your
Mothers ? You *Theeues* of *Wit*, *Cheators* of Arte,
traitors of fchooles of *Learning : murderers* of
Schollers. More worthy you are, to vndergoe the
Romane *Furca* like flaues, and to be branded ith
fore-head deeper then they that forge teftaments
to vndoe Orphants : Such doe but rob children
of goods that may be loft : but *you* rob Schollers
of their Fame, which is deerer then life. You are

not worth an Inuectiue, not worthy to haue your
names dropp out of a deferuing pen, you fhall
onely bee executed in Picture : (as they vfe to
handle Malefactors in France,) and the picture
(though it were drawne to be hung vp in *another
place*) fhal leaue you impudently-arrogãt to your
felues, and ignominioufly-ridiculous to after ages :
in thefe collours, are you drawne.

The true picture of thefe Falconers.

—————— *There be Fellowes*

*Of courfe and common bloud ; Mechanicke
          knaues,* Proh superi
quantum-
pectora cælæ
Noctis Habēt.
Whofe wits lye deeper buried then in graues,
And indeede fmell more earthy ; whofe creation
Was | but to giue a Boote or Shooe good fafhion.
Yet thefe (throwing by the Apron and the Awle)
Being drunck with their own wit, caft vp Scribimus
indocti, doctiq ;
          their gall
Onely of yncke : and in patchd, beggerly Rimes,
(As full of fowle corruption, as the Times)
From towne to towne they ftrowle in foule, as poore
As th'are in clothes : yet thefe at euery doore,
Their labors Dedicate. But (as at Faires)
Like Pedlars, they fhew ftill one fort of wares
Vnto all commers (with fome filde oration)
And thus to giue bookes, now's an occupation.

One booke hath ſeauen ſcore patrons : thus deſart

Is cheated of her due : thus noble art

Giues Ignorance (that common ſtrumpet) place,

Thus the true ſchollers name growes cheap & baſe.
&c.

Iacks of the Clock-houſe.

A new and cunning drawing of money from Gentlemen.

Chap. 6.

THere is another Fraternitie of wandring Pilgrims who merrily call themſelues *Iackes of the Clocke-houſe*, and are verry neere allyed to the *Falconers* that went a Hawking before. The Clarke of *Erebus* ſet downe their names too in his Tables, with certain bréefe notes of their practiſes : and theſe they are.

The Iacke of a Clocke-houſe goes vppon Screws, and his office is to do nothing but ſtrike : ſo does this noiſe, (for they walke vp and downe like Fidlers) trauaile with *Motions* ; and whatſoeuer their *Motions* get them, is called ſtriking.

Thoſe Motions are certaine *Collections*, or wittie Inuentions, ſome-times of one thing, and then of an other (there is a new one now in rime, in praiſe of the *Vnion*). And theſe are fairely written and engroffed in Vellum, Parchement, or Royall paper, richly adorned with / compartiments, and fet out with letters both in gold and in various coullours.

This labour being taken, the Maifter of the Motion hearkens where fuch a Nobleman, fuch a Lord, or fuch a Knight lyes, that is liberall: hauing found one to his liking, The Motion (with his Patrons name fairely texted out, in manner of a Dedication,) is prefented before him : he receiues it, and thinking it to be a work onely vndertaken for his fake, is bounteous to the giuer, efteeming him a Scholler, and knowing that not without great trauaile, hee hath drawne fo many little ftragling ftreames into fo faire and fmoothe a Riuer : whereas the Worke is the labour of fome other (copied out by ftealth), he an impudent ignorant fellow, that runnes vp and downe with the Tranfcripts; and euery Ale-houfe may haue one of them (hanging in the bafeft drinking roome) if they will bee but at the charges of writing it out. Thus the liberallitie of a Nobleman, or of a Gentleman is abufed : thus learning is brought into fcorne and contempt : Thus men are cheated of their bountie, giuing much for that (out of their free mindes) which is common abroad, and put away for bafe prices. Thus villanie fome-times walkes alone, as if it were giuen to Melan-cholly, and fome-times knaues tie themfelues in a knot, becaufe they may be more merry, as by a mad fort of Comrades whome I fee leaping into the Saddle, anon it will apeare.

Rancke-Riders,

The manner of Cozening Inn-keepers.
Poft-maifters and Hackny-men.

Chap. 7.

THere is a troope of Horfemen, that runne vp and downe the whole kingdome : they are euer in a gallop, their bufineffe is weightie, their iournies many, their / expences greate, their Innes euerie where, their lands no where : they haue onely a certaine Free-holde cald Tyberne (fcituate neere London, and many a faire paire of Gallowes in other Countries befides,) vppon which they liue verie poorely till they dye, and dye for the mofte part wickedly, becaufe their liues are villanous and defperate. But what race fo euer they runne, there they end it, there they fet vp their reft, there is their laft halte, whether foeuer their iourney lyes. And thefe horfemen haue no other names but ranck Riders.

To furnifh whome foorth for any iourney, they muft haue Riding futes cut out of thefe foure peeces.

1. The Inne-kéeper or Hackney-man, of whome they haue horſes, is cald A *Colt*.

2. He that neuer alights off a rich Farmer or country Gentleman, till he haue drawne money from him, is called *The Snaffle*.

3. The money ſo gotten, is *The Ring*.

4. He that feedes them with mony is called *The prouander*.

Theſe Ranck-riders (like Butchers to Rumford market) ſildome goe vnder ſixe or ſeauen in a company, and theſe Careeres they fetch.   Their purſſes being warmly lined with ſome purchaſe gotten before, and they theſelues well booted and ſpur'd, and in reaſonable good outſides, arriue at the faireſt Inne they can chooſe, either in Weſt-minſter, the Strand, the Cittie, or the Suburbes.

Two of them who haue cloathes of purpoſe to fitte the play, carrying the ſhew of Gentlemen : the other act their partes in blew coates, as they were their Seruingmen, though indeede they be all fellowes. They enter all durted or duſtied (according as it ſhall pleaſe the high way to vſe them) and the firſt bridle they put into the Colts mouth (thats to ſay the Inkeepers) is at their comming in to aſke alowde if the footeman be gone backe with the horſes? tis anſwered yes.   Heere, the *Ranck-riders* lye three or foure daies, ſpending moderately

The manner of Brideling a colt.

enough, yet abating / not a penny of any reckoning to ſhew of what houſe they come : in w̄ ſpace
their counterfeit followers learne what countryman
the maiſter of the houſe is, where the Hoſtlars
and Chamberlaines were borne, and what other
countrie Gentlemen are gueſts to the Inne? which
leſſons being preſently gotten by heart, they fal in
ſtuddy with the Generall rules of their knauerie :
and thoſe are, firſt to giue out, that their Maiſter
is a Gentleman of ſuch and ſuch meanes, in ſuch
a ſhire (which ſhall be ſure to ſtand farre enough
from thoſe places where any of the houſe, or of
other gueſts were borne,) that hee is come to
receiue ſo many hundred poundes vppon land
which he hath ſolde, and that hee meanes to Inne
there ſome quarter of a yeare at leaſt.

This Braſſe money paſſing for currant through
the houſe, hée is more obſerued and better attended, is worſhipped at euerie word : and the
eaſier to breake and bridle the *Colt*, his *Worſhip*
will not ſit downe to Dinner or ſupper, till the
Maiſter of the houſe be placed at the vpper end
of the boord by him.

In the middle of Supper, or elſe verie earely
in the following morning, comes in a counterfeit
footeman, ſweatingly, deliuering a meſſage that
ſuch a Knight hath ſent for the head-Maiſter of
theſe Rancke-ryders, and that hee muſt bee with

him by fuch an houre, the iourney being not aboue
twelue or foureteene miles. Vpon deliuerie of this
meffage, (from fo deere and noble a friend) he
fweares and chafes, becaufe all his horfes are out
of Towne, curfeth the fending of them backe,
offers any money to haue himfelfe, his couzen
with him, and his mē but reafonably horft. Mine
hoft being a credulous Affe, fuffers them all to
get vppe vpon him, for hee prouides them horfes
either of his owne (thinking his Gueft to be a
man of great accompte, and beeing loath to loofe
him, becaufe hee fpends well) or elfe fendes out to
hire them of his neighbours, paffing his word for
their forthcomming / with in a day or two. Vp
they get and away Gallop our Ranck-riders, as
far as the poore Iades can carry them.

The two daies being ambled out of the worlde,
and perhaps three more after them, yet neither
a fupply of Horfe-men or Foote-men, (as was
promifed) to be fet eye vppon. The lamentable
In-keeper (or Hackney man, if he chance to be
Sadled for this iourney too) loofe their Colts teeth,
and finde that they are made olde arrant Iades:
Search, then runnes vp and downe like a Conftable
halfe out of his wittes (vppon a Shroue-tuefday)
and hue and cry followes after, fome twelue or
foureteene miles off, (round about London); which
was the fartheft of their iourney as they gaue out.

But (alas!) the horfes are at pafture foure fcore or
a hundred miles from their olde mangers : they
were fould at fome blinde drunken theeuifh faire,
(there beeing enow of them in company to faue
themfelues, by their Toll-booke,) the Seruing-men
caft off their blew coates, and cried *All fellowes* :
the money is fpent vpon wine, vpon whores,
vpon fidlers, vpō fooles (by whom they wil loofe
nothing) and the tyde beeing at an ebbe, they are
as ready to practife their fkill in horfe-manfhip to
bring Coltes to the faddle in that Towne, and to
make Nags run a race of three-fcore or a hundred
miles of from that place, as before they did from
London.

Running at the Ring.

THus, fo long as *Horfeflefh* can make them
fat, they neuer leaue feeding.   But when
they haue beaten fo many high-waies in feuerall
countries, that they feare to be ouer taken by
Tracers, then (like Soldiers comming from a
Breach) they march faire & foftly on foot, lying
in garrifon as it were, clofe in fome out townes, til
the foule Rumor of their Villanies (like a ftormy
durty winter) be blown ouer : In which time of
lurking in ẙ fhel, they are not idle neither, but
like fnailes they venture abroad tho the / law hath
threatned to rain downe neuer fo much punifhmēt

vpon them : and what do they ? they are not bees,
to liue by their owne painfull labors, but Drones
that muſt eat vp the ſweetneſſe, and be fedde with
the earnings of others : This therefore is their
worke. They careleſly inquire what gentleman of
worth, or what rich Farmers dwell within fiue,
fix or feauen miles of the Fort where they are
inſconc'd (which they may do without ſuſpition)
and hauing gotte their names, they ſingle out
themſelues in a morning, and each man takes a
feuerall path to himſelfe : one goes Eaſt, one *Weſt*,
one North, and the other South : walking either
in bootes with wandes in their handes, or other
wiſe, for it is all to one purpoſe. And note this
by the way, that when they trauell thus on foot,
they are no more call'd *Ranck-riders* but *Strowlers* ;
a proper name giuen to Country platers, that (without Socks) trotte from towne to towne vpon the
hard hoofe.

Being arriu'd at the Gate where the *Gentleman*
or *Farmer* dwelleth, he boldly knocks, inquiring
for him by name, and ſteppes in to ſpeake with
him : the ſeruant ſéeing a faſhionable perſon, tells
his Maiſter there is a Gentleman deſires to ſpeake
with him : the maiſter comes and ſalutes him, but
eying him well, ſaies he does not know him : No
Sir, replies the other (with a face bolde ynough)
it may be ſo, but I pray you, Sir, will you walke

a turne or two in your Orchard or Garden, I
would there conferre: Hauing got him thether,
to this tune he plaies vppon him.

How the snaffle is put on.

SIr, I am a Gentleman, borne to better meanes
then my prefent fortunes doe allow me: I
ferued in the field, and had commaunde there,
but long peace (you knowe Sir) is the Cancker
that eates vp Souldiers, and fo it hath mee.   I lie
heere not far off, in the Country at mine Inne,
where ftaying vppon the difpatch / of fome bufi-
nefle, I am indebted to the houfe in moneys, fo
that I cannot with the credit of a Gentleman
leaue the houfe till I haue paide them.   Make mee
fir fo much beholden to your loue as to lend me
fortye or fiftie fhilings to beare my horfe and
my felfe to London; from whence within a day
or two, I fhall fend you many thanks with a
faithful repayment of your curtefie.

The honeft Gentleman, or the good natur'd
Farmer beholding a perfonable man, fafhionably
attir'd, and not carrying in outward coullors, the
face of a cogging knaue, giues credit to his words,
is forry that they are not at this prefent time fo
well furnifhed as they could wifh, but if a matter
of twenty fhillings can ftead him, he fhall commaund it, becaufe it were pittie any honeft

Gentleman fhould for fo fmall a matter mifcarry. Happilye they meete with fome Chap-men that giue them their owne afking; but howfoeuer, all is fifh that comes to net; they are the moft con-fcionable market folkes that euer rode betweene two paniers, for from fortie they will fall to twentie, from twenty to ten, from ten to fiue : nay thefe mountibanckes are fo bafe, that they are not afhamed to take two fhillings of a plaine hufbandman, and fometimes fixe pence (which the other giues fimply and honeftly) of whome they demaunded a whole fifteene.

In this manner doe they digge filuer out of mens purfes, all the day, and at night meet together at the appointed *Rendeuouz*; where all these *Snaffles* are loofed to their full length, the *Ringes* which that day they haue made are worne. The *Prouender* is praifed or difpraifed, as they finde it in goodneffe, but it goes downe all, whilft they laugh at all.

And thus does a Common-wealth bring vp children, that care not how they difcredit her, or vndoe her : who would imagine that Birdes fo faire in fhewe, and fo fweete in voice, fhould be fo dangerous in condition? but Rauens thinke carryon the daintieft meate, and villains / efteeme moft of that money which is purchaft by bafenes.

The Vnder Sheriffe for the county of the *Caco-*

demōs, knowing into what arrearages thefe Rank-
riders were runne for horfe-flefh to his maifter, (of
whome he farmed the office) fent out his writs to
attach them, and fo narrowly purfued thē, that
for all they were wel horft, fome he fent poft to
the gallowes, and the reft to feuerall iayles : After
which, making all the haft he pofibly could to get
to London againe, he was way-layd by an army
of a ftrange & new found people.

Moone men.

*A difcouery of a ftrange wild people, very dangerous
to townes and country villages.*

CHAP. VIII.

A *Moone-man* fignifies in Englifh, a mad-man,
becaufe the Moone hath greateft domination
(aboue any other Planet) ouer the bodies of Fran-
tick perfons.   But thefe *Moone-men* (whofe Images
are now to be carued) are neither abfolutely mad,
not yet perfectely in their wits.   Their name they
borrow from the Moone, becaufe as the Moone
is neuer in one fhape two nights together, but
wanders vp & downe Heauen, like an Anticke,
fo thefe changeable-ftuffe-companions neuer tary
one day in a place, but are the onely, and the
onely bafe Ronnagats vpon earth.   And as in the

Moone there is a man, that neuer ftirres without a bufh of thornes at his backe, fo thefe *Moone-men* lie vnder bufhes, & are indéed no better then Hedge creepers.

They are a people more fcattred then Iewes, and more hated : beggerly in apparell, barbarous in condition, beaftly in behauior : and bloudy if they meete aduātage. A man that fees them would fweare they had all the yellow Iawndis, or that they were Tawny Moores baftardes, for no Red-oaker man caries a face of a more filthy / complexion ; yet are they not borne fo, neither has the Sunne burnt them fo, but they are painted fo : yet they are not good painters neither, for they do not make faces, but marre faces. By a by-name they are called Gipfies, they call themfelues Egiptians, others in mockery call them *Moone-men*.

What a moone man is.

If they be Egiptians, fure I am they neuer difcended from the tribes of any of thofe people that came out of the Land of *Egypt* : *Ptolomy* (King of the Egiptians) I warrant neuer called them his Subiects: no nor *Pharao* before him. Looke what difference there is betwéene a ciuell cittizen of Dublin & a wilde Irifh Kerne, fo much difference there is betwéene one of thefe counterfeit Egiptians and a true Englifh Begger. An Englifh Roague is iuft of the fame liuery.

They are commonly an army about foure-fcore His order in ftrong, yet they neuer march with all marching on their bagges and baggages together, but foote or ierning open horse. (like boot-halers) they forrage vp and downe countries, 4. 5. or 6. in a company. As the fwizer has his wench and his Cocke with him whē he goes to the warres, fo thefe vagabonds haue their harlots, with a number of litle children following at their héeles : which young brood of Beggers, are fometimes cartied (like fo many gréene geefe aliue to a market) in payres of panieres, or in doffers like fresh-fifh from Rye ẏ comes on horfebacke, (if they be but infants.) But if they can ftradle once, then afwell the fhee-roagues as the hee-roagues are horft, feauen or eight vpon one iade, ftrongly pineond, and ftrangely tyed together.

One Shire alone & no more is fure ftil at one time, to haue thefe Egiptian lice fwarming within it, for like flockes of wild-géefe, they will euermore fly one after another : let them be fcattred worfe then the quarters of a traitor are after hées hang'd drawne and quartred, yet they haue a tricke (like water cut with a fwoord) to come together in-ftantly and eafily againe : and this is their pollicy, which way foeuer the formoft ranckes lead, they / fticke vp fmall boughes in feuerall places, to euery village where they paffe; which ferue as enfignes to waft on the reft.

Their apparell is od, and phantafticke, tho it be neuer fo full of rents : the men weare
fcarfes of Callico, or any other bafe _{His Furniture.} ftuffe, *hanging* their bodies like Morris-dancers, with bels, & other toyes, to intice the coûtrey people to flocke about them, and to wounder at their fooleries or rather rancke knaueryes. The women as ridiculoufly attire themfelues, and (like one that plaies the Roague on a ftage) weare rags, and patched filthy mantles vpermoft, when the vnder garments are hanfome and in fafhion.

The battailes thefe Out-lawes make, are many and very bloudy. Whofoeuer falles into _{His manner} their hands neuer efcapes aliue, & fo _{of night.} cruell they are in thefe murders, that nothing can fatisfie thē but the very heart-bloud of thofe whom they kill. And who are they (thinke you) that thus go to the pot ? Alaffe ! Innocent Lambs, Shéep, Calues, Pigges, &c. Poultrie-ware are more churlifhly handled by them, thē poore prifoners are by kéepers in the counter it'h Poultry. A goofe comming amongft them learnes to be wife, that hee neuer wil be Goofe any more. The bloudy tragedies of al thefe, are only acted by ꝝ Womē, who carrying long kniues or Skeanes vnder their mantles, do thus play their parts : The Stage is fome large Heath : or a Firre bufh Common, far from any houfes : Vpō which cafting them-felues

into a Rıng, they inclofe the Murdered, till the
Maffacre be finifhed. If any paffenger come by,
and wondring to fee fuch a cõiuring circle kept
by Hel-hoũdes, demaund what fpirits they raife
there ? one of the Murderers fteps to him, poyfons
him ẘ fweete wordes and fhifts him off, with this
lye, ẙ one of the womẽ is falne in labour. But if
any mad *Hãlet* hearing this, fmell villanie, & rufh
in by violence to fee what the tawny Diuels are
dooing, thẽ they excufe the faƈt, lay the blame on
thofe that are the Aƈtors, & perhaps (if they fee /
no remedie) deliuer them to an officer, to be had
to punifhment : But by the way a refcue is furely
laid ; and very valiantly (tho very villanoufly) do
they fetch them off, & guard them.

The Cabbines where thefe Land-pyrates lodge
in the night, are the Out-barnes of Farmers &
Hufbandmen, (in fome poore Village or other)
who dare not deny them, for feare they fhould
ere morning haue their thatched houfes burning
about their eares : in thefe Barnes, are both their
Cooke-roomes, their Supping Parlors, and their
Bed-chambers : for there they dreffe after a beaftly
manner, what foeuer they purchaft after a théeuifh
fafhion : fometimes they eate Venifon, & haue
Greyhoundes that kill it for thẽ, but if they had
not, they are *Houndes* them-felues & are damnable
Hunters after flefh : Which appeares by their vgly-

fac'd queanes that follow them : with whom ın thefe barnes they lie, as Swine do together in Hogfties.

Thefe Barnes are the beds of Incefts, Whore-domes, Adulteries, & of all other blacke and deadly - damned *Impieties* ; here His qualities whilst he lies intrenched. growes the Curfed *Tree of Baftardie*, that is fo fruitfull: here are writtē the *Bookes* of al *Blafphemies*, *Swearings* & *Curfes*, ẙ are fo dread-full to be read. Yet the fimple country-people will come running out of their houfes to gaze vpō them, whilft in the meane time one fteales into the next Roome, and brings away whatfoeuer hée can lay hold on. Vpon daies of paftime & libertie, they Spred them-felues in fmal companies What peeces of desperate seruice hee ventures vpō. amōgft the Villages : and when young maids & batchelers (yea fometimes old doting fooles, that fhould be beatē to this world of villanies, & forewarn others) do flock about thē : they then profeffe fkil in Palmeftry, & (forfooth) can tel fortunes : which for the moft part are infallibly true, by reafon that they worke vppon rules, which are groūded vpon certainty : for one of them wil tel you that you fhal fhortly haue fome euill luck fal vpon you, & within halfe an houre after you fhal find your pocket pick'd, or your purfe / cut. Thefe are thofe *Egiptian Grafhoppers* that eate vp the fruites of the Earth, and deftroy

the poore corne fieldes : to fweepe whofe fwarmes
out of this kingdome, there are no other meanes
but the fharpnes of the moſt infamous & baſeſt
kinds of puniſhment.   For if the vgly body of this
Monſter be fuffred to grow & fatten it felfe with
mifchiefs and diforder, it will haue a neck fo
Sinewy & fo brawny, that the arme of ẙ law will
haue much ado to ſtrike of ẙ Head, ſithence euery
day the mēbers of it increafe, & it gathers new
ioints & new forces by *Priggers, Anglers, Cheators,*
Morts, Yeomens Daughters (that haue taken fome
by blowes, & to auoid fhame, fall into their Sinnes:)
and other Seruants both men & maides that haue
beene pilferers, with al the reſt of that Damned
Regiment, marching together in ẙ firſt Army of
the *Bell-man,* who running away from theyr own
Coulours (ẘ are bad ynough) ferue vnder thefe,
being the worſt.   *Lucifers Lanꞌprizado* that ſtood
aloof to behold the muſtrings of thefe Hell-hoūds,
took delight to fee them Double their Fyles fo
nimbly, but held it no pollicy to come neere thē
(for the Diuell him-felfe durſt fcarce haue done
that.)   Away therefore hee gallops, knowing that
at one time or other *they would all come to* fetch
their pay in Hell.

The Infection

Of the Suburbs.

Chap. IX.

THe *Infernall Promoter* béeing wearied ẘ riding vp & downe the Country, was glad when he had gotten the Citty ouer his head, but the Citty being not able to hold him within the freedome, becaufe he was a Forreiner, the gates were fette wide open for him to paffe through, & into the *Suburbes* hee went. And what faw hee there? More Ale-houfes than there are Tauernes in all *Spayne* & *France*. Are they fo dry in the *Suburbs*? Yes, pockily dry. What faw he befides?

Hée / faw the dores of notorious *Carted Bawdes*, (like Hell-gates) ftand night and day wide open, with a paire of Harlots in *Noctes atque dic patet laniæ* Taffata gownes (like two painted pofts) *Ditis.* garnifhing out thofe dores, beeing better to the houfe then a *Double figne*: when the dore of a poore Artificer (if his child had died but ẘ one Tokē of death about him) was clofe ram'd vp and Guarded for feare others fhould haue beene infected: Yet the plague that a Whore-houfe layes vpō a Citty is worfe, yet is laughed at: if not laughed at, yet not look'd into, or if look'd into, *Wincked* at.

The Tradefman hauing his houfe lockd vp, loofeth his cuftomers, is put from worke and vndone : whilft in the meane time the ftrumpet is fet on worke and maintain'd (perhaps) by thofe that vndoe the other: giue thankes O wide mouth'd Hell! laugh *Lucifer* at this, Dance for ioy all you Diuells.

Belzebub kéepes the Regifter booke, of al $\tilde{y}$ Bawdes, Panders & Curtizans : & hee knowes, that thefe Suburb finners haue no landes to liue vpon but their legges: euery prentice paffing by them, can fay, *There fits a whore* : Without putting them to their booke they will fweare fo much themfelues : if fo, are not Counftables, Church-wardens, Bayliffes, Beadels & other Officers, Pillars and Pillowes to all the villanies, that are by thefe committed? Are they not parcell-Bawdes to winck at fuch damned abufes, confidering they haue whippes in their owne handes, and may draw bloud if they pleafe? Is not the Land-lord of fuch rentes the Graund-Bawde? & the Dore Kéeping miftreffe of fuch a houfe of finne, but his Vnder-Bawd? fithence hee takes twenty pounds rēt euery yeare, for a vaulting fchoole (which frō no Artificer liuing by the hardneffe of the hand could bee worth fiue pound.) And that twenty

pound rent, hée knowes muſt bée preſt out of
petticoates : his money ſmells of ſin : the very
ſiluer lookes pale, becauſe it was earned by luſt.

How happy therefore were Citties if they had
no Suburbes, ſithence they ſerue but as caues,
where monſters are / bred vp to deuowre the
Citties them-ſelues? Would the Diuell hire a
villaine to ſpil bloud? there he ſhall finde him.
One to blaſpheme? there he hath choice. A
Pandar that would court a matron at her praiers?
hées there. A cheator that would turne his owne
father a begging? Hées there too : A harlot that
would murder her new-borne Infant? Shée lies
in there.

What a wretched wombe hath a ſtrumpet, which
being (for the moſt) barren of Children, is notwithſtãding the onely *Bedde* that breedes vp theſe
ſerpents? vpõ that one ſtalke grow all theſe mis-
chiefes. *Shee* is the Cockatrice that hatcheth all
theſe egges of euills. When the Diuell takes the
Anatomy of all dãnable ſinnes, he lookes onely
vpon *her* body. Whẽ *ſhe* dies, he ſits as her
Coroner. When *her* ſoule comes to hell, all
ſhunne *that* there, as they flie from a body ſtruck
with the plague here. *She* hath her dore-kéeper,
and *ſhe* herſelfe is the Diuells chãber-maide. And
yet for all this, that ſhée's ſo dangerous and deteſt-
able, when ſhe hath croak'd like a Rauẽ on the

Eues, then comes fhe into the houfe like a Doue.
When her villanies (like the mote about a caftle)
are rancke, thicke, and muddy, with ftanding long
together, then (to purge herfelf) is *fhe* dreined out
of the Suburbes (as though her corruption were
there left behind her) and as a cleere ftreame is
let into the Citty.

What armor a harlot weares comming out of the
Suburbes to befiege the Citty within the wals.

VPon what perch then does fhe fit? what part
plaies fhe then? onely the *Puritane.* If
before fhe ruffled in filkes, now is fhe more ciuilly
attird then a Mid-wife. If before fhe fwaggred in
Tauernes, now with the Snaile fhe ftirreth not out
of dores. And where muft her lodging be takē vp,
but in the houfe of fome cittizē, whofe known
reputation, fhe borrowes (or rather fteales) putting
it on as a cloake to couer her deformities? Yet
euē in that, hath fhe an art too, for he fhalbe
of fuch a profeffion, that all cōmers / may enter,
without the dāger of any eyes to watch thē. As
for example *fhe* wil lie in fome *Scriueners houfe,*
& fo vnder the collour of comming to haue a
Bond made, fhe herfelfe may write *Nouerint*
vniuerfi. And tho the law threaten to hit her
neuer fo often, yet hath fhe fubtile defences to
ward off the blowes. For, if *Gallants* haūt the

houfe, then fpreds fhe thefe collours : *fhe* is a
captaine or a lieutenãts wife in the *Low-coũtries*,
& they come with letters, from the fouldier her
hufband.   If *Marchants* refort to her, then hoiftes
fhe vp thefe *fayles*, fhe is wife to the Maifter of a
fhippe, & they bring newes ỹ her hufbãd put in
at the *Straytes*, or at *Venice*, at *Aleppo*, *Alexandria*,
or *Scanderoon*, &c.   If *fhop keepers* come to her,
with *what do you lack*, in their mouthes, thē fhe
takes vp fuch & fuch commodities, to fend them
to Rye, to Briftow, to Yorke, &c. where her
hufband dwells.   But if the ftreame of her fortunes
runne low, and that none but *Apronmen* lanch forth
there then keepes fhe a pollitick tempfters fhop,
or fhe ftarches them.

Perhaps fhee is fo pollitick, that none fhalbe
noted to board her : if fo, then fhe failes
vpõ thefe *points* of the cõpaffe : fo foone How a citty punck Rang-eth.
as euer fhe is rig'd, and al her furniture
on, forth fhe lancheth into thofe ftreetes that
are moft frequēted : where the firft man that fhe
meetes of her acquaintance, fhal (without much
pulling) get her into a Tauerne : out of him fhe
kiffes a breakefaft & then leaues him : the next
fhe meetes, does vpon as eafie pullies, draw her to
a Tauerne againe ; out of him fhe *cogs* a dinner,
& then leaues him : the third man, *fquires* her to a
play, ẘ being ended, & the wine offred & taken

(for fhe's no Recufant, to refufe any thing) him
fhe leaues too : and being fet vpon by a fourth,
him fhe anfwers at his own weapō, fups with
him, & drincks *Vpfie Freeze*, til the clok ftriking
Twelue, and the Drawers being drowzy, away
they march arme in arme, being at euery foot-
ftep fearful to be fet vpō by the *Band* of
Halberdiers, that lie fcowting in rug gownes
to cut of fuch mid-night ftraglers. But the
word / being giuen, & *who goes there*, with *come
before the Conftable*, being fhot at them, they vaile
prefently & come, fhe taking vpon her to anfwer
al the *Bil-men* and their *Leader*, betweene whome
& her, fuppofe you heare this fleepy Dialogue :
where haue you bin fo late ? *at fupper forfooth
with my vncle here (if he be wel bearded) or with
my brother (if the haire bee but budding forth) and
he is bringing me home.* Are you married? *yes
forfooth* : whats your hufband ? *fuch a Noble-mans
man, or fuch a Iuftices clarke,* (And then name fome
Alderman of London, to whom fhe perfwades
herfelfe, one or other of the bench of browne
billes are beholding) where lye you ? *At fuch a
mans houfe : Sic tenues euanefcit* in *Auras :* and
thus by ftopping the Conftables mouth with fugar-
plummes (thats to fay,) whilft fhe poifons him with
fweete wordes, the punck vanifheth. *O Lanthorne
and Candle-light*, how art thou made a blinde Affe ?

becaufe thou haft but one eye to fee withall : Be
not fo guld, bee not fo dull in vnderftanding : do
thou but follow aloofe thofe two tame Pigeons, &
thou fhalt finde that her new *Vncle* lies by it al
that night, to make his kinfe-woman one of mine
Aunts : or if fhee bee not in trauell all night, they
fpend fome halfe an houre together : but what doe
they ? marry, they doe that, which the Conftable
fhould haue done for them both in the ftreetes,
thats to fay *commit, commit,*

You *Guardians* ouer fo great a Princeffe as the
eldeft daughter of King *Brutus* : you *twice twelue
fathers* and gouernours ouer the Nobleft Cittie, why
are you fo careful to plant Trees to beautifie your
outward walks, yet fuffer the goodlieft garden
(within) to be ouer-run with ftincking wéedes?
You are the proining kniues that fhould loppe off
fuch idle, fuch vnprofitable and fuch deftroying
branches from the Vine : The beames of your
Authoritie fhould purge the ayre of fuch infection : your breath of Iuftice fhould fcatter thofe
foggy vapors, and driue them out of your gates
as chaffe toffed abroad by the windes.

But / ftay : is our walking fpirit become an
Orator to perfwade ? no, but the *Bel-man* of
London with whom he met in this perambula-
tion of his, and to whom hée betraied himfelfe
& opened his very bofome, (As hereafter you

ſhall heare,) is bould to take vpon him that
ſpeakers Office.

Of Ginglers.

*Or the knauery of Horſe-Courſers in
Smith-field diſcouered.*

CHAP. X.

A T the end of fierce battailes, the onely *Rendeuouz* for lame ſouldiers to retire vnto,
is an Hoſpitall : and at the end of a long Pro-
greſſe, the onely ground for a tyred Iade to runne
in, is ſome blind country faire, where he may be
ſure to be ſold.   To theſe Markets of vnwhole-
ſome Horſe-fleſh, (like ſo many Kites to féede
vpon Carion) doe all the Horſe-courſers (that
rooſt about the Citty) flie one after another.   And
whereas in buying all other commodities, men
ſtriue to haue the beſt, how great ſo euer the
price be, onely the Horſe-courſer is of a baſer
minde, for the woorſt horf-fleſh (ſo it be cheape)
does beſt goe downe with him.   He cares for
nothing but a fayre out-ſide, and a hanſome ſhape
(like thoſe that hyre whores, though there be a
hundred diſeaſes within) : *he* (as the *other*) ventures
vpon thē all.

The firſt leſſon, therefore, that a Horſe-courſer
takes out, when he comes to one of theſe Markets,
is to make choyce of ſuch Nags, Geldings, or

Mares, efpecially, as are fatte, fayre, and well-fauor'd to the eye: and becaufe men delight to behold beautifull coullors, and that fome coulours are more delicate (euen in beafts) then others are, he will fo néere as he can, bargaine for thofe horfes that haue the daintieft complexion: as the Milke-white, the Gray, the Dapple-Gray, the Cole blacke with his proper markes (as the white ftarre in the forehead, the white / héele, &c.) or the bright Bay, with the like proper markes alfo. And the goodlier proportion ẙ beaft carries or the fayrer markes or coulour that hee beares, are or ought to bee watch-words as it were to him that afterwards buyes him of the horfe-courfer, that he bee not coozend with an ouer-price for a bad peny-worth: becaufe fuch Horfes (belonging for the moft part to Gentlemen) are feldome or neuer folde away, but vpon fome fowle quality, or fome incurable difeafe, which the Beaft is falne into. The Beft coulours are therefore the beft Cloakes to hide thofe faults that moft disfigure a Horfe: and next vnto coulour, his Pace doth often-times deceiue and goe beyond a very quick Iudgement.

Some of thefe *Horfe-hunters*, are as nimble Knaues in finding out the infirmities of a Iade, as a Barber is in drawing of téeth: and albeit (without cafting his water) hee does more readily

reckon vp all the Aches, Crampes, Crickes, and
whatfoeuer difeafe elfe lyes in his bones, and for
thofe difeafes feemes vtterly to diflike him; yet if
by looking vpon the Dyall within his mouth, he
finde that his yeares haue ftruck but fiue, fixe, or
feauen, and that he prooues but young, or that
his difeafes are but newly growing vpon him, if
they be outward; or haue but hayre and fkin to
hide them, if they bee inward; let him fweare
neuer fo damnably that it is but a Iade, yet he
will be fure to faften vpon him.

So then, a *Horfe-courfer* to the *Merchant*, (that
out of his found iudgement buyes the faireft, the
beft-bred, and the nobleft Horfes, felling them
againe for breede or feruice, with plainneffe and
honefty,) is as the *Cheator* to the faire *Gamefter* :
hee is indeed a meere Iadifh *Nonopolitane*, and
deales for none but tyred, tainted, dull, and
difeafed horfes. By which meanes, if
his picture bee drawne to the life, you
fhall finde euery *Horfe-courfer* for the
moft part to bee in quality a coozener, by profeffion a knaue, by his cunning a Varlet, in fayres
a Hagling Chapman, in the Citty a Cogging
diffembler, and / in . Smith-field a common for-
fworne Villaine. Hee will fweare any thing, but
the fafter hee fweares, the more danger tis to
beleeue him : In one forenoone, and in felling a

The picture
of a Horfe-
courser.

Iade not worth fiue Nobles, will hee forfweare himfelfe fifteene times, and that forfwearing too fhall bée by *Equiuocation.* As for example, if an ignorant Chapman comming to beate the price, fay to the Horfe-courfer, your nagge is verie olde, —or thus many yeares olde, and reckon ten or twelue : hee claps his hand prefently on the buttocke of the beaft, and praies he may bee damb'd if the Horfe be not vnder fiue, meaning not that the horfe is vnder fiue yeares of age, but that he ftandes vnder fiue of his fingers, when his hand is clap'd vppon him. Thefe *Horfe-courfers* are called *Iynglers*, and thefe *Iynglers* hauing laide out their money on a company of Iades at fome drunken fayre, vp to London they driue them, and vppon the Market day into Smithfield brauely come they prauncing. But leaft their Iades fhould fhew too many horfe trickes in Smith-field, before fo greate an Audience as commonly refort thither, their maifters doe therefore Schoole them at home after this manner.

How a Horfe-courfer workes vpon a Iade in his
own Stable, to make him feruiceable for
a couzening Race in Smith-field.

THe Glanders in a horfe is fo filthy a difeafe, that he who is troubled with it, can neuer keep his nofe cleane: fo that when fuch a foule-

noſed Iade happens to ſerue a Horſe-courſer,
hee hath more ſtrange pils (then a
Pothecarie makes) for the purging of
his head : he knowes that a horſe with
ſuch a qualitie, is but a beaſtly companion to trauell vppon the high way
with anye Gentleman.

How a Horse-
courser may
coozen his
chap-man
vvith a horse
that hath the
Glanders.

Albeit therefore that the Glanders haue played
with his Noſe ſo long, that hee knowes not how
to mend himſelfe, / but that the diſeaſe beeing
ſuffered to runne vppon him many yeares together, is grown inuincible, yet hath our Iingling
Mountibancke Smithfield-rider a tricke to cure
him, fiue or ſixe waies, and this is one of them.

In the verie morning when hee is to bee rifled
away amongſt the Gamſters in Smithfield, before
hee thruſt his head out of his Maiſters Stable, the
Horſe-courſer tickles his noſe (not with a Pipe
of Tobacco) but with a good quantitie of the beſt
Neeſing powder that can bee gotten : which with
a quil being blown vp into the Noſtrills, to make
it worke the better, he ſtands poaking there vp
and downe with two long feathers plucked from
the wing of a Gooſe, they beeing dipt in the iuice
of Garlick, or in any ſtrong oyle, and thruſt vp to
the verie top of his head, ſo farre as poſſibly they
can reach, to make the pore dumbe beaſt auoide
the filth from his noſtrils ; which hee will doe in

great aboundance : this being done, he comes to
him with a new medicine for a ficke horfe, and
mingling the iuyce of Bruzed Garlike, fharpe
biting Muftard, and ftrong Ale together, into both
the Noftrils (with a Horne) is powred a good
quantitie of this filthy Broth ; which by the hand
being held in by ftopping the noftrils clofe together, at length with a little neezing more, his
nofe will be cleaner then his Maifters the Horfe-
courfer, and the filth bee fo Artificially ftop'd that
for eight or ten houres a Iade will holde vp his
head with the prowdeft Gelding that gallops
fcornefully by him, and neuer haue neede of
wiping.

This is one of the Comedies a Common horfe-
courfer playes by himfelfe at home, but if when
hee comes to act the fecond part abroad, you
would difgrace him, and haue him hiffd at for not
playing the Knaue well, then handle him thus :
If you fufpect that the Nagge which he would
Iade you with, bee troubled with that or any
other fuch like difeafe, gripe him hard about the
wefand pipe, clofe toward the roofe of the tongue,
and holding him / there fo long and fo forcibly,
that he cough twice or thrice, if then (after you
let goe your holde) his chappes begin to walke
as if he were chewing downe a Horfe-loafe, fhake
hands with old *Mounfier Cauiliero Horf-Courfer,*

but clap no bargain vpon it, for his Iade is as full of infirmitie, as the maifter of Villanie.

Other Gambals that Horfe-courfers practife vpon Fowndred Horfes, olde Iades, &c.

Smithfield is the ftage upon which the *Moũti-bank Englifh Horfe-courfer* aduãncing his banner, defies any difeafe that dares touch his Prancer: Infomuch that if a horfe be fo olde, as that foure legs can but carry him, yet fhall he beare the markes of an Nag not aboue fixe or feauen yeares of age ; & that counterfeit badge of youth, he weares thus : The *Horfe-courfer* with a fmal round yrõ made very hot, burnes two black holes in the top of the two out-moft teeth of each fide the out-fide of the Horfes mouth vpon the nether teeth, & fo likewife of the teeth of the vpper chap, which ftand oppofite to ỹ nether, the qual-litie of which marks is to fhew that a horfe is but yong: but if the iade be fo old that thofe teeth are dropt out of his head, thẽ is there a tricke ftill to be fumbling about his olde chaps, & in that ftroaking his chin, to pricke his lips clofely with a pin or a naile, till they be fo tender, that albeit he were a giuen horfe none could bee fuffered to looke him in the mouth (which is one of the beft Calenders to tell his age) but a reafonable

fighted eie (without helpe of fpectacles) may eafily
difcouer this Iugling, becaufe it is groffe and
common.

If now a Horfe (hauing beene a fore Trauailer)
happē by falling into a colde fweate to bee
Foundred, fo that (as if hee were drunck or had
the ftaggers) hee can fcarce ftand on his legges,
then will his maifter, before hee enter into the lifts
of the field againft all commers, put him into a
villanous chafing, by ryding him vp and downe /
a quarter or halfe an houre, till his limbes bee
thoroughly heated; and this hee does, becaufe fo
long as hee can difcharge that falfe fire, or that
(being fo collerickly hotte) hee tramples onely
vppon foft ground, a very cūning *Horfema* fhal
hardly find where his fhoo wrings him, or that
hee is *Fowndred.* And (to blinde the eyes of the
Chapman) the *Horfe-courfer* will bee euer tickling
of him with his wand, becaufe hee may not by
ftanding ftill like an Affe, fhew of what houfe hee
comes.

If a *Horfe* come into the fielde (like a lame
foldier) Halting, hee has not *Crutches* made for
him, as the foldier hath, but becaufe you fhall
thinke the *Horfes* fhooemaker hath feru'd him like
a Iade, by not fitting his foote well, the fhooe fhall
bee takē off purpofely from that foote which halts,
as though it had beene loft by chance : And to

proue this, witneſſes ſhall come in, if at leaſt
twenty or thirty damnable oathes can be takē,
that the want of the Shooe is onely the cauſe of
his *Halting*.   But if a *Horſe* cannot be luſtie at
legges, by reaſon that either his hoofes bee not
good, or that there be Splents, or any other *Eye-
ſore* about the nether Ioynt, the *Horſ-courſer* vſes
him then as *Cheating Swaggerers* handle *Nouices* :
what they cannot winne by the Dyce, they will
haue by *Foule play* : & in that foule manner
deales hee with the poore horſe, ryding him vp
and downe in the thickeſt & the durtieſt places,
till that durt, like a ruffled boote drawne vppon
an ill-fauor'd gowtie legge, couer the Iades infirmitie from the eyes of the *Buyer*.

How a Horſe-courſer makes a Iade that
has no ſtomach, to eate
Lamb-pye.

A Lbeit *Lamb-pie* be good meat vpō a table,
yet it is ſo offenſiue to a *horſes* ſtomach,
ẏ he had rather be fed a moneth together with
muſtie oates, thã to taſte it : Yet are not all *Horſes*
biddē to his *Lamb-pie-Breakefaſts* but / onely ſuch
as are dyeted with no other meate : and thoſe are
Dull, Blockiſh, Sullen ; and heauie footed Iades.
When-ſoeuer therefore a *Horſe-courſer* hath ſuch
a *Dead commoditie*, as a *Lumpiſh ſlow Iade*, that

goes more heauily then a Cow when fhee trots, and that neither by a fharpe bitte nor a tickling fpurre he can put him out of his lazie and dogged pace, what does hee with him then? Onelye he giues him *Lamb-pie.* That is to fay, euery morning when the *Horfe-courfer* comes into the Stable, he takes up a tough round cudgell, and neuer leaues fencing with his *Quarter ftaffe* at the poore *Horfes* fides and buttockes, till with blowes hee hath made them fo tender, that the verry fhaking of a bough will be able to make the horfe ready to runne out of his wittes. And to keep the horfe ftill in this mad mood, becaufe he fhall not forget his leffon, his maifter will neuer come neer him, but he will haue a fling at him: If he doe touch him, hee ftrikes him: if he fpeakes to him, there is but a worde and a blow: if he doe but looke vpon him, the *Horfe* flings and takes on, as though he would breake through the walles, or had bene a *Horfe* bredde vp in Bedlam amongft mad-folkes. Hauing thus gotten this hard leffon by heart, forth comes he into *Smithfield* to repeat it, where the *Rider* fhall no fooner leap into the faddle but the *Horfe-courfer* giuing the Iade (that is halfe fcarred out of his wits already) three or foure good bangs, away flies *Bucephalus* as if yōg *Alexander* wer vpon his backe. No ground can holde him, no bridle raine him in; he gallops away

as if the Deuill had hired him of fome Hackney-man, and fcuds through thicke and thinne,
as if crackers had hung at his heeles. If his
taile play the wag, and happen to whifke vp and
downe (which is a figne that he does his feates of
Actiuitie like a *Tumblers* prentice by compufilon
and without taking pleafure in them) then fhall
you fee the *Horfe-courfer* laie about him like a
thrafher, till with blowes he made him carry his
taile to his Bottocks : which / in a Horfe (contrary
to the nature of a Dog) is an argument that he
hath mettall in him and Spirrit, as in the other it
is the note of cowardife.

Thefe and fuch other bafe iuglings are put in
practife, by the *Horfe-courfer* ; in this maner
comes he arm'd into the field : with fuch bad
and deceiptfull cōmodities does he furnifh the
markets. Neither fteps he vpon the diuels ftage
alone, but others are likewife Actors in the felfe-
fame Scene, and fharers with him : for no fooner
fhall money be offred for a Horfe, but prefently
one *Snake* thrufts out his head and ftings the buyer
with falfe praifes of the Horfes goodneffe : An
other throwes out his poifoned hooke and whifpers
in the Chapmans eare, that vpon his knowledge
fo much or fo much hath bene offred by foure or
fiue, and would not be taken : and of thefe *Rauens*
there be fundry nefts, but all of them as blacke in

foule as the *Horſe-courſer* (with whome they are
yoaked) is in conſcience. This *Regiment* of *Horſe-
men* is therefore deuided into foure *Squadrons. viz.*

1. When *Horſe-courſers* trauaile to country faires,
they are called *Iynglers.*

2. When they haue the leading of the *Horſe* &
ſerue in Smithfield, they are *Drouers.*

3. They that ſtand by and conycatche the Chapman either with *Out-bidding, falſe-praiſes, &c.* are
called *Goades.*

4. The boyes, ſtriplings, &c., that haue the
ryding of the Iades vp and downe are called
Skip-iacks.

Jacke / in a Boxe.

*Or a new kinde of Cheating, teaching how to change
golde into Siluer, vnto which is added a Map, by
which a man may learn how to trauell all ouer
England and haue his charges borne.*

Chap. ii.

Ow many *Trees* of *Euill* are growing in this
coũtrie? how tall they are ? how Mellow is
their fruit? and how greedily gathered ? ſo much
ground doe they take vp, and ſo thickly
doe they ſtand together, that it ſeemeth *Terra malos
homines nunc
educat.*
a kingdom can bring forth no more of
their nature : yes, yes, there are not halfe ſo many

Riuers in Hell, in which a foule may faile to damnation, as there are *Black Streames* *Noxia mille* *modis Lacera-* of *Mifchiefe* and *Villany* (befides all thofe *bitur vmbra.* which in our Now-two Voyages we haue ventured fo many leagues vp, for difcouerie) in which thoufandes of people are continually fwimming, and euerie minute in danger vtterly to be caft away.

The *Horfe-courfer* of hell, after he had durtyed himfelfe with ryding vp and downe *Abufes of* *race-running* Smithfield, and hauing his beaft vnder *glanced at.* him, gallopped away amaine to beholde a race of fiue myles by a couple of *Running-Horfes*, vppon whofe fwiftneffe great fummes of money were laide in wagers. In which Schoole of *Horfe-manfhippe* (wherein for the mofte part none but Gallants are the Studients) hee conftrued but ftrange Lectures of *Abufes* : he could make large Comments vppon thofe that are the *Runners* of thofe *Races*, and could teach others how to lofe fortie or fiftie pound pollitickly in the forenoone, and in the after noone (with the felfe-fame Gelding) to winne a thoufand markes in fiue or fixe miles riding. He could tell how Gentlemen are fetch'd in and made younger brothers, and how your *new Knight* comes to be a Couzen of this Race. He could drawe the true pictures of fome fellowes, that dyet thefe *Running Horfes*, / who for a bribe of fortie or fiftie fhillings can by a falfe *Dye* make their owne Maifters loofe a hundred pound a race. He could fhew more craftie *Foxes* in this wilde-goofe chafe thē there are white *Foxes* in *Ruffia*, & more ftrange Horfe trickes plaide by fuch Riders, then *Bankes* his curtall did euer practife (whofe Gamballs of the two, were the honefter.)

But becaufe this fort of Birdes haue many feathers to loofe, before they can feele any colde, he fuffers them to make their owne flight, knowing that prodigalls doe but ieft at the ftripes which other mens rods giue them, and neuer complaine of fmarting till they are whip'd with their owne.

In euerie Corner did he finde Serpents ingendering: vnder euerie roofe, fome impyetie *Vix sunt* or other lay breeding: but at laft per- *homines hoc* ceiuing that the moft part of men were *nomine dignis,* by the forcerie of their own diuelifh *quāq; lupi læuæ plus feritatis habēt.* conditions transformed into Wolues, and being fo changed, were more brutifh & bloody, then thofe that were Wolues by nature: his fpleene leap'd againft his ribbes with laughter, and in the height of that ioy refolued to write the villanies of the world in *Folio*, and to dedicate them in priuate to his Lord and Maifter, becaufe hee knew him to bee an open-handed patron, albeit he was no great louer of fchollers.

But hauing begunne one picture of a certaine ſtrange Beaſt, (called *Iack in a Boxe*) that onely (becauſe the Cittie had giuen money already to ſee it) hee finiſhed : and in theſe colours was Iacke in a Box *Iack in a Boxe* drawn.   It hath the described. head of a man (the face well bearded) the eyes of a *Hawke*, the tongue of a *Lap-wing*, which ſaies *heere it is*, when the neſt is a good way off : it hath the ſtomacke of an *Eſtrich*, and can diſgeſt ſiluer as eaſily, as that Bird dooth Yron. It hath the pawes of a *Beare* inſtead of handes, for whatſoeuer it faſtneth vppon, it holdes : From the middle downe-wardes, it is made like a *Grey-hound*, and is ſo ſwift of foote, that if it once get the Start of you, a whole *Kennel of Hounds* cannot / ouertake it.   It loues to hunt dry-foote, and can *Scent* a *Traine* in no ground ſo well as the Cittie, and yet not in all places of the Cittie. But he is beſt in *Scenting* betweene *Ludgate* and *Temple-barre* :   and tis thought that his next hunting ſhall bee betweene *Lumbard-ſtreete* and the *Gold-ſmithes Rowe* in *Cheape-ſide* :   Thus much for his outward parts, now you ſhall haue him vnrip'd, and ſee his inward.

This *Iacke in a Boxe*, or this Deuill in mans His exerciſe. ſhape, wearing (like a player on a Stage) good cloathes on his backe, comes to a *Golde-ſmithes* Stall, to a *Drapers*, a *Haberdaſhers*,

or into any other fhop where he knows good ftore
of filuer faces are to be feene.   And there drawing
foorth a faire new box, hammered all out of *Siluer
Plate,* hee opens it, and powres foorth twentie or
forty *Twentie-fhilling-peeces in New-golde.*   To
which heape of *Worldly-Temptation,* thus much
hee addes in words, that either *he him-felfe,* or
fuch a Gentleman (to whom he belongs) hath an
occafion for foure or fiue daies to vfe fortie pound.
But becaufe he is verie fhortly, (nay he knowes
not how fuddenly) *to trauaile to Venice,* to *Ieru-
falem* or fo, and would not willingly be disfurnifhed
of *Golde,* he dooth therefore requeft the Cittizen
to lend (vpon thofe *Forty twenty fhilling peeces*)
fo much in white money (but for foure, fiue or
fixe daies at moft) and for his good-
will he fhall receiue any reafonable
fatisfaction.   The *Cittizen* (knowing
the pawne to be better thē a Bond)
powres downe fortie pound in filuer;
the other drawes it, and leauing fo much golde in
Hoftage, marcheth away with *Bag* and *Baggage.*

*sitiens fugien-
tia captat
Flumina: quid
rides ? mutato
nomine, de Te
Fabula
narratur.*

Fiue   daies   being   expired,   *Iacke in a box,*
(according to his Bargaine) being a man of his
word comes againe to the Shop or ftall (at which
hee angles for frefh Fifh) and there cafting out his
line with the filuer hooke, thats to fay, pouring
out the forty pound which hee borrowed, The

Citizen fends in, or fteps himfelfe for the *Boxe*
with the *Golden deuill* in it : it is opened, and the
army of angels / being muftred together, they are
all found to bee there. The *Box* is fhut agen and
fet on the Stall, whilft the Cittizen is telling of his
money : But whilft this muficke is founding, *Iacke
in a Boxe* actes his part in a dumb fhew thus ; hee
fhifts out of his fingers *another Boxe* of the fame
mettall and making, that the former beares, which
fecond Boxe is filled onely with *fhillings* & being
poized in the hand, fhall feeme to cary the weight
of the former, and is clap'd down in place of the
firft. The Citizen in the meane time (whilft this
Pit-fall is made for him) telling the fortie poundes,
miffeth thirtie or fortie fhillinges in the whole
fumme, at which the *Iacke in a Boxe* ftarting
backe (as if it were a matter ftrange vnto him)
at laft making a gathering within himfelfe, for his
wits, hee remembers (he faies) that hee laid by fo
much money as is wanting (of the fortie poundes)
to difpatch fome bufineffe or other, and forgot to
put it into the Bag againe; notwithftanding, hee
intreates the Citizen to keepe his golde ftill, hee
will take the white money home to fetch the reft,
and make vp the Summe, his abfence fhall not bee
aboue an houre or two : before which time he
fhall bee fure to *heare* of him; and with this the
little *Diuell* vanifheth, carrying that away with

him, which in the end will fend him to the
Gallowes, (thats to fay his owne golde) and fortie
pound befides of the Shop-keepers,
which hee borrowed, the other béeing
glad to take forty fhillings for the
whole debt, and yet is foundly box'd for his
labour.
Multa potenti-
bus desunt
multa.

This *Iacke in a boxe*, is yet but a Chicken, and
hath laide verie few Egges : if the Hang-man
doe not fpoyle it with treading, it will prooue an
excellent Henne of the Game. It is a knot of
Cheators but newly tyed, they are not yet a
company. They flie not like Wilde-Geefe (in
flockes) but like Kites (fingle) as loath that any
fhould fhare in their pray. They haue two or
three names, (yet they are no *Romaines*, but errant
Rogues) for fome-times they call themfelues *Iacke
in a boxe*, but / now that their infantrie growes
ftrong, and that it is knowne abroad, that they
carrie the Philofophers ftone about them, and are
able of fortie fhillings to make fortie pound, they
therefore vfe a deade March, and the better to
cloake their villanies, doe put on thefe *Mafking
fuites* : viz.

1. This art or fleight of changing golde into
filuer, is called *Trimming*.

2. They that practife it, terme them-felues
Sheepe-fhearers.

3. The Gold which they bring to the Cittizen, is cald *Iaſons Fleece*.

4. The ſiluer which they pick vp by this wandring, is *White-wooll*.

5. They that are Cheated by *Iacke in a Boxe*, are called *Bleaters*.

Oh Fleete-ſtreete! Fleete-ſtreete! how haſt thou bene trimd, waſhed, Shauen and Polde by theſe deere and damnable Barbers? how often haſt thou mette with theſe *Sheep-ſhearers*? how many warme flakes of wooll haue they pulled from thy Back? yet if thy Bleating can make the flockes that graze nere vnto thee and round about thee, to lift vp their eyes, and to ſhunne ſuch Wolues and Foxes, when they are approaching, or to haue them worryed to death before they ſucke the blood of others, thy misfortunes are the leſſe, becauſe thy neighbours by them ſhall be warned from danger.

Many of thy Gallants (O Fleete-ſtreete) haue ſpent hundreds of poundes in thy preſence, and yet neuer were ſo much as drunke for it ; but for euerie fortye pound that thou layeſt out in this Indian commoditie (of gold) thou haſt a *Siluer Boxe* beſtowed vpon thee, to carry thy Tobacco in, becauſe thou haſt euer loued that coſtlye and Gentleman-like Smoak. *Iacke in a Boxe* hath thus plaide his part. There is yet another Actor to ſtep vpon the ſtage, and he

feemes to haue good fkil in Cofmography, for he
holdes in his hand a Map, wherein hee hath layde
downe / a number of Shires in England,
and with fmall pricks hath beaten out
a path, teaching how a man may eafily,
(tho not verry honeftly) trauell from Country to
Country, and haue his charges borne; and thus
it is.

How to tra-
uaile without
charges.

He that vnder-takes this ftrange iourney, layes
his firft plotte how to be turned into a *Braue man*,
which he findes can be done by none better then
by a *trufty Tailor* : working therefore hard with
him, till his fuite be granted, Out of the Cittie,
beeing mounted on a good gelding, he rides vpon
his owne bare credit, not caring whether he trauell
to meete the Sunne at his Ryfing or at his going
downe. He knowes his Kitching fmokes in euery
Countie, and his table couered in euery Shire. For
when he comes within a mile of the Towne where
hee meanes to catche Quailes, fetting Spurres to
his horfe, away he gallops, with his cloake off (for
in thefe *Befeigings* of Townes hee goes not armd
with any, his Hatte thruft into his Hofe, as if it
were loft, and onely an emptie paire of *Hangers*
by his fide, to fhew that hee has bene difarmed.
And you muft note, that this Hot-fpurre does
neuer fet vppon any places but onely fuch, where
hee knowes (by intelligence) there are ftore of

Gentlemen, or wealthy Farmers at the leaſt. Amongſt whome when hee is come, hee tels with diſtracted lookes, and a voice almoſte breathleſſe, how many Villanies ſet vppon him, what golde & ſiluer they tooke from him, what woods they are fled into, from what part of *Englãd* he is come, to what place he is going, how farre he is from home, how farre from his iornies end, or from any Gentleman of his acquaintance, and ſo liuely perſonates the lying *Greek (Synon)* in telling a lamentable tale : that the mad *Troianes* (the Gentlemen of the towne,) beleeuing him, & the rather becauſe he carries the ſhape of an honeſt man in ſhew, and of a Gentleman in his apparrell, are liberall of their purſes, lending him money to beare him on his iourney : to pay which he offers either his bill or bond (naming his lodging / in London) or giues his word (as hées a Gentleman), which they rather take, knowing the like misfortũe may be theirs at any time.

And thus with the feathers of other birdes, is this *Monſter* ſtuck, making wings of ſundry faſhions, with which he thus baſely flies ouer a whole kingdom. Thus doth he ride from Towne to Towne, from Citty to City as if he were a *Lãd-lord* in euery ſhire, and that he were to gather *Rents* vp of none but *Gentlemen.*

There is a *Twin-brother* to this *Falſe galloper,*

and hee cheats *Inne-keepers* onely, or their *Tapſters*,
by learning firſt what Country-men they are, and
of what kindred: and then bringing counterfeit
letters of commendations from ſuch an Vncle,
or ſuch a Coozen (wherin is requeſted, that the
Bearer thereof may bee vſed kindely) hee lyes in
the Inne till he haue fetcht ouer the Maiſter or
Seruant for ſome mony (to draw whome to him
he hath many hookes) and when they hang faſt
enough by the Gills, vnder water *Our Sharke* diues,
and is neuer ſeene to ſwimme againe in that Riuer.

Vppon this Scaffold, alſo might be mounted a
number of *Quack-ſaluing Empericks*, who ariuing
in ſome Country towne, clappe vp their *Terrible
Billes*, in the Market-place, and filling the Paper
with ſuch horrible names of *diſeaſes*, as if euery
diſeaſe were a Diuell, and that they could coniure
them out of any Towne at their pleaſure. Yet theſe
Beggerly *Mountibancks* are meare Coozeners, and
haue not ſo much ſkill as Horſeleeches. The poore
people not giuing money to them to be cured of any
infirmities, but rather with their money buying
worſe infirmities of them.

Vppon the ſame poſt, doe certaine ſtragling
Scribling Writers deſerue to haue both their
names and themſelues hung vp, inſteed of thoſe
faire tables which they

Trauelling
Emperickes.

Strowling
schoole-
maister.

hang vp in Townes, as gay pictures to intice Schollers to them : the Tables are w[r]itten with fundry kindes of hands, but not one finger of thofe hands (not one letter there) / drops from the Penne of fuch a falfe wandring Scribe. He *buyes* other mens cunning good cheape in London, and fels it deere in the Country. Thefe Swallowes bragge of no qualitie in them fo much as of *fwiftneffe.* In *foure* & *twenty houres,* they will worke foure and twenty wonders, and promife to teach thofe, that know no more what belongs to an A. then an Affe, to bee able (in that narrow compaffe) *to write as faire* and as faft as a country Vicar, who commonly reads all the Townes Letters.

But wherefore doe thefe counterfeit Maifters of that *Noble Science of Writing,* kéepe fuch a florifhing with the borrowed weapons of other Mens Pennes ? onely for this to gette halfe the Birdes (which they ftriue to catch) into their hands, thats to fay, to bee *payde* halfe the money which is agréed vpon for the Scholler, and his neft being halfe fild with fuch Gold-finches, he neuer ftayes till the reft be fledge, but fuffers *him* that comes next, to beate the bufh for the other halfe. At this Careere the Ryder that fet out laft from Smith-field, ftop'd : and alighting from *Pacolet* (the horfe that carried him) his next iourney was made on foote.

The Bel-mans ſecond
Night-walke.

Chap. XII.

S Ir *Lancelot* of the infernall Lake, or the
Knight *Errant* of Hell, hauing thus (like
a yong country gentleman) gone round about the
Citty, to ſee the *ſights* not onely within the walles
but thoſe alſo in the *Subburbes,* was glad when hee
ſawe night hauing put on the vizard *Induta nigris*
that Hell lends her (cald darkenes) to *vestibus,*
currum insilit
leap in to her Coach, becauſe now he *Nox.*
knew he ſhould meete with other ſtrange birdes
and / beaſts fluttring from their neſts, and crawling
out of their dennes.   His prognoſtication held
currant, and the foule weather (which hee fore-
told,) fell out accordingly.   For *Canale-light* had
ſcarce opend his eye (to looke at the Citty like
a gunner ſhooting at a marke), but fearefully
(their féet trembling vnder thẽ) their *Noctis & erebi*
eyes ſuſpitiouſly rouling from euery *progenies sunt*
Dolus, Metus,
nooke to nooke round about them, & *Miseria,Fraus,*
Querelæ, &c.
their heads (as if they ſtood vppon *Cic. in Lib.* 3
De Nat.
oyled ſkrewes) ſtill turning back be- *Deorum.*
hinde them, came créeping out of hollow-trées,
where they lay hidden ; a number of couzning

Bankrupts in the fhapes of Owles, who when the Marfhall of light, the funne, went vp and downe to fearch the Citty, durft not ftir abroad, for feare of béeing houted at and followed by whole flockes of *vndon creditors.*

But now when the ftage of the world was hung *· Nox verenda,* in blacke, they ietted vppe & downe *verenda, &c.* like proud *Tragedians.* O what thankes they gaue to Darkneffe! what * fonges they balladed out in praife of Night, for beftowing vpon them fo excellent a cloake wherein they might fo fafely walke muffled! Now durft they, as if they had beene Conftables, rappe alowd at the dores of thofe to whom they owed moft money, & braue them with hie wordes, tho they payd them not a penny.

Now did they boldly ftep into fome priuiledged Tauerne, and there drinke healthes, dance with Harlots, & pay both Drawers and Fidlers after mid-night with other mens money, & then march home againe feareleffe of the blowes that any *fhowlder-clapper* durft giue thē. Out of another Neft flew certaine *Murderers* and *Theeues* in the fhapes of *Skreech-owles,* who, being fet on by the Night, did beate with their bold and vēturous fatall wings at the very dores whereas, in former times, their villanies had entred.

Not farre frō *Thefe,* came crawling out of their

bufhes a company of graue & wealthy *Lechers* in the fhapes of *Glowe-wormes*, who with gold, Iyngling in their pockets, / made fuch a fhew *Sapiens in munera venit adultor, Præbuit ipsa sinus, nec polisti metuunt Deos nec hos respicere Deos opinor.* in the night, that the dores of Common *Brothelryes* flew open to receiue them, tho in the day time they durft not paffe that way, for feare that noted *Curtizans* fhould challenge them of acquaintance, or that others fhould laugh at them to fee *white heads* growing vpon *greene ftalkes*.

Then came forth certaine infamous earthy minded *Creatures* in the fhapes of *Snailes*, who all the day time hyding their heads in their fhells, leaft boies fhould ẘ two fingers point at them for liuing bafely vpō the *proftitutiō* of their wiues bodies, cared not now, before *candle-light*, to fhoote out their largeft & longeft *Hornes*.

A number of other monfters, like *Thefe*, were feene (as the funne went downe) to venture from their dēnes, only to ingender with *Darkneffe* : but *candle lights* eyefight growing dimmer & dimmer, and hee at laft falling ftarke blind, *Lucifers* Watchman went ftrumbling vp and down in the darke.

How to weane Horfes.

EVery dore on a fudden was fhut, not a candle ftood peeping through any window, not a *Vintner* was to be féene brewing in his Cellor, not a drunkerd to be met réeling, not a Moufe to be heard ftirring : al ẏ Citty ſhewed like one Bed, for all in that Bed were foũdly caft into a fléepe. Noyfe made no noife, for euery one that wrought with the hamer was put to filence. Yet notwithſtãding when euen the Diuel himfelfe could haue béene contẽted to take a nap, there were few *Innkeepers* about ẏ towne but had their fpirits walking. To watch which fpirits what they did, *our Spy*, that came lately out of ẏ *Lower countries*, ſtole into oné of their Circles, where lurking very clofely, hée perceiued ẏ whẽ all the guefts were profoundly fléeping, when Cariers were foundly fnorting, & not fo much as the Chamberlaine of the houfe but was layd vp, fuddenly out of his bed ftarted an *Hoftler*, who hauing no apparell on but his ſhirt, a paire of ſlip-ſhooes on his / feete, and a *Candle* burning in his hand like olde *Ieronimo* ftep'd into the ftable amõgft a number of poore hungry Iades, as if that night he had beene to ride poaft to ẏ Diuell. But his iorney not lying that way till fome other time, he neither bridled nor fadled any of his foure-footed guefts that ftood there at racke and manger, but feeing them fo late at fupper, and knowing that to ouer-eate them-felues would fill them full of difeafes, (they being fubieƈt to aboue a hundred & thirty

Mutat Quies habitat.

The knauery of Hostlars.

already) hée firſt (without a voyder) after a moſt vnmanerly faſhion tooke away, not onely all the Prouander that was ſet before them, but alſo all the hay, at which before they were glad to lick their lippes. The poore Horſes looked very rufully vpon him for this, but hee rubbing their teeth onely with the end of a *Candle* (in ſteed of a Corrall) tolde them, that for their Iadiſh trickes it was now time to weane them : And ſo wiſhing them not to bee angry if they lay vpon the hard boards, cõſidering all the beddes in the houſe were full, back againe hee ſtole to his Coach, till breake of day : yet fearing leaſt the ſunne ſhould riſe to diſcouer his knauery, vp hee ſtarted, & into the ſtable he ſtumbled, ſcarce halfe awake, giuing to euery Iade a bottle of hay for his breake-faſt ; but al of them being troubled ẇ the greazy tooth-ach could eate none, which their maiſters in the morning eſpying ſwore they were either ſullen or els that prouender pricked them.

This Hoſtler for this peece of ſeruice was after-wards preferred to be one of the Groomes in *Belzebubs* ſtable.

Another Night-peece drawne in fundry collours.

SHall I fhew you what other bottomes of mifchiefe, *Plutos* Beadle faw wound vpon the blacke fpindels of the Night, in this his priuy fearch? In fome ftreetes he met Mid-wiues running, till they fweat, & following them clofe at heeles, he fpied them to be let in, at the backe dores of houfes, feated either in blind lanes, or in by-gardens: / which houfes had roomes builded *Matronaq;* for the purpofe, where young Maides, *rara pudica est.* being bigge with child by vnlawful Fathers, or young wiues (in their hufbands abfcence at fea, or in the warres) hauing wraftled with *Sæpè solent* batchilers or maried men, til they caught *aura multa* falls, lay fafely til they wer deliuered of *subesse malâ.* them. And for reafonable fummes of mony, the baftards that at thefe windows crept into the world, were as clofely now and ** Pectora* then fent prefently out of the * world, or *tantis obsessa* *malis,* els were fo vnmannerly brought vp, that *Non sunt ictu* *ferienda leui.* they neuer fpake to their owne parents that begot them.

In fome ftreetes he met feruants in whofe breft *Quit prodere* albeit the arrowes of the plague ftuck *tanta relatu* *Funera.* halfe way, yet by cruell maifters were they driuen out of dores at mid-night and conuaid to Garden-houfes, where they either died before next morning, or elfe were carried thither dead in their coffins, as tho they had lien ficke there before and there had dyed.

Now and then at the corner of a turning hee fpyed feruants purloyning fardels of their maifters goods, and deliuering them to the hands of common ftrumpets.

This dore opend, and *Luft* with *Prodigality* were heard to ftand clofely kiffing : and (wringing one another by the hand) foftly to whifper out foure or fiue good-nights, till they met abroad the next morning.

A thoufand of thefe comedies were acted in dumb fhew, and onely in the *priuat houfes* : at which the Diuells meffenger laught fo loud that *Hell* heard him, and for ioy range foorth loude and luftie *Plaudities.* But beeing driuen into wonder why the *night* would fall in labour, and bring foorth fo many Villanies, whofe births fhe practifed to couer (as fhe had reafon) becaufe fo many *watchmen* were continually called and charged to haue an eye to her dooings, at length he perceiued that *Bats* (more vgly and more in number then thefe) might flye vp and downe in darkeneffe : for tho with their Letherne Wings they fhould ftrike the verry billes out of thofe *Watchmens* handes, fuch leaden plummets were commonly / hung by fleepe at all their eyelids, that hardly they could be awakned to ftrike them agen.

On therefore he walkes, with intent to haften home, as hauing fil'd his Table Bookes with fufficient notes of intelligence. But, at the laft, meeting with the *Bell-man,* and not knowing what he was becaufe he went without his *Lanthorne* and fome other implements : for the man in the *Moone* was vp the moft part of the night and lighted him which way foeuer he turned : he tooke *him* for fome churlifh *Hobgoblin,* feeing a long ftaffe on his necke, and therefore to be one of his owne fellowes. The *Bel-ringer* Smelling what ftrong fcent he had in his nofe, foothed him vp, and queftioning with him how he had fpent his time in the citty, and what difcouery of *Land-villanies* he had made in this *Iland voiage* : ỹ *Mariner of hell,* opened his *chart,* which he had lined with all abufes lying either *Eaft, Weft, North, or South* : he fhewed how he had *pricked* it, vpon what *points* he had *faild,* where he *put* in : vnder what *height* he kept him-felfe : where he went a *fhore,* what ftrãge *people* he met : what *land* he had *difcouered,* and what commodities he was *laden* with from thẽce. Of all which the *Bell-man* drawing forth a perfect *Map,* they parted : which *Map* he hath fet out in fuch collors as you fee, tho not with fuch cunning as he could wifh : the paines are his owne, the pleafure, if this can yeelde any pleafure, onely *yours*, on whome he beftowes it : to *him* that embraceth his labours, he *dedicats* both them and his loue : with *him* that either knowes not *how*, or cares not to entertaine them, he will not be angry, but onely to Him fayes thus much for a *farrewell*.

———————*Si quid Nouifti rectius iftis,*
Candidus imperti : Si non, His vtere mecum.

FINIS.

A STRANGE HORSE-RACE.

1613.

NOTE.

For my exemplar of 'A Strange Horfe Race,' I am indebted to the Huth Library. There is another in the British Museum. In the former there are a number of (apparently) contemporary margin scribblings by a "Will. Colborne," whose autograph is on the title-page, chiefly explanations of meanings of words—*e.g.*, 'dignifie' = 'make worthy'; 'victors' = 'conquerors'; 'fupported' = 'borne vp'; 'exultations' = 'liftings vp'; 'infolence' = 'pryde, difdayne'; 'that Celebration' = 'famous folemnyty'; 'incite' = 'move, ftrive or provoke'; 'adorne' = 'beautefye'; 'influence' = 'flowing in'; 'rifle' − 'fearch, take away by violence'; 'afpiring' = 'climbing vp'; 'ambitious' = 'defirous of honour, or of ftriuing for p'ferment'; 'equipage' = 'furnyture'; 'auftere' = 'rough'; 'admiration' ≤ 'wonderment, reuerence'; 'benedictions' = 'prayfings'; 'epilogue' = 'conclufion'; 'fhe is Times Herald' = 'Fame is Tymes Herald'; 'irruption' = 'breaking in'; 'ftigmaticall' = 'knauifhe'; 'prepofter-ous' = 'diforderd, froward, [illegible word,] fetting ye cart before ye H[orfe].' One or two have been shorn by the binder. See 'Glossarial Index,' *s.v.*

'A Strange Horfe Race' is given in succession to the 'Belman' volumes, as being of kin with them. The following is the collation : Title-page—epistle-dedicatory pp. 2—second epistle pp. 2—contents 1 p. (*verso* blank)—and pp. 43 (last *verso* blank), A 2—G.

A. B. G.

A

Strange Horſe-Race,

At the end of which, comes in

THE CATCH-POLES
MASQVE.

AND AFTER THAT

The Bankrouts Banquet :

VVhich done, the Diuell, falling
*ſicke, makes his laſt will a*nd *Teſta-*
ment, this preſent yeare.

1613.

Aliquid latet, quod non patet.

VVritten by Thomas Dekker.

LONDON,
Printed for *Ioſeph Hunt*, and are to bee ſold at his
Shop in Bedlem, neere *Moore-field Gate.*
1613.

TO THE VERY

WORTHY, IVDITIOVS,
AND VNDERSTANDING
Gentleman, THOMAS VVAL-
THAL Efquire.

IF I put into your hands a homely peice of Worke (neither fo good as you deferue, nor fo rich as I do wifh it) I muft entreat you to blame the vanitie of our times, which are fo phantafticall, that they couet Stuffes, rather flight, to feede the eye with fhew, then Subftantiall for enduring. Let the Fafhion be *French,* it is no matter what the Cloth be. I haue therefore not (with the *Sturgeon*) fwomme againft the ftreame ; But followed the Humorous Tides of this Age, and (like *Demo-critus*) haue falne a Laughing at the world, fithence it does nothing but mocke it felfe. But feeing no creature is fo wife as man, nor any fo foolifh, my Wits haue heere beene at charges to feaft either fort. A mixt Banquet of Sweete and Sowre, Fulfome, and VVholefome, *Seria cum Iocis |*

ſtands furniſhed before them. In this *Horſe-Race* there is no cheating, my Building (as many Richmens great houſes) is not onely to keepe Rats, and Spiders in it, but euery Roome (though all be but meane) hath ſome picture to delight you. The Platforme being narrow, I could raiſe no lofty Stories ; for when the Ditty is light, the Aire muſt not be Graue ; A *Crow* is not to build ſo high as an *Eagle* : as the Face of my Inuention was drawne, ſuch I could not choſe but proportion out the Body. Yet the Picture hath loſt ſome of the Cullors I gaue it.

I know you loue to Reade, becauſe you know to Cenſure ; Reade, this I pray as I writ it —(willingly,) and Cenſure, as I ſend it—(in Loue). Beare with the hard-fauourdneſſe of the Title. The value of a Diamond is not leſſened by the roughneſſe when it is Vncut. It can bee no ſhame to gather a Violet, growing cloſe to the ground. Had I better, you ſhould enioy it ; ſuch as it is if you entertaine, I ſhall reſt.

Moſt affectionately deuoted,

Yours,

Thomas Dekker.

Not to the Readers : but to
the Vnderſtanders.

E that writes, had need to haue the Art
of a ſkilfull Cooke ; for there muſt be
thoſe Condimenta (ſeaſonings) in his
pen, which the other caries on his
tongue : A thouſand palats muſt bee pleaſed with
a thouſand ſawces : and one hundred lines muſt
content fiue hundred diſpoſitions. A hard taſke :
one ſayes, it is too harſh : another, too ſupple :
another too triuiall : another too ſerious. The firſt
reades, and mewes : the ſecond reades, and railes :
the third reades, and rackes me : the fourth reades,
and rends me. He is tyed to a ſtake like a Beare to
be baited that comes into Paules Church-yard to bee
read. So that bare Readers (I meane not threed-
bare) are not Lectores, but Lictores, they whip
Bookes (as Dionyſius did boyes) whereas to Vnder-
ſtanders, our libri, which we bring forth, are our
Liberi (the children of our braine) and at ſuch
hands are as gently intreated, as at their parents :
at the others, not.

The Titles of Bookes are like painted Chimnies in

great Countrey-houſes, make a ſhew afar off, and catch Trauellers *eyes ; but comming nere them, neither caſt they ſmoke, nor hath the houſe the heart to make you drinke.* | *The Title of this booke is like a* Ieſters face, *ſet (howſoeuer he drawes it) to beget mirth : but his ends are hid to himſelfe, and thoſe are to get money. Within is more then without ; you ſhall not finde the kirnell, vnleſſe you both cracke and open the ſhell.* Aliquid latet, quod non patet : *Digge vnder the right tree, and it is ten to one but you take vp gold : for in this (as in all other my former* Noꞓturnis lucubrationibus*) I haue ſtroue to feed the mind, as well as the body ; If one leafe make you laugh, the next ſettles your countenance. Tart meates go eaſily downe, being ſtrewd with ſugar : as muſicke in* Tauerns *makes that wine go downe merily, till it confound vs, which (if the* Fidlers *were not there) would hardly be taſted. So for the ſake of the ſawce which I haue tempered for this diſh, you may (perhaps) eate the meat, which otherwiſe you would not touch.*

The maine plot of my building is a Moral laby-rinth *; a weake* thred *guides you in and out : I will ſhew you how to* enter, *and how to* paſſe through, *and open all the* Roomes, *and all the priuate walkes, that when you come to them, you may know where you are : and theſe they be* ——

Yet I will not ; I know it is more pleaſure to finde out the conceitfull-deceits of a Paire of Tarriers, *then to haue them diſcouered. That pleaſure be yours, the* Tarriers *are mine.*

Fare-well.

The / Contents of this Booke.

A / Strange Horſe-race.

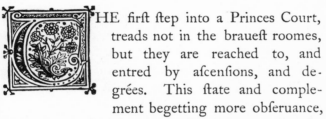

HE firſt ſtep into a Princes Court, treads not in the braueſt roomes, but they are reached to, and entred by aſcenſions, and de- grées. This ſtate and comple- ment begetting more obſeruance, delectation, aſtoniſhment, and reuerence : by the ſame line are leſſer ſquares drawne. For if you come into a Gold-ſmiths, or Lapidaries ſhop, and deſire to buy the faireſt Iewels: the cunning Artizan tempts you firſt with ſlight ones, and then bewitcheth you with coſtlier, and (for the vp-ſhot) ſtrikes your eye with admiration, by gazing at the beſt of all. So that as no man, (how wretched ſoeuer) can comparatiuely be miſerable, becauſe the palſie-lame hand of *Fortune* can throw him to no baſeneſſe and deiection ſo low, but hee ſhall fall vpon ſome other as low as

himfelfe. Euen likewife on the contrary part, are
there no obieĉts of triumph, (as mafkes, prefentations, banquets, and fuch like) how glorious foeuer
of themfelues, but may haue their fplendor and
dignity heightned by a comparatiue traducing of
things in the fame ranke and qualitie.

Giue me leaue therefore, firſt to make a flourifh
with my pen, and cleare the way, (as a Fencer
doth in a May-game) for more roome, vntill the
Mafquers come in : fo fhall you know the caufe
of that coſt, and the fumptuoufneſſe of the
Banquet ; to which I wifh no man to be too
fawcy in preſſing in, leſt he pay more déere for
his fweet meates (the banquet being prepared in
hell) then the dreſſing and Cookery of one Pea-
cocke, / and two Pheafants coſt in one of the
Kings of *Tunis* his Kitchin, which amounted to
an hundred duckets. What talke I of an hundred
duckets? Nay, leſt he be more peppered then
thofe Mafons, Bricke-layers and Carpenters were,
that builded thofe Pyramids in *Egypt*, during their
worke about one of which *Pliny* brings in a bill of
a 1800. Talents, that were laid out for Scallions,
Onions, Garlicke, and Léekes onely, befides Bread
and Cheefe, which he fcores not downe: for belike
the *Gypfey-Kings* left that vnpaid.

But before either this *Mafque*, or *Suger-feaſt*
come marching in their true and moſt fweet ſtate,

I inuite you (for variety) to behold a *Race*, on foot, and horfe, with fome triumphing in Chariots, after the *Roman* fafhion : to fet forth which of ours in their thundring velocity, lightning-like violence, and earth-quaking, whorrying, fo liuely, that (if it were poffible) the noyfe fhould make you mad, as the fight could make you merry : I will (as I held it fit, before) giue you feuerall pictures of *Races*, that in former Ages ran themfelues out of breath, to the end that the now-dead colours of the one, may fet off the braue, frefh, and amazeable-ftarting pageantry of thefe our other. When the *Romans* were Lords ouer the world, and their Emperours maifters ouer them, no glory was wanting to illuftrate their triumphes, after the fubduing of ftrange Nations, nor any coft fpared in popular prefentations, to binde vnto them, and bewitch the hearts of their owne people, after their victorious re- *Blondus de Roma Triumphante.* turning home. Thofe that did triumph, Chariot Races for Triumph. fate in Chariots guilded all ouer, drawne fometimes by white horfes ; fo was *Auguftus* : fomtimes with Elephants, fo was *Pompey.* To excell whom in that pride, *Cæfar* *Tranquil. Suetonius.* had his Chariot of triumph drawne The manner of Roman Triumphes. by forty Elephants : fome haue béene drawne by Harts, and fo was *Aurelianus*. In thefe Chariots, with the Emperours, fate their fonnes, as heires to their fathers glory; and after them followed the *Roman* Souldiers, crowned with garlands, as partners in their Emperours honours. Before the Chariots went the Captiues, (Kings, Quéenes, and others) / chained, the fpoyles taken in warres, borne aloft to defpite them; and more to dignifie the Conquerour, pictures and counter-fets of all the Citties, Mountaines, Riuers and Battailes, from whence they came victors, were drawne in Enfignes to the liuelieft portrature, all fupported before the Triumpher.   And in this laft manner did *Germanicus Cæfar* enter into *Rome*, *Cor. Tacit.* in a triumphall Chariot, loden with fiue *lib.* 2. *annal.* of his children, after the victories gotten againft the *Cherufie*, *Chatti*, and *Angrinari*, with all other Nations inhabiting to the riuer *Albis*, as *Corn. Tacit.* fets downe in the fecond of his *Annalles.*

Now, left thefe higheft exaltations of *Fortune* fhould make their Emperours fwell into too much infolence, and fo into a fcorning of their fubiects; the Souldiers, themfelues, yea and the common Plebeians that ftood vpon ftalles to behold thefe fights, would commonly (in hate of fuch honours, and in abatement of fuch pride that might bréed in their Emperours) as they march in all that pompe, caft bitter afperfions vpon them.   As for example : When *Ventidius Baffus* came home in

a *Parthian* triumph, the Souldiers aloud
cryed out thus in mockery of him ;
*Behold, he who lately rub'd horſes heeles,
is now your glorious Conſull.* And at another time
to the people thus : *O you Citizens of
Rome, keepe your wiues at home in your
ſhops, you are beſt : for now we haue
brought you your bald - pate Whore-
maiſter :* their Emperour hauing, at that time,
more néed of a periwig, then a Barber.

*Qui Mulos
fricabat
fractius est
Cōsul.*

*Romani seruate
vxores, Mæ-
chum calvum
vobis adduci-
mus.*

Theſe beames of worldly felicity ſhon about
the heads of their Princes : let vs now ſée what
pleaſures the *Roman* people enioyed.

For them were built Theaters, and Amphitheaters, in ſome of which might ſit
fourcſcore thouſand people together ;
the Theaters themſelues being ſome
of ſtone, ſome of wood, curiouſly
adorned with columnes, and Images of their
Emperours : ſome guilded all ouer, ſome mouing
vpon whéeles, to avoyd the heate of the Sunne.
All of them ſpacious, all ſumptuous : In theſe
they ſomtimes ſaw playes tragicall, or comicall, /
with all ſorts of muſicke, *Doricke, Chromaticke,*
ſoft and delicate, *Lidian, Nypolydian*
mournfull, fit for Tragedies : and to
theſe ſorts of muſicke they had all ſorts of
Dauncing ; And *Hyporchema* (in time of a peſti-

In the *Roman*
Theaters were
alwaies their
Scænici Ludi,
stage-playes.

Grecian
musicke.

lence) a daunce to *Apollo* in the Campe; the *Pyrichian*, which was a daunce in Armour: In the Chamber (as wee now haue) dances, with wanton gefticulation. All which, as well *Muficke* as *Daunces*, they borrowed from the *Greekes*.

Plutarch, in Moralib.

Then had they both in *Circo*, & *Theatris*, (their *Race* and *Theaters*) fights both on foot and horfebacke; fometimes Man to Man, now and then Men and Beafts in countring together, three hundred *Gladiators*, or Sword-players, fighting at one time at fharpe, with equall number. In which paftimes *Gordianus* the Emperour, to feede the people to the full, confumed twelue dayes, euery dayes prefentation varying from each other; As fword-playing, Wraftlings in diuerfe kindes, cafting of Dartes and Speares, Chariot-chaces, Huntings, and fuch like; In one day to a hundred Fencers, thrufting out a hundred and fifty of the fierceft *Lybian* beafts; in another a thoufand, which they were to kill with their fwords, or to hazard their owne liues: for he maintained a large and thicke wood, ftrongly defenfible, in which ran two hundred wilde Harts, thirty vn-back'd fierce horfes of *Brittaine*, a thoufand fheepe, ten Roebuckes, which he caufed to be guilded all ouer;

Trãquillus Suetonius.
Sword-players.
Sword-playing, Hunting, and the fighting of beasts in the Roman Amphitheaters.

thirty wilde Affes, a hundred and fifty wilde Boares, two hundred Ibices, and two hundred wilde *Heluetian* Goates : vpon all which he cryed hauocke to the people, to haue them torne in peeces in one folemne feftiuall meeting.

The like did *Philippus Arabs* the Emperour, at two feuerall times; the firft at the celebration of the *Circumcifion Games* (fo called of *Circus*, the place where they were per- formed) At which time he turned out *Ludi Circēses, cuius ludi Originem.* two and thirty Elephants, twenty Tygers, an hundred *Hyenaes*, one *Rhynoceros*, three- fcore tame Lyons, and ten curle-mained *Virgil, lib. 5, describit.* Lyons, ten Panthers, thirty Leopards, and ten fierce Horfes to be cut in péeces.

The fecond time was at the celebration of thofe games, which were held but once in a hundred yeares : and thereupon were called *Ludi Seculares*, (of *Seculum*, an age of a man, which was then counted an hundred yeares) their *Solemnization* being in honour of *Apollo* and *Diana*. Againft which day a Cryer went vp and downe the Citty of Rome with this note : *Whofoeuer will fee games, which no man aliue hath euer feene, nor* *Venite ad Ludos quos* *any man liuing fhal euer fee more, now* *nemo mortalem* *let them come.* At which time, the Rites *vidit, neque visurus est.* due to that Celebration béeing performed, and the people of *Rome* in infinite numbers affembled to-

gether, he caufed to bee hunted (befides the beafts
before named, to as great or a greater number) ten
horned Elkes more, by no other perfons, then by two
thoufand *Fencers*, armed onely with their Swords

Vide Plin. in their hands, the beafts running loofe,
Lib. 18. madding and roaring vp and downe.

Thus haue you feene the *Roman* Emperours
in their Chariots of Triumphs, after which the
people further rewarded them with Statues, or
Images made to the life, fome in maffy gold,
fome in filuer, fome in braffe, and fome in marble,
vpon which were infculped and richly cut out,
all their Battailes, Conquefts, and Triumphes :

Aureis post- and befides thefe Statues, they had alfo
modum succes- at firft Crownes of Gold fent them, and
serunt,
Laureæ: erant- thofe were after changed to Garlands of
que & virtutis
& honoris Laurell, the honour of both being all
eiusdem
præmia. one. The common people receiued
Gellius.
after their combats, fights, victories, &c.
(to incite them likewife to hunt after fame, &
Garlands giuen military renowne) wreathes & Coronets
to the Romans. to adorne their temples. The horfemen and Charioters being by this time wearied,
giue way for the infantery to come vp, and try
The first sort how nimbly they beftir their héeles.
of Rūners were
called *Stadio-* In which *Races* on foot, not onely the
dromi. *Romanes*, but alfo the *Greekes, Troians,*
Athenians, Macedonians, and many other Nations

excelled for their incredible fwiftneffe : I thinke
the wilde Irifh are beft at it in thefe latter times.
This kinde of exercife had three changes in it:
For fome, vpon whofe heads the wagers were
layd, ftood breaft-wife in a direct line, at a marke,
and ran onely to a / goale propofed and
left there : others being at the goales _{The fecōd sort were called} *Diaulodromi.*
end before their fellowes, wan no glory
by it, vnleffe they could againe recouer the marke
from which they firft fet forth.

The third *Race* was to run and returne to
and fro, from the marke to the goale, without
intermiffion, by the fpace of eight
changes, and neuer vnder fixe : and he _{The third sort were called} *Dolichodromi.*
that could hold out his winde fo long,
to be firft at the bounds where he began his race,
carryed away both garland and prizes.

My Mufe could heere leaue running at *Bafe*
thus vpon earth, and ftretching her wings forth
to a more noble expanfion, foare aloft _{Races in heauen.}
vp into the *Celeftiall Habitations,* and
from thence bring news, what race the Sun runs
in his *Zodiacall Circle,* where he fets _{The Suns Race.}
out euery morning, and where he refts
euery night : at what houfes he ftayes (being 1 2
in number) and how long he tarries, in what
part of the world he fhortens his *Careeres,* and
in what part hee enlargeth it : his fires burning

at all times alike, but not alike in all places : by
Sol fons lucis. whofe heate all Countries do propa-
gate and bring forth bleffings to their
inhabitants; but no Country can boaft fhe pos-
feffeth all, becaufe what one wants, another fhould
fupply, and fo euery land to be beholden one to
another : then to fhew, that al-be-it he runs not
in a perfect *Orbicular Circle*, but that fometimes
he runs fide-wife with an oblique carriage of his
body, yet his courfe is conftant: his horfes,
(*Pirois, Eous, Æthon,* and *Phlegon*) as they are
foure in number, making foure great *Stoppes*, or
Careeres in Heauen, which beget foure *Changes*
or foure *Renouations* of time vpon earth, that is
1 Spring. to fay : the *Vernall, Æftiuall, Autumnall*
2 Sommer. and *Brumall*, they keeping euer their
3 Autum.
4 Winter. day (like iuft *Debitors*) onely a few
minutes difference. But fo much reuerence do I
owe to the Diuine ftudy of the tranfcendently-
learned *Aftronomer*, that I lay downe heere this
Buckler, knowing him moft worthy to take it vp.

From tracing therefore any further the wheeles
The Moones of this *Illuminous Chariot*, wherein the
Race. *God of the day* rides, our *Protean Mufe*
altering the fhape of her courfe, a little lower
could / ftand and difcouer how the *Queene of the
night* (the *Moone*) is, (with a fwifter whirling then
the *Sunne* her brother) whiried vp and downe in

a coach of filuer, & there fhew likewife, why
fometimes fhe fits *Horned*, fometimes
Halfe-faced, fometimes *Full* and perfectly
Round: then, where that *Light* is locked
vp that is taken from our fight; and by what
meanes, and how fo quickely it is againe reftored.

The Sun the
cause of the
Moones vari-
able shapes.

  Then could I without helpe of her light, flip
in a moment into the *Seas*, and faile
onely by that Star, whofe influence now
guides my pen. There could I defcribe
what warlike *Races* the *Winds* held with the
Waters : their *Wraftling, Running, Retiring*, and
Chafing this way and that way, like two great
Princes ftriuing for *Superiority*, and confounding,
by their contention, not themfelues, but thofe
vnder them.

The Race of
the windes
& the Waters.

  Quicquid delirant Reges, plectuntur Achiui.

  But becaufe you fhall not bee weary by being
weather-beaten in Tempefts: fuppofe the Windes
haue fpent their Malice (like Rich-men, vndon by
going to Law in defending vniuft Actions). But
the *Seas* fwell ftill by a Naturall pride
which the *Moone* (their Miftreffe) puts
into them, becaufe their Nature being
quarrellous, they rage (like Roaring
Boyes vpon the Land) that they can
faften no oppofite to go together bi'th eares

The Sea flowes
when the
motion of the
Moon is
downewards
and neerer
to it.

withall, the next they meete they iuftle, and
that's the *Earth* : there they purpofe to begin
another *Race* ; for their *Waues* run (like Mad-
men out of Bedlam) beyond their bounds vp into
the *Land*, doing what they can to fwallow it ; and
that fhewes (me-thinkes) like an vnthrifty riotous
Heire, wafhing away (in Tauernes) the poffeffions
of his father, and his owne Patrimony, whilft the
carefull old man feekes to keepe all within compaffe ; as the walles of the Earth ftriue to hold
the vnruly Waters within their owne dominions,
and to bar them entrance into her owne : for all
their buftling, and for all their billowes, we are
now leap'd fafe on fhore.

Whilft thus I ftand vpon the foft and un-
remoueable habitation of our great Grand-mother
(the *Earth*) Another *Race*, / is prefented

The Race of
the Elements to mine eie, for I could heere defcribe,
in Mans body.
how the foure Elements, (like fo many
wheeles in a Clocke) are proportioned to more

1 Earth.   diuerfe waies, and with ftrange turnings,
2 Water.
3 Aire.   yet all to meete in one delicate tune
4 Fire.   within *Mans body*.   And then, if any
one of thofe foure *Protectors*, bée predominant
aboue the other, and fo fet the reft together by
the eares, how then the bloud hath his Race,
and runnes into difeafes, and the fhortning of
that Race is to ftumble at Deaths Dore.   Againe,

if I fhould rifle this Treafure-houfe of liuing Creatures, and looke into the depth of it, I could bring you to thofe hidden *Races of* The Race of *Minerals*, and *Mettals*, which the *Sunne* Minerals. neuer fees, yet can they not liue without him: there fhould you behold a *Mine of Lead*, The ambition labouring to turne it felfe into *Tynne*, of Lead. and fo to rife to preferment ; but like a poore Man, that workes day and night to grow rich, hee ftriues with impoffibilities, and is at the yeares end no better then at the biginning. There fhould you behold a *Mine of* The ambition *Tynne*, (fifter to *Siluer*) vfing all the of Tynne. Art fhe can, to be transform'd into her fifters fhape, and to carry a beauty as faire as her's ; but like a Rich Man, that hauing enough, and being well to liue, yet practifeth vnlawfull courfes to encreafe his ftate, as his, fo her doings do feldome profper: There likewife fhould Ambition of you behold a *Mine of Siluer*, ambitioufly Siluer. afpiring to bee as glorious *Gold*: but fhe workes like an Alchimift, watches long, and loofes her labour ; yea, though fhee were able to paffe through thofe twelue gates.

1 *Calcination.*

2 *Diffolution.*

3 *Separation.*

4 *Coniunction.*

Ripley:
Chanon of
Bridlington.

  5 *Putrifaction.*
  6 *Congelation.*
  7 *Cibation.*
  8 *Sublimation.*
  9 *Firmentation.*
 10 *Exaltation.*
 11 *Multiplication.* /
 12 *Proiection.*

And fo come to weare in a Ring, the very
Phylofophers Stone, yet the triall of her
beauty would bee when her painting
came to the Touch.   Laft of all, you fhould
there likewife behold (the eldeft child of the
Sunne) *A Mine of Gold,* who being King of
Mettals, neuer afpires to bee higher, becaufe
it knowes, there is none aboue him.

Touching *Minerals* of bafer quality let vs not
caft our eye vpon them, hauing enriched our
Lading with the beft :   hoyft now vp Sailes,
therefore from hence and away ; for thefe *Races*
(if I fhould meafure the fhorteft of them to his
end) would weary me too much, and appeare,
yrkefomely, too long, like that iourney of *Philip-
pides,* who ranne one thoufand, two hundred and
forty furlongs (which makes 155 miles) (from
Athens in *Greece* to *Lacedemon*) in two daies, if
Polyhiftor lies not.

Gold hath no ambition.

I could here be content after this weary Voyage, round about the vaſt compaſſe of the world (dis-patcht, as you ſée, by my Sea-chariots, within a little time,) now to fixe vp *Herculean Pillars*, and write vpon them *Non vltra*. But our Muſe is ambitious, and (to her) *Non ſufficit Orbis*, ſhe muſt on againe.   For ſhe hath one Race   A freſh yet to Run, which (for Antiquity) is as   Race. Reuerend, (for Perſons) as Renowned, (for the Contention) as Glorious, and (for the Victory) as Memorable, as any that euer yet haue bene in the World.

It is (becauſe you ſhall weary your eyes with ſtaring no longer) A Race or Challenge   Vertue & betwixt the Vertues that dwell in the   Vice run. little world (*Man*) and the Vices to whom hee giues free entertainement; they are all ready to preſent their Troupes, and to do their Deuoire: But before they enter the liſts, (ſome on horſe-backe, ſome on foote, ſome in Chariots) I will play the Herauld to marſhall them in order, ac-cording to their quality and worth, and ſend them forth, marching in braue equipage before you.

The *Vertues* are not Mounted, and haue Few Followers; they haue no Plumes, and   Vertue is ſo, no Pride; their Attire is decent,   ſeldoſne ſober, girt to them, and ciuill: their   mounted. Faces graue, auſtere in very ſwéeteneſſe, ſwéete

in aufterity; faireft when they are neereft; louely
a farre off, and all open; vfed to no
Her picture. mafke, their pace demure, maieftically-
humble, conftant and comely.

The *Vices* are Gallant Fellowes, they are
Vice is euer Mounted, and haue no fmall Fooles to
mounted. their Followers: they haue Plumes, like
Eftridges, and Perfumes like *Mufke-cats*, (fo ftrong)
they are foone fmelt out: for Attire, they carry
Lordfhips on their backes, a Knights liuing in
their Bréeches, & a Shop-kéepers wealth in a
Hat-band, Garters, and Shoe-ftrings;
Her picture. Their Faces light, anticke, impudent,
difdainefull, amoroufly bewitching, fhadowed now
& then, but not poffible alwaies to be couered:
As a Fools face can neuer be hid.

The *Vertues* will go fometimes from you (when
anon you fee them) but the *Vices* will ftill come
with their Faces towards you, for if you looke
narrowly vpon their backes, if they fhew but them
to you firft, you will ftraight turne taile to them
too, & no more care a pin for their company,
vnleffe you be mad; I will giue you an example of
fome of them, that carry their heads higheft: thus,

The *Hole i' th' Counter*, is the *Backe of Riot*;
The backe if a *Prodigall* lay there in Hunger and
part of Riot. Cold, but fiue fuch moneths no worfe
then the laft great Froft was, in a deere yéere,

and in a Plague-time when no body would come at him ; and this hée fhould fuffer before hee bound himfelfe for euer to his *Mercer,* being fure, elfe, to fuffer it after-wards : I doe not thinke but my Gallant would loue a warme Freze Jerkin better than a fuite of cut Sattin, and choofe rather (like a Horfe) to draw béere, then to weare rich trappings like an Affe, for which his bones pay fo derrely. So

Head-ach is the Backe of *Drunkennes* : if the *Head-ach* would knocke our Coxcombs foundly, fo foone as wee cry out Drawer in a Tauerne, we fhould neuer quarrel with ỹ Watch, / nor breake downe Baudy-houfe-windowes at mid-night. _{The backe part of drunk-ennesse.}

But beft finnes, like the worft faces, are moft and euer painted, and that's the reafon they fo bewitch vs, for it is a good eye can fee their deformity : Hearke,

The Trumpets fownd, they are ready for the Lifts : behold, they enter ; you perhaps (that are but Standers-by) may miftake them, and therefore I will defcribe them, as they either begin the *Race* or end it. _{The Race beginnes.}

The firft that runs, is *Blafphemous Infolence,* a *Turke,* (for you muft vnderftand, that of all Nations, fome are at this *Race*) he will be firft, becaufe he will be _{The character of a proud *Turke.*}

firft; his looks are full of Darings, his voyce
thunders out Braues ; hee laies downe Threates
infteed of Wagers, hee fcornes to Wage any thing
vpon an euen Lay, for if terror or tyrany can
win it, he will haue All; By his fide comes his
Surgeon (called Infidelity) the horfe he rides on
is fwift Vengeance, his two Pages are Fyre and
Sword.

    A Chriftian Lady runs againft him, her name
Innocent Humility : if fhe get to the Race-end, fhe
is promifed a paire of wings, befides the prize ;
her looks are modeft, her words few, to her-felfe
(as fhee fets forth) fhe praies: fhe has onely one
Maid waites vpon her, called *Sufferance* ; they
both run on foote : Sée, fee, the *Turke* flies like
a winged Dragon, the Chriftian flies too, like a
Doue, yet with nobler fpeed ; fhée has now gotten
the better way of him, and is gone beyond him,
and fée ! Rage and Haft to difgrace her, in her
fpéed, haue caft him from his Horfe, his
owne Horfe kickes and tramples on the
Maifter. The Chriftian Lady runs in
pitty to faue him : but he curfing Her,
and calling onely vpon his owne Sur-
geon (Infidelity) fhee (for want of fkill) poifons
his wound in fteed of curing it ; he's dead : his
Surgeon rips his body, to fearch what was perifhed
within him (vpon fo flight a fall, as fhe tearmes

The *Turks*
owne ven-
geance pre-
par'd for
others, cō-
founds him-
selfe.

it) and (fee!) his heart is turned into a Flint:
Blacke, and Hardened as Marble, & lying drown'd
in the bloud of a thoufand poore *Hun-*
garians, yet all that could not foften it. *Hungary ouer-run by the Turkes.*
The Wager they ranne for was / a Gar-
land of Palme-trees held vp by a Lady at the
Goales end (whofe name is *Eternity*) and by her
giuen to the Chriftian Conqueror, with the Wings,
befides, which were promifed her, if fhee fainted
not in her Race. When the whéels of Defire
are once fet a going, the more weights you hang
vpon them, the fafter turne they about, for lo!
all the Opponents in this Race-running haue done
what they came for in a moment, whilft you were
bufy about the firft Challenger and Defendant,
fo great was their Feruor: but I haue the Roll
here of the perfons and their names, and albeit
you haue loft the fight of them in Action, you
fhall not loofe the fport of it in my Relation.

The fecond that ran, and made the braueft
fhow, was a yong Gallant, his name, *Prodigalities Race.*
Prodigallity, loued of many Ladies for
his good gifts, and followed by many rich Citizens
fons, who were preferd vnto him by their fathers
Mony: he fat in a Chariot, open on *The Character of a Prodigall.*
euery fide, foure Horfes drew him,
(*Rafhneffe*, *Luxury*, *Folly*, and *Hanger-on*) his
Coach-man being drunke, A Whore whipped

him for-ward, and made all Fly; at the backe
of the Chariot, two leaped vp, & were drawne
after him, *viz.* : *Beggery* and a *Foole*, whofe
gefture of making mouthes and anticke faces
was excellent fport to the fpectators: he ran a
fwift and thundring pace; after him and clofe
by him rid many Merchants, Mercers, and Silke-
men, who had laid great Wagers on his head,
but he gaue them all the flip, and was before
hand with them ftill.

The Defendant whom he challenged, was a
polliticke Belgicke, his name *Hans-thrift*
Thrifts Race. (a Dutchman) vigilant in his courfe,
futtle in laying his wager, prouident in not
venturing too much, honeft to pay his loffes,
induftrious to get more (twenty fundry waies)
if hee fhould happen to bee cheated of all; his
Horfe was not fo fwift as fure, his Attire not
curious, but rich & neate: they fet out both
together, but before *Prodigallity* came halfe way
of his iourney, *Thrift* got the ftart of him, out-
went, out-wearied, out-fpent him; tother loft all,
this won what the other loft.

Prodigality / vpon this difgrace hid his head, but
incountring when he went away, with
Difcontēt the
mother of
Treafon. a crue of *Male-contents*, they fchooled
him, and they fpoyled him; for in a
hote bloud hee prefently grew defperate, and fwore

to vndertake (for raifing of his fortunes) the plots of Treafon, to blow vp kingdomes, to murder Kings, and to poyfon Princes : *A malo in peius.* But the Hang-man hearing their whifpering, fet vp a paire of gallowes in his way; at which hee ran full-but, fell downe, brake his necke, and neuer fince could kéepe any good quarter.

The third that came fneaking in was a leane ill-faced fhotten-herring-bellied-rafcall ; his nofe dropped as foone as he entred *The Character of a Niggard.* into the *Race*, whofe filth, becaufe it would fcoure, and fo faue fope, hee wrapt vp in as filthy a hand-kercher : his apparell was cut out of 6 or 7 religions, and as they turned, that turned. He ftole one onely coale of fire from *Prodigality*, which hee toft betwixt his hands to warme them : he had in his pocket (to victuall him for this voyage) two dried cobs of a red herring, referued by a fifhmonger at the fiege of *Famagofta*, & then afterward laid on a dung-hil, and the cruft of a bifket that had béen twice at the weft *Indies*. This *Thing* was a *Vfurer*, cald *Niggardlineffe*; he had no page, but two Brokers (out of their loue to him, hoping to get by it) came along with him vpon their owne charge.

Againft this wretch, (in braue defiance) ftept forth an old Lord (that is now no Courtier; for hee kéeps a place in the *Hospitality pictured.*

Countrey, & all the chimnies in it fmoke: he fpends his money as he fpends the water that paffeth to his houfe, it comes thither in great pipes, but it is all confumed in his kichin,) his name *Hofpitality*. It is a graue & reuerend countenance ; he weares his beard long of purpofe, that ÿ haires being white, and ftill in his eie, he may be terrified frõ doing anything vnworthy their honor : his apparrel is for warmth, not brauery : if he thinke ill at any time, he prefently thinks wel : for iuft vpon his breaft he wears his *Reprehenfion*.   As a iewel comprehends much treafure in a little roome ; and as that nut-fhell held all *Homers Iliads* fmally written in a / péece of *Vellum*.   So, though the trée of his vertues grow high, and is laden with goodly fruit, yet the top-bough of all, and the faireft Apple of all he counteth his *Hofpitality* : His bread was neuer too ftale, his drinke was neuer fowre, no day in the yeare was to them that are hungry, *A fafting day*, yet he obferues them all : Hee giues moderately euery houre, but in reuerence of one feafon in the yeare, all that come may fréely take.

And this is (as the Booke doeth remember)

The cold frofty feafon of December :

Chaucer in the
Franklins   *Phœbus* waxed old, and hewed like *Latoun*
tale.

That afore in his hot Declination

Shone as the burned gold, with ftreames bright,
But now in *Capricorne* adowne he light:
Whereas he fhone full pale, I dare well feyne,
The bitter froftes with the fleet and raine
Deftroyed hath the greene in euery yerd:
Ianus fitteth by the fire with double berd,
And drinketh of his Bugle-horne the wine,
Befote him ftandeth the Brawne of the tufked fwine.

The horfe he fate vpon was gray and aged,
like his maifter, but weake by reafon
of yeares; yet his heart good, and
knew the way to many holy places,
whither hee had often carried his Lord,
They that vphold hospitality are in these daies weake, because few.
and therefore fcorning now he fhould incounter
fo ignoble an oppofite as he faw ftand brauing,
hee breathed a kinde of quicke fire in and out at
his fnoring noftrils, in figne he had quickned
his old courage, and that he wifhed to ftand on
no ground till this worke were ended. Forward
therefore, both parties fet: *Hofpitality*
had thoufands following him, with
fhouts, heartnings, plaudits, and praifes:
Niggardlinesse & Hospitality run.
At *Niggardlineffe* euery man laughed, euery man
difdained him, none clapped him on the backe,
but his two trunch-men (the Brokers) the tother
rode like a prince with all eyes throwne vpon him
in admiration: but this poore ftarueling ran as if

a ſcar-crow had flowen : it was not / a running,
but a kinde of falſe ſcuruy Amble, or rather
Hobling, which put him into ſuch a heate (he
neuer in all his life ſweating before) that hee
melted all his tallow, which at the moſt was not
able to make a piſſing Candle ; and ſo the ſnuffe
of his life went out ſtinking.   Before hee dyed,
he gaue his keyes to the Brokers, and made them
his heires, with charge to bury him there in the
high-way, onely to ſaue charges, and to ſtrip off
his cloathes, which he made them ſweare they
ſhould ſell : *Et hic finis priami,* and with that
word he lay as dead as a dogge.   His heires
performed his will, and going home merily, to
ſhare his wealth, which they knew to be infinite,
they found nothing in the houſe but two peny
Halters : (for all his money hee had buried vnder
the earth in a field) the ſight of this ſtruck cold
to their hearts : and ſo (ſeeing their owne Father,
as it were, had cozened them) the *Brokers* went
both away like a cupple of *Hounds* from the
dogge-houſe in a ſtring together, and lye buried
at the grate which receiues the common *Sewer* in
the midſt of *Hounds-ditch.*   *Hoſpitality* had the
honour of the day, and went away crowned with
poore mens *Benedictions.*

The next *Contenders* that followed theſe, were
an *Engliſh* Knight and a *Spaniſh :* the *Don* was

a temperate and very little féeder, and no drinker, as all *Spaniards* are ; the Knight had béene dub'd onely for his valour in that feruice : to it they went both, horfed alike, manned alike, braue alike, the

The Spaniard temperate in dyet, the English a glutton.

Spaniard not fo gawdy, but more rich. *Sir Dagonet* had fcarce fet fpurs to his *Bucephalus*, but with healths which he tooke out of euery commanders fift, drinking to his boone voyage, he fell ficke, & his horfe, both of the *Staggers*, of which hee neuer recouered : hee had (befides his Page) fome *Voluntaries* that attended

A drunkards followers.

him, that is to fay, the *drowfie* and *decayed Memory* ; the one filled his glaffes, the other his Tobacco-pipes. *Shortneffe of Life* held his bridle, and helped him ftil off. The *Diego* was a dapper fellow, of a frée minde and a faire, bounteous of his purfe, but fparing / in his Cups, as fcorning to make his belly a wine-celler, therefore the more nimble ; and hauing nothing in him but fire, (as the other nothing but the contrary Element) hee flew before the winde like a gallant Pinnace vnder fayle, and held out his *Race* to the end, leauing

Plures occidit crapula, quam gladius.

the *Englifh-man* dead-drunke, in leffe then a quarter of the way.

Then came in two by two, other Troopes, whofe onfets, and ouer-throwes, honours, and

difgraces, darings, and dauntings, merit an ample Chronicle, rather then an *Abftraɛt*; of
all which the *Braggadochio-vices* ftill got the worft: the *Vertues* departing in Triumph, but not with any infulting. And thus the glory of this *Race* ended.

Now, as after the cleare ftreame hath glided away in his owne current, the bottome is muddy and troubled. And as I haue often féene, after the finifhing of fome worthy Tragedy, or Catastrophe in the open Theaters, that the Sceane after the Epilogue hath béene more blacke (about a nafty bawdy Iigge) then the moft horrid Sceane in the Play was: The Stinkards fpeaking all things, yet no man vnderftanding any thing; a mutiny being amongft them, yet none in danger: no tumult, and yet no quietneffe; no mifchifs begotten, and yet mifchiefe borne: the fwiftneffe of fuch a torrent, the more it ouerwhelmes, bréeding the more pleafure.

So after thofe Worthies and Conquerours had left the field, another Race was ready to begin, at which, though the perfons in it were nothing equall to the former, yet the fhoutes and noyfe at thefe was as great, if not greater. They marched in no order, and that made them féeme comely; Handfomeneffe in them had beene a difgrace, the worfe they fhewed, the better they were liked; They could do nothing ill, becaufe they could doe nothing well, and were therefore commended, becaufe there was in them nothing commendable : Such praife as / they brought, they caried away; and this it was.

The firft Troope that came thronging in, were a company of braue ftaring fellowes, that looked like *Flemings*, for they were as fat as butter, and as plumpe in the face as Trumpeters are when their chéekes fwell like bladders. No horfes could bee hired for them : for (as Gallants doe Citizens) they were fure to breake their backes : they were all Foot-men therefore, and ran very heauily (like men going to hanging) becaufe if they fhould fall, their bellies making them leape heauy, they were fure to breake their neckes. Thefe termed themfelues *Epicures*, and all that heard them beleeued it : for their *Guts* was their *God*, their *Heads, Hogfheads* of wine, their *Bodies, Cages* for wild-fowle, and their *Soules* nothing elfe but the fteame and breath of roafted *Capons* ferued vp piping hot. Thefe ran into a thoufand mens *Debts*, but ran fo farre one from another, (for feare of breaking *Ribbes* if they had iuftled) that they would be fure neuer to run in any certaine danger.

The laft *Race* they ran (for you muft know they had many) was from a cry of *Sergeants*: yet in the end the Law ouer-tooke them, and after

Belly-gods.

Of Epicurus, from whom sprang that Sect.

a long, fweaty, and troublefome *Race*, ouer-threw
and layd them in the duft ; they dyed in prifon,
and were buryed in filence.

After them came in a pert *Lawyer*, puffing and
blowing (one that for putting a wrench
A Lawyer and
his conscience into the *Lawes* mouth, to force her to
run. fpeake any thing, was pitched ouer the
barre) and hee ran really : but with whom thinke
you ? againft his owne *Confcience* : but in the *Race*
(fweat and fweare, do what he could) fhe gaue
him the flip, tired him extreamely, and was ftill
out of his reach the length of *Gracious ftreet*, at the
leaft ; yet the *Lawyer* was a goodly man, ftrong,
and full of action, and / his Confcience nothing in
the world to fpeake of.

The next was one that fhould haue beene a
fcholler, and was indéed, and he ran
A Vicar. horrible faft after foure Benefices all at
one time : they held him nobly to it a long fpace ;
but with much adoe hee got beyond them, and
wonne what he ran for : Mary hee caught fuch
an incurable cold (by reafon of his purfineffe) that
hee loft his voyce prefently, and grew by degrees,
fo hoarfe, that he neuer fpake after to any great
purpofe, all his lights were fo ftopped.

At laft comes fkipping in a terfe, fpruife,
A Taylor runs neatified Capricious *Taylor*, new leaped
with Pride. from his Shop-boord ; and the Diuill

could not perfwade him, but hee would runne
with *Pride*, and with none elfe. *Pride* was for
him, and tooke hold of him prefently, *Horfes*
were offered to them both : No (fayd the Taylor)
I will not bee fet on Horfe-backe, I will not
ride, nor be ridden : *Pride* fcorned any courtefie
more then he. To it they go then ; *Pride* got
ftill before him, and he followed her at an ench
like a mad-man, tooth and nayle. In the end
hee had her at his backe : *Pride* then (for anger
that any fhould out-ftrip her) made fuch extreame
hafte, that fhee caught a fall. The *Taylor* (hauing
many gallant parts of a Gentleman about him)
looking afide, and feeing his Incounterer downe,
came brauely to her, offering to take her vp;
which fhe difdaining, allowed him a yard before
her, which hee was content to take, and to it
they go againe : *Pride* followed him clofe, and
comming home vp to him, fpyed her aduantage
(being neere the *Races* end) and leaping forward,
hit him full at the heart, and fo ouerthrew him.
Inraged at which, hee drew out a *Spanifh* weapon,
and would haue runne it through her ; fhee put
him by, and cut his combe, which fo cut his
heart (to fee a woman his confufion) / that hee
was neuer his owne man afterward. But he
fayd hee wrought his owne woe himfelfe, and
confeft it was his owne feeking to meddle

with her ; and therefore fuch bread as he brake,
was but broken to him againe, yet fwore (if a
man might beleeue him) that though he funke
into hell for it, he would, at one time or other,
fawce her.

This quarrell made peace ; for the vn-rauelling
of this bottome, was the laft thréed that ended
all. You now fee what voyage this fhip of fooles
(in which thefe laft were imbarked) hath made.
Heere caft they Anchor, and leap on Shore.

A preparation to the Mafque enfuing,
and the caufe therof.

FAME, who hath as many tongues as there
are mouthes in the world, hearing of the
honourable defeature giuen by thofe worthy
Champions to their ignoble (but infulting) ene-
A newes spred. mies, could not choofe (becaufe fhee
is a woman) but prattle of it, in all
places, and to all perfons ; infomuch that the
Courts of Kings rang of it, Cities made bone-
fires for it, the Country had almoft broke all
their bels about it : at euery Croffe it was proclaimed, at euery Market, one word went about
the price of victuals, and fiue about that : *Barbers*

had neuer ſuch vtterance of a newes, *Booke-ſellers*
ſold more ſhéetes then Linnen-drapers; Carriers
could load their horſes with no Packes but of
This: No Ship went to Sea, but ſome part of the
fraight was this victory: It was written of at
home, diſperſed in / letters abroad, and ſung to a
new Tune euery where. Omitting theſe hither
parts of *Chriſtendome*, ſhe (*Fame* I meane) taking
her Trumpet (becauſe ſhe is *Times Herald*) flew
with it ouer the *Mediterranean-ſea* into *Aſia*, firſt
into *Turkey*, ſo to *Caldæa*, *Perſia*, *Hircania*, *Aſſiria*,
Armenia, and then getting vp higher ouer the
Caſpian ſea, away ſhee poaſted to the *Tartars*, and
Cathayans, then to the *Chynois*, and other *Eaſt
Indians*, ſo backe againe ouer the *Arabian Sea*,
into *Arabia Fælix*: then croſſing ouer *Numidia*,
her next cut was into *Barbary* in *Affrica*, from
thence downe to *Noua Guinea*; and from thence
croſſing the *Lyne* into the *Ethyopian ſea*, away
ſwoopes ſhee by *Braſill*, and ſo beates her *Wings*
in the *Weſt Indies*, whoſe heate being ready to
melt her, (as the *Eaſt Indies* did before) ouer the
Lyne againe ſhe ſcuds to *Noua Hiſpania*, & ſo
to the *Northward* of *America*; then homeward
through *Florida*, taking *Virginea*, *Noua Francia*,
Norembega, and all thoſe *Septentrionall Countries*
in her paſſage, and ſo croſſing the *Deucalidonian
ſea*, hauing beaten her ſelfe almoſt to death in

proclaiming and trumpeting lowdly the *News*; fhe pantingly ariues where fhee fet forth, pruning and peecing vp her flagging and broken *Wings*.

The *winds* caching her breath in all kingdoms, through which fhe went, were as great with it as her felfe, & ready to burft vntill they were deliuered. Neuer was fuch puffing & blowing, fuch bluftring & roaring, fince they threw downe *Babel* : fo that with their ftrugling who fhould cry out firft, they were all brought a bed of it at one time : for all of them breaking by force into the bowels of the earth, and by that irruption tearing her very foundation with an vniuerfall earth-quake, the maffy frame was cleft & riuen afunder, and fo the terror of the report was by the wherrying *winds* fhot (as if with a thunder-bolt from heauen) and neuer tarryed, or met any rub, till it burft open the *Gates* of Infernall *Erebus*.

The / *Grand-Sophy* of the *Satanicall Synagogue*, at the very found of it belchd out a groane, the rebound of which (like one bandogs whyning in *Paris* Garden, fetting all the Kennels a barking) left all the *Stygian* Hel-hounds in a moft clamorous howling. The difmall confort hauing (with a worfe noife then the grating and crafhing of Iron when it is a fyling) ended thefe *Blacke Sants*, & fhooke their gaftly heads foure or

The naturall cause of an earth-quake.

The Diuel put in feare when Good-men prosper.

fiue times together, & with chaines ratling at their
heeles, (as if fo many blacke Dogs of New-gate
had beene mad in a Tauerne there) ran bellowing
All, about their *Father of Mifchiefe*, to know what
Qualme came ouer his ftomake. He (darting an
eye vpon them, able to confound a thoufand Coniurers in their owne Circles, though with a wet
finger they could fetch vp a little Diuell) and with
an *Vlulation*, (his chin almoft burfting his breaft-
bone with a Nod) from which, fum'd out a breath
(blacker then fea-coale fmoake out of a Brew-
houfe chimney) which if their withered chaps had
bin there, yawning to fucke it downe was of
power to haue turned ten thoufand old Beldams
in *Lapland* into the rankeft Witches, Hee thus
grumbled : *Hel's vndone*, Why, yelped all the reft?
An *Armada* (quoth he) cannot faue vs, <small>Hels Army</small>
our Legions (in the world next aboue <small>defeated.</small>
vs) are ouerthrowne by that *Stigmaticall Virago
Vertue* : All thofe Battalions that warred vnder
ẙ cullors of our Red & fiery Dragō are de-
baufhed : Suffer this bracke into our *Acheronticke
Territories* & hotter *Affaffinations* will euery day
pel mel maule vs. Al about him cryed they
would neuer endure it.

Whilft this indigefted mifchiefe lay broyling on
their ftomackes, roome was made for an *Intelligencer* newly arriu'd vpon thefe ftronds of Horror.

It was one of thofe nimble *Vmbratici Dæmones,* as inuifible as the Aire, & (like Aire) neuer out of our company, one of thofe *Gnomi,* whofe part *Theophraftus Paracelfus* takes fo terribly, prouing / that whether we fw[i]mme, or are on land, or in the woods, or in houfes, wee are ftill haunted with a fpirit or two at leaft, neither hurtfull nor doing good ; and fuch a one was This : *Belial Belzebub* of *Bara-thrum,* had lately employed this Pur-feuant of his about ferious bufineffe ; in which hauing done nothing, and dreading but forry paiment for his labour, hee knew not how better to efcape the Furies, then by forging fome egregious lies, by the fame Anuile, that all hell was now ftriking (that's to fay, touching the late victorie of the *Vertues*) and fo to bee thought hee had fpent all his time in that intelligence.

Paracelsus de gnomis.

Furies are Hels Beadels, three in number : *Alecto, Tyfi-phone,* and *Mægera* : to the number of those three Passions which carry vs head-long, *viz.* Anger, Couet-ousnesse, and Luxury. *Lactantius de vero cultu.*

He therefore being toffed, (the throng was fo great) vpon their glowing flefh-hookes, from one to one, till hee came before the grand *Cacodemon,* (his Maifter) who fate in a chaire all on fire, downe fell my little fpirit flat at his clouen feete : and then, the Captaine of Damnation, (hauing firft fpit out foure or fiue Blafphemies, which one of his Gentlemen

Blasphemy the diuels spittle.

Vſhers ſtill trod out) hee gnaſhed his teeth, and aſked if the newes were current : it was replied, yes.

Nay (cries this *Goblin*) to vnclaſpe a booke of my further trauels, let mee bee hung in chaines of yce (as you are in fire, if I lie) and bee bound to eate flakes in the Frozen *Zone* for a thouſand yeares, if the Gloabe of the Terreſtriall world bee not new Moulded, the Ball of it hath none of the Old Stuffing : not an inch of knauery can now bee had for loue or money ; if you would giue a Million of Gold you cannot haue a Courtier in debt, if you would beſtow a thouſand pounds worth of Tobacco on a Souldier but to ſweare a Garriſon-oth, hee would die ere hee drunke it ; beſides all Rich-men are liberall, Poore men not contentious, Beggars not drunke, Lawyers not couetous, rich heires not riotous, Cittizens not enuious, clownes moſt religious.

No / more, cryed the *Tartarian Tarmagant* ; The tother ſtop'd in his Careere, and it was time ; for this laſt Cannon, ſhot *Schel-lum Waſſerhand* through both his broad ſides. The fall of this Mil-ſtone had almoſt burſt his heart, he ſigh'd nothing but flaſhes of fire, ſpit nothing but flakes of brim-ſtone, weep'd nothing but ſcoopes-full of ſcalding-water ; for now he ſaw the *Dilaceration* of his

Schellum in Dutch, a Theiſe : *Waſſerhand* a Fauning Cur, Names fitting for the Diuell.

owne *Luciferan Kingdome,* and the exaltation of
his enemies ; out of his prefence hee commanded
all. They breake their Neckes for haft ; he bawld
for Muficke ; Ten thoufand foules were prefently
fet a yelling : hee tooke no pleafure in't. Hee felt
himfelfe damnably heart-burnt, pangues worfe then
the tortures of euerlafting death fell vpon him,
and no hope of his Recouery ; which made an
inexpreffible howling in hell.

No Amendment being in him, hee cals for
Phyfitions : not one would come neere him, they
knew his payment too well ; for *Potecaries* they
were futtle enough, and cared not for his cuftome.
He then roard out for a cunning Scriuener to
make his *Will* : one was at his Elbow
prefently. Him he hugd in his armes,
and cry'd out, Welcome my Sonne ;
thou now fhalt for euer bind mee vnto thee.
S^r. *Satrapas Satan,* then goes on and tels him,
Hee's falne into a low and miferable eftate, his
cafe is defperate, and therefore being vtterly
giuen ouer, hee fends for him to make his *Laft
Will and Teftament,* and fo *Signior Scriuano*
begins, and galops as faft with his Pen,
as *Monfieur Diabolo* could with
his chaps. The *Will*
was this.

The Notary dwels in Hel-streete in *Paris.*

The / Diuels laſt Will and
TESTAMENT.

BEHEMAH *Dornſchweyn*, Prince of all that lyes betwéene the Eaſt and the Weſt, the North and the South; Mighty both on the Sea, and on the Land, chiefe Vayuode of Vſury, Symony, Bribery, Periury, Forgery, Tyrrany, Blaſphemy, Calumny, &c. (My Vaſſails and Deputies, with all their Petty Officers vnder them) Patron of all that ſtudy the blacke and *Negromanticke Arts* ; Father of all the Roaring Boyes ; The Founder and Vpholder of Paintings, Dawbings, Plaiſterings, Pargettings, Purflings, Ceruſings, Cementings, Wrinkle-fillings, and Botchings vp of old, decayed, and weather-beaten Faces ; being confounded, and tormented in euery limbe : but hauing my Memory and Wits freſh and liuely, doe make

The Diuill is *Behemah*, an *Elephant* for ſtrength to ouercome and *Dornſchweyn*, a *Porcupine* for quils, he ſhoots daily at our ſoules.

A *Vayuode* is a chiefe Ruler: an Attribute giuen to great Men in those parts of *Morauia* and *Transalpine Hungary*.

this my *laft Will and Teftament* in manner and forme following :

Inprimis, I will bequeath the World (whereof
The Legacies. I am Prince) with all the Pleafures,
Inticements, and Sorcerous Vanities thereof, to bee equally diftributed amongft / my
To his children. Sons and Daughters ; and becaufe (of my owne knowledge) I find very many of them, to be damnable and wicked, I lay vpon all fuch a fathers heauy curfe ; not caring though they hang in hell, becaufe they haue run a villanous, impious, prepofterous, and diuelifh Race.

Item. To all thofe Ladies, Gentlewomen, and
A Legacy to Ladies. Cittizens wiues, (being fet downe by their Names in my Black-book) to whofe houfes & company I haue bene welcome at mid-night, my Will is ꝼ they all, fhall mourne.

Item. I further will and bequeath to my louing
A Legacy to Vsurers. and deereft friends, the Vfurers of this Citty, all fuch moneis as are now, or fhall heereafter bee taken aboue the rate of 10. ith hundred.

Item. My Will is, that euery Gentleman who
A Legacy to Gallants, that follow him. ferues mee, fhall bee kept in his Chaine, yea, the worft that hath followed mee, let him goe in a blacke fuite of Durance.

Item. Whereas I haue many Bafe Daughters lurking about ꝼ Suburbs, I giue to thē Carbuncles a peece, the biggeft that can be goten. And to thofe Matrons (that for my fake haue bene euer déere to thofe my faid Daughters) I giue to each of them a bottle of the fame *Aqua-vitæ*, whereof I my felfe drinke.

A Legacy to Puncks of the Cittie.

A Legacy to Baudes.

Item. I giue my inuifible cloakes to all Bank-routs, becaufe they made them, but to one Poet onely (called *Poet Comedy*) I giue my beft inuifible Cloake, becaufe it onely fits his fhoulders better then mine owne, but chiefly for that hee will trim it vp well, and line it with *Come not neere me*, or *ftand off*; And becaufe he is a flip of mine owne grafting, I likewife bequeath to him my beft Slippers, to walke and play with his Kéepers nofes.

A Legacy to Bankrouts.

Item. I giue to all Officers that loue mee, a brace of my owne Angels to hang about their neckes, as a remembrance of mee.

A Legacy to Officers that loue him.

Item, / my Wil is, that all the Brokers in Long-lane be fent to me with all fpéed poffible, becaufe I haue much of them laid to pawne to me, which will, I know, neuer be redeemed, and what I giue to them fhall bee in Hugger-Mugger; and for their brethren (the reft of their Iewifh Tribe in the Synagogue of *Hounf-ditch*) let thē be affured they fhall not bee

A Legacy to Brokers.

forgotten, becaufe I heare they pray for mee howrely : I pitty thefe poore difpifed foules, becaufe if they fhould miffe mee, I know what would become of them.

Item. I giue toward the mending of the High-
A Legacy for waies, betweene New-gate and Tyburne,
repairing the all the grauell that lies in the Kidneys,
way to Ty-
burne. Reynes and Bladders, of Churles, Vfurers, Baudes, Harlots, and Whoore-maifters, and rather then thofe Grauel-pits, fhould grow fcanty, I will that they bee fupplied continually.

Item. I giue to all Iailors and Kéepers of
A Legacy to prifons, to euery one of them, the foule
Iaylors. of a Beare (to bee rauenous) the body of a Woolfe (to be cruell ;) the fpeech of a Dog (to be churlifh ;) the Tallons of a Vulture (to bee griping,) and my countenance to beare them out in their office, that they may looke like diuels vpon poore prifoners :

Item. My Will is, that if any Roaring Boy
A Legacie to (fpringing from my Race) happen to be
Roaring Boies. Stabd, fwaggering, or fwearing three-pil'd oathes in a Tauerne, or to bee kild in the quarrell of his Whoore ; let him bee fetched hither (in my owne Name) becaufe heere he fhall be both lookt too, and prouided for.

Laftly, I make and ordaine (by this my *laft Will and Teftament*) a common Barretour to

bee my Executor ; and two Knights, who are
my fworne feruants and are of the Poft;
(their Names and feruice being naild A Legacie to the Diuels Ouer-seers.
vpon Pillers in *Weftminfter* Pallace)
I make them, (al-be-it they / are pur-blind) my
Ouerfeers, and for their paines therein, I will bequeath to each of them a great round Pearle, to
be worne in their eyes, becaufe I may be ftil in
their fight, when I am gone from them.

And to teftify that this is my laft and onely
Will which fhall ftand, I fubfcribe my Name
vnto it, thereby Renouncing, Retracting, Reuo-
cating, Difanulling, & quite Cancelling, all former
Wils whatfoeuer by mee at any time or times
made : In witneffe whereof all the States *Infernall* ;
Avernall, Acheronticke, Stygian, Phlegetonticke and
Peryphlegitonticke, haue likewife fubfcribed, in the
yeare of our *Ranging* in the World, 5574.

Mounfieur Nouerint (being a man, whofe con-
ditions were too well knowne) had Although there be, *Vestigia nulla retrorsa* out of Hell, yet you must know hee had a conueiance for that pur-pose, to haue ingresse and egresse.
nothing faid to him at this time, be-
caufe the Diuell was very bad, and had
no ftomacke to talke of old Reckonings
(for *Vniuerfe* was in his debt) but had
his payment, and was glad he got away.

Now, as it often happens to rich Cur- Rich mens false alarums.
mudgeons, that after they haue fettled
their eftates on their death-beds, (as they verily

feare) and that their wiues gape day and night to
be widdowes, that from their hufbands coffin they
may leape into a Coach and be Ladies, their
fonnes and heires curfing as faft (as the mothers
pray) vntill the great Capon-bell ring out, the
daughters weeping (when they know their portions) onely becaufe they are not marriageable, or
if mariageable, becaufe ere they mourne in blacke,
they haue not Suiters to make them merry, & the
kindred as greedy (for their parts) to fee the wind-
ing fheete laid out, that they may fetch their fat
Legacies, & then (oh terrible then !) ẏ old Fox
reuiues, fals to his fleepe, cals for his victuals,
feeles himfelfe mend, remembers his bags, cries
out for his keies, feales vp his mony, no talk of
a Wil, no hope of a Widdow, no fharing of his
wealth ; Euen the felfe-fame Pill tooke this *Diego*
Dæmonum, and recouered vpon it.

For / all his children, acquaintance, and feruants,
ftanding round about him, howling and crying for
him, behold ! this howling of theirs made him
almoft out of his wits; that madneffe quickened
his fpirits, his fpirits made him rowze vp himfelfe,
with that rowzing hee began to looke into what
danger he was falne, and by looking into it, to
deuife plots againe to raife it.

Heereupon, a Synode was called of all the
fubtilleft and plaugieft prates in Hell, (of which

there are good ſtore) : *Magog Mammon*, there dis-
couers his diſeaſe, the cauſe of it, and the perill ;
his feare is that his Kingdome would now bee
ſorely ſhaken, and his ſorrowes, becauſe all they
ſhould be ſure to ſmart for it more then he himſelfe, hee therefore craues their infernall counſell.

They ſit, they confer, they conſult, and from
that conſultation (after many villanous proiects
told on their hornes like dung vpon Pitch-forkes,
and ſmelling worſe) this Aduice was hatched, and
had fethers ſtucke on the backe, the reſt were
pluckt naked ; And this it was, That *Minotaure
Polyphem* (the Sire of all thoſe Whelpes barking
thus in the Kennels of Hell) ſhould forth-with
put fire into his old Bones, and fall to threſhing
of their Damme, to get more Hell-hounds, (braue
yong little Diuels) whom hee may (like Tumblers)
hoyſt from one Fiends ſhoulder vp to another,
and ſo pop them into the world : And they againe
going to Bull, with other blacke Goblins, may
ingender, what monſters they pleaſe to ſet all the
world and all the people in it out of tune, and
the worſe Muſicke they make, the more ſport it
is for him.

This Act was Filed vpon Record : moſt Voyces
carried it away ; the Councell flowed currant, the
Court is adiourned, and the great *Beglherby* of
Lymbo fals hotly / to his buſineſſe. Now you muſt

vnderſtand, that the Diuell being able to get children faſter then any man elſe, had no ſooner
touched his old *Laplandian Gueneuora*, but ſhee
as ſpeedily quickned ; and no ſooner quickned,
but was deliuered, and lay in, and had at this
Litter or *Burden*, two twins.

 Dabh, *Aldip Alambat* : their father gaue them
their names, the one was called *Hypo-*
crifie, the other *Ingratitude*. *Hypocrifie*
was put to nurſe to an *Anabaptiſt* of
Amſterdam, but *Ingratitude* was brought
vp at home. In a ſhort time they
battend, and were plumpe as fat Chop-
bacons they were, and toward to practiſe
any trickes that were ſhewed them.

Dabh, the Hyæna that digs dead men out of graues to deuoure them. *Aldip Alambat*, is a ravenous or furious Woolfe. *Ingratitude*, & Hypocrisy borne.

 So that béeing ripe for maiſters, *Hypocrifie* was
preſently bound to a Puritane Taylor,
by his Nurſe, and did nothing but make
Clokes of Religion for to weare, of a thouſand
colours. Hee ran away from the Taylor, and
then dwelt with a Vizard-maker, and there hee
was the firſt who inuented the wearing of two
faces vnder a hood. After this hee trauelled into
Italy, and there learned to embrace with one arme,
and ſtabbe with another : to ſmile in your face,
yet to wiſh a ponyard in your boſome : to proteſt,
and yet lye : to ſweare loue, yet hate mortally.

Hypocrisyes cloake-maker.

 From *Italy* hee came into the *Low-countries*,

where he would not talke, vnleffe hee dranke with him, and call you *Myn Leeuin Broder,* with a full glaffe, onely to ouer-reach you in your cups of your bargaine.

Out of *Germany* hee is againe come ouer into *England,* his lodging is not certaine : For (like a whoore) hee lyes euery The picture of an hypo-crite. where. Hée fometimes is at Court, and is there excéeding full of complement ; hee goes fometimes like a threed-bare Scholler, with lookes humble, as a Lambes, and as innocent, but his heart prouder then a *Turkes* to a *Chriftians.*

Hee / hath a winning and bewitching prefence, a fweete breath, a muficall voyce, and a *Fistula dulce canit, &c.* warme foft hand. But it is dangerous to keepe company with him, becaufe he can alter himfelfe into fundry fhapes. In the Citty hee is a Dogge, and will fawne vpon you : In the fields hee is a Lyons Whelpe, and will play with you : In the Sea hee is a Mer-mayd, and will fing to you. But that fawning is but to reach at your throat : that playing is to get you into his pawes, and that finging is nothing elfe but to fink and confound you for euer.

This picture of *Perdition* (*Hypocrifie*) was not drawne fo fmoothly, fo cunningly, and Ingratitude pictured. fo enticingly, but his brother (*Ingrati-tude*) though there went but a paire of Sheares

betweene them, was as vgly in fhape, and as
blacke in foule : hee was a Fiend in proportion,
and a Fury in condition. It is a monfter with
many hands, but no eyes : It catcheth at any
thing, but cannot fee the party from whom it
receiues. This is that fellow made all the Diuels
at firft, and ftill fupplyes their number continually.

This is that *Lethargy* that makes vs forget our
Maker, and neuer to thanke him for
whatfoeuer he beftowes on vs : for no
eftate is content with his ftate. If wee
are poore, wee curfe ; If rich, wee
grumble it comes in no fafter ; If hard-fauoured,
wee enuy the beautifull ; If faire, it is our trée
of damnation, and for money euery flaue
climbes it.

*Lethargia est
mentis alien-
atio & rerum
prope omnium
obliuio.*

This is that *Torpedo*, which if we touch, a
Numbneffe ftrikes all our ioynts, and
wee haue no féeling one of another.
This is hee which maketh one forget
God and his country, the King and his kindred,
only to pleafe the great Diuell his father. He that
this day hath beene comforted with thy fire, fed
with thy bread, relieued with thy purfe, and kept
from being lowfie by thy linnen, to / morrow will
bee ready to fet the fame houfe on fire ẙ hid him
from cold, for thy bread to giue thee ftones ; for

*Torpedinem
piscem, si quis
attirit, torpēt
membra.*

the money thou lenteſt him, to ſell thee (like a *Iudas,*) and for thy linnen, which wrapped him warme, glad to ſee thee in danger to goe naked. Thus haſt thou this *Gorgon* in his liuely colours: becauſe therefore that the odiouſneſſe of this beaſt *Ingratitude,* ſhould ſtill be in our eye, God hath *Hierogliphically* figured it in many of his creatures.

A *Gorgon* is a beaſt euer looking downe-ward, it eateth ſerpents, is ſcaly as a dragon, toothed as a ſwine : it hath wings to flye, the breath is venemous, the eyes fiery, and ſtrike be-holders dead. All which properties belong to the Diuell. *Æsop. Fab. 5.*

The *Viper* is an Embleme of it, whoſe yong-ones gnaw out the belly in which they are bred. So is the *Mule,* whoſe panch being full with ſucking, ſhe kickes her dam. So is the Iuy, which kils that by which it climbes : and ſo is fire, which de-ſtroyes his nouriſher.

The tongue of *Ingratitude* is the ſting of that frozen Snake, which wounds the boſome that gaue it heate and life.

The hands of *Ingratitude* are thoſe Tubbes full of holes, which the daughters of *Danaus* fill vp with water in hell, and as faſt as it is powred in, it all runs out againe.

An ingratefull man therefore is not like *Nero,* that gathered flowers out of *Ennius* his heape of dung, but like the *Cantharides* that ſuckes poyſon out of the ſweeteſt flower.

Cantharidum succos, dante parente bibas. Ouid. in Ibim.

D. III.   46

Not without great wifedome did that old
Serpent, (the *Anthropophagizde Satyr*)
cloath his Hellifh brood of his in
humane fhapes: for you fee how bene-
ficiall their feruice may bee to him, and
how maleuolent they are likely to be to
man: for thefe are thofe *Ichneumons* that
creepe in at our mouthes, and are not
fatisfied only firft with deuouring whats within vs,
and then to eate quite through our bodyes, but
the food which they luft after, is to rauen vpon
the foule.

My purpofe was (when the grand *Helca* had
gotten thefe / two Furies with nine liues), onely
to haue drawne the Curtaines of her Childe-bed,
in which fhee lay in, and to haue fhewne no
more but the well-fauoured faces of her paire of
Monkyes; But you fee, from her withered Teates
I haue brought them to their cradles, from the
cradle caried thē to Nurfe; & from thence followed them till they were able to doe feruice in
the world. How they haue fped, you heare, and
how they are likely to profper, you may iudge.

But you muft thinke that their father, after
hee had begun to digge, and feeing his
labours thriue, would not fo giue ouer:
For the old Counteffe *Canidia*, (his
wife) being a teeming *Lamia*, after fhe was

[marginal notes:]

The Man-eating-mon-ster. *Anthro-pophagi* were *Scythians* (now *Tartars*) so called for eating men. & drinking bloud in their sculs. *Polyhistor.*

Canidia a witch of whom *Hor.* writes.

deliuered of the two firſt *Lemures*, (*Hypocriſie* and *Ingratitude*) did within ſhort time after, bring forth others, as *Schiſme*, *Atheiſme, Paganiſme, Idiotiſme, Apoſtacy, Impenitency, Diffidence, Preſumption*, and a whole generation of ſuch others ; of whom the father needes not bee iealous that the Sorcereſſe their mother playd falſe with him, euery one of them béeing like him in viſage, and carrying in their boſomes his villanous conditions ; For as he himſelfe goes prowling vp and downe for his Prey, ſo do theſe take after him, and play their parts ſo well, that all Hell roares with laughing, and rings with giuing them plaudits.

Lamia a letcherous spirit, that neuer takes rest. *a spectre.*

A Race of vnhapy children.

For theſe Furies haue in the Church bred *Contentions*, in Courts *Irreligion*, in the Citty *Prophanation*, in the Countrey ignorance of all goodneſſe ; and in the World, a knowledge of the moſt flagicious Impieties.

At the birth of euery one theſe Monſters, were particular Triumphes, but aboue all the reſt, one had the glory to be graced with a Maſque, and it was at an vpſitting, when the *Goſſips* and many great *States* were there preſent.

It / was a *Morall Maſque*, a *Miſticall Maſque*, and a *Conceited*, ſet out at the coſt of The Masque. certaine *Catch-pols*, who were witty in the Inuention, liberall in the Expence, quicke in the Performance, and neate in the putting off.

The *Mafquers* themfelues were braue fellowes, bare-faced, not néeding, nor caring for any Vizards (their owne vifages béeing good enough, becaufe bad enough), they were not afhamed of their doings. Euery one of them came in with fome property in his right hand, appliable to the name of a *Catch-poll*, and to the nature of the *Catch-pols Mafque* : For one had a Fifhermans Net, another an Angling rod, another a trée like a Lime-bufh, another a Welfh-hooke, another a Moufe-trap, another a handfull of Bryers, and fuch like : and euery one of thefe had a baite, and a Soule nibling at euery baite. In their left hands they held whips, vpon their heads they wore Anticke crownes of Feathers plucked from Rauens wings, Kites and Cormorants, (béeing all Birds of Rapine and Catching:) And on their bodyes loofe Iackets of Wolues fkinnes, with Bafes to them of Vultures, whofe heads hang dangling downe as low as their knées, which made an excellent fhew. Their legges were buttoned vp in *Gamafhes*, made of Beares paws, the nailes fticking out at full length.

They who fupplyed the places of *Torch-bearers*, carryed no Torches, (as in other Mafqueries they doe) but (their armes being

The Masquers.

Their Masquing apparrell.

The Torch-bearers.

ftript vp naked to their elbowes) they griped
(in either hand) a bundle of liuing Snakes, and
Adders, which writhing about their wrifts, fpit
wild fire and poyfon together, and fo made excellent fport to the affembly.

They had a *Drum*, after which they marched
(two & two) & that was made of an old *Caudron*,
the head of it being couered / with the fkins
of two flead *Spaniſh Inquiſitors*, and
a hole (for vent) beaten out at the Their Drum.
very bottome : the Drum-ftickes were the fhin-
bones of two *Dutch-Free-booters* : So that it
founded like a *Switzers Kettle-drum*.

The Muficke ftrucke vp, and they daunced ;
in their dauncing it was an admirable The Masquers
fight to behold, how the Soules that lay Daunce.
nibbling at the baites, did bobbe vp and downe :
and ftill as they did bite, the whippes lafhed them
for their liquorifhneffe. The fwallowing of the
baytes was (to thofe Soules) a pleafure, and their
fkipping to and fro, when they were whipped,
made all Hell fall into a laughing. One of thofe
baytes was *Promotion*, the fecond was *Gold*, the
third *Beauty*, the fourth *Reuenge*, the fift *a pipe
of Tobacco* : and fuch rotten ftuffe were all the
reft.

The Daunce was an infernall *Iriſh-hay*, full of
mad and wilde changes, which (with the *Maſquers*)

vaniſhed away as it came in, (like vnto *Agryppaes* ſhadowes.)

Now becauſe (in naming this the *Catch-pols Maſque*) ſome ſquint-eyd Aſſe, (thinking he can ſée quite through a load of Mill-ſtones) will goe about to perſwade the credulous world, that I meane thoſe Sergeants and Officers who ſit at Counter-gates. No, there is no ſuch traine layd, no ſuch powder, no ſuch linſtocke in my pen to giue fire : they are *Boni & legales homines*, good fellowes, and honeſt men : that name of *Catch-poll* is ſpitefully ſtucke vpon them by a by-name : for to theſe *Catch-pols*, that are now vnder my fingers, doth it properly, naturally, and really belong, and to none other.

If thoſe two ſet of Counters compell a man to caſt vp his Reckoning, what he owes, and how much hee is out, yet they catch no man, except the Law put them on, / and it is their office. No, no, *Paulo Maiora Canamus.* Thoſe *Catch-pols* whom wee deale with, are of a larger ſtampe, of a richer mettall, and of a coine more currant. I will therefore firſt tell you what a *Catch-poll* is, and then you may eaſily picke out what thoſe gallants are whom we call ſo.

A *Catch-poll* is one that doth both catch and
What a *Catch-poll* is. poll : who is not content onely to haue the ſheepe, but muſt ſheare it too ; and

not fheare it, but to draw bloud too. So then by this *Etymology* of the word, any one that finifterly wrefts and fcrues *Monopolies* into his hands, to fill his Coffers, (though his owne confcience whifpers in his eare, that hee beggers the Common-wealth) and his Prince neuer the better for it : but the poore Subiects much the worfe : Hee is a *Grand Catch-poll.* Their Species.

Any one that takes Bribes, and holds the Scales of Iuftice with an vn-euen hand, laying the rich mans caufe (be it neuer fo bad) in the heauy fcale, and the poore mans (be it neuer fo good) in the light one, hée is a *Catch-poll.*

A *Paftor*, that hauing a Flocke to féede, fuffers them to breake into ftrange fields, lets them ftray he cares not how ; be dragged away by the Wolfe, he regards not whither : féeth them ficke and difeafed, and will not cure them : hee is a *Catch-poll.*

So is a Lawyer, that fleas his Clyent, and doth nothing elfe for him.

So is an Alder-man, if he rob the poore Widow, or friendleffe-forfaken Orphant.

So is a Soldier, that makes bloud, rapes, luft and violence his proper ends ; and not Gods quarrell, his Princes right, or the honour of his Country.

So is a Citizen, that cozens other men of their

goods, and fels bad ware in a blind fhop, to honeft Cuftomers, of / which they neuer are able to make the one halfe: yet if they breake their day, hee will let them rot in prifon rather then releafe them.

And laftly, that Prentice, who robs his maifter, and fpends his fubftance vpon Harlots; hée is a *Catch-poll* as egregious as the beft.

Out of thefe *Rankes* were thofe *Hot-fhots* (the *Mafquers*) drawne, whom I leaue to double their *Files* by themfelues, becaufe I fée the *Reare-ward* comming vp, and I muft likewife teach them their *Poftures.*

THE / BANKROVTS
BANQUET.

WHAT is a Maſque without a Banquet?
And what is a Banquet if it bee not
ſerued vp in State?

To heighten therefore the Solemnity
of this Child-beds vp-ſitting, as alſo to curry
fauour, with the Blacke King of *Neagers*, (their
Lord and Maiſter), another crew, of as boone
Companions as the former, as fat in the purſe and
as lauiſh in ſpending, but more carefull of beeing
blazoned to the world, for what they did, and
therefore all of them hiding their heades, laid
their monies together, and preſented a Strange,
Rare, Curious, and moſt Sumptuous Banquet, to
Donzell Diauolo. Inuiting not onely himſelfe,
but alſo his new-deliuered Spouſe (Queene of the
Grimme *Tartars*, the *Troglodites*, who eate Serpents,
the foode of Diuels, the *Cimerians*, the *Sodomites*,
and the *Gomorrhæans*) and with her, the great
Diabolicall Conuenticle there aſſembled together.

D. III.   47

To ftoppe all thefe mouthes with Sugar-plumes,
you/muft needs thinke, would afke a huge charge;
but they who vndertake the coft, refpected not
the expence, for they had not onely coyne of their
owne enough, but they had fhragd others too of
theirs, and being hunted from corner to
corner in the world, hither (into the
Iland of the *Bermudes* haunted as all
men know with Hogs and Hobgoblings)
came they for fhelter, for heere they
know they are fure, from hence none dare fetch
them : they are called *Bankrouts.*

Bermudes called the Iland of Diuels, by reason of the grunting of Swine, heard from thence to the Sea.

And becaufe the Catch-pols proportiond out a
Deuice refponfible to their Name and Quality ;
thefe Bankrouts (treading in the fame fteps of
Ambition) Martiald vp a Banquet, rellifhing likewife of their name, carriage and condition. So
that, although they had hooked into their hands,
all forts of Wares, Goods, Commodities, and
Merchandize, out of the true Owners fingers,
and had laid them far enough from their reach ;
yet would they ferue this Banquet to the Table,
neither in Plate, in Chriftall, in *Chyna* difhes, glaffe
or any other furniture, but in a Stuffe, deerer to
them (and more deere to others) then any of the
Mettals recited. For they to get wealth into their
Fifts, not making a feare, nor confcience to feale
to any Parchements ; in Sealed Difhes, therefore

was their Banquet brought in. And thus the Bankrouts themſelues (to adde more State to the Ceremony) came marching with their *Suckets*, &c. in order.

Firſt, the vpper end of the Table was furniſhed with the heauieſt, coſtlieſt, and cunningſt *Bondes* that could be got, for loue, wit, or mony ; and they were heaped vp with Cynamon Comfits, (Cynamon being an extreme *Bynder* ;) and of this Banquetting Diſh was ſuch ſtore, that it ran cleane through the Board.

The Bankrouts banquet.

Bondes, a binding meate.

Next, came in *Bils Obligatory*, (a thouſand in a cluſter) and they were filled with *Conſerues* of *Slowes*, and other / Stipticke ſweete-meates.

Bils, binders too.

After theſe in moſt Iuditiall manner, and with great pompe and charge, were *Statutes* ſerued vp : and they were laden with *Candyed Eringoes* ; of purpoſe to put ſpirit into him that ſhould eate of this diſh, and to keepe him vp, becauſe, if hee ſinke or grow ſicke with chewing downe or ſwallowing of *Statute*, he'es gone and little hope of recouery.

Statutes dangerous meats.

Iuſt in the taile of thoſe, were brought to the Table a goodly company of *Defeazances*, and they held delicate Flakes of White and Red Iellies, being both Reſtoratiue, and very looſing to the ſtomake, and good againſt

Defeyſance cõfortable to the ſtomacke.

thofe Binding and Reftringent difhes, which came
in firft : at the vpper end of the Table this difh
fhould haue bene ferued vp, but it had a mis-
chance.

After all this, a *Capias* with a *Latitat*, went
from one to one, but none touched
Latitats no
sweetnesse in thofe difhes, yet they were heaped
them.   full to the brim with *Sugar-pellets*, and
cakes of *Gynger-bread* piled round about them;
But the *Pellets* when they were fhot did fcarce
hit, and the *Gynger* fo bit their tongues,
Hot in the
mouth and and fet their mouths in a heat, that none
biting.   at the Table toucht them, but fhifted
them one from another.

At the laft, *Attachments* appeared in their like-
Attachments a neffe, and they were fild into bottels of
heady-drinke. *Hypocras*, and other ftrong Wines; able
to lay hold of a man, as fuddenly as he laies hold
of them, and to make him (if hee drinke hard of
them) to bee carried away, and bid good-night
Land-lord.

Next thofe difhes, were brought in, a number
Outlaries are of *Outlaries*, thwackt with *Purging-*
terrible Purges. *comfits* ; for they are able to make a
man flye ouer nine hedges.

And below them ftood *Iudgements*, full of new
Iudgements lie bakt *Diet-bread*, and therefore hard for
heauy in the
stomacke.   the ftomacke to difgeft.

But / clofe by them were placed *Executions*, which cloyed euery ones ftomacke there ; *Executions* a very sowre meate and vnwholsome. for they were *Tarts* of feuerall Fruites, ftucke with *Mufke-comfits* of purpofe, to fweeten the mouth, if any fhould happen to lay his lippes to [fo] fowre a difh.

The laft Banquetting-ftuffs (faue one) were *Ne exeat Regnum*, and thofe were heaped *Ne exeat Regnum* good to stay a running. to the top with *Annif-feed-comfits*, being exceeding good to procure Long-winds, if a man haue a minde, or bee forced to Run his Country.

The laft of all were *Protections*, fome larger than other ; and when thefe came in, a fhoute was given, for all the *Bankrouts* *Protections* wholesome & comfortable. flung vp their caps, and bid their Guefts *profaces*, for now they faw their Cheere. In thofe *Protections* lay *March-panes*, which fhewed like *Bucklers*, ỹ long *Orange-comfits* ftanding vp like *Pikes*, & in the midft of euery *March-pane* a goodly fwéet *Caftle*, all the bottomes being thickely ftrewed with *Careawaies*. And this was the *Bankrouts Sybariticall Banquet.*

The queint cafting of the difhes fo brauely, all in wax was wondred at, the working, tempering, moulding, and fafhioning of the Swéete-meates were commended, the conceipt of Furnifhing the Table extolled, the coft well liked off, and the

Beftowers, not reward with common thankes ; for the *Grand-Signior* of the triple-world called the *Bankrouts* his *White Sonnes*, and fwore a Damnable Oath, that hee himfelfe would haue an Eye ouer them.

And fo, after hee and his *Bafhaes*, had cramd their guts, they rofe, euery Officer being charged to looke to his place, that no more fuch terrors may fhake the fteepe hils that fupport his Kingdome; and with fuch leffons, they flye feuerall waies, fwift, and as horrid as whirle-windes. A muffe being made amongft the poorer fort in Hell, / of the fweete-meate-fcraps, left after the Banquet.

The *Feafters* being difperfed, the maifters of the *Feaft*, (the *Bankrouts*) held in a knot together : it was told them, there was beating at the gates to fpeake with them. All went to fee : and who was it but the *Comfit-maker*, that trufted them with his ftuffe, and brought a bill of three-fcore and odde pounds, requefting to haue his money. His *Pay-maifters* told him this was no world to part from money, but to get as much as euery man could into his owne hands : other men did fo, and fo would they, their elders read them that leffon, and they muft take it out. If he would take two fhillings in the pound, they would pay him downe vpon the naile : If not, they were refolued to try the vtmoft, and therefore bid him go fhake his eares.

The poore rotten-tooth'd Comfit-maker, at thefe out-of-tune-notes, was ready to run out of his wits: Hee rapt at the gates, fwore, curfed, and railed; Are you men (cryed he out) or diuels? How fhall I pay my Sugar-marchant? How my Grocers? How my Bakers? How my worke-men? How my Orange-women, if you pay me thus with flips? Into halters flip you all; you haue robbed me, vndone me, beggered me, and left nothing in my fhop but one box of bitter Almonds, and I would they were burning red-hot in your bellies too.

The more fowre his language was, the more fweet it was to them: for they did but laugh to heare him curfe, and went their wayes: He féeing no remedy, fwore hée would rattle all hell about their eares if they bob'd him off thus: And fo betwéene fcolding and whining, he thus tooke his peny-worths of them in words, though not in filuer.

If (faid he) you were poore, and had it not, I would neuer afke you a peny, if you _{Men that are} were forced to breake by any / late _{forc'd to break are to be} fhip-wracke at fea, or by the villany _{pittied.} of *Debito*[r]*s* on the land, or by the frownes of the world, or the falfeneffe of feruants, I fhould pawne my fhirt from my backe to releiue you; but you burft vpon knauery, cheating, and roguery.

You that thus vndermine your owne eftates, *An inuectiue with other mens)* your felues, are like *against volun-* *tary and* trées ftanding in your next neighbours *cosening* *bankerouts.* ground, which you climbe in the darke, & gathering the fruit (like théeues) run away with it by Moone-fhine. But if your ftates were weake for want of ability to pay, then are you thofe trees that (in your owne ground) are beaten with ftormes, whofe apples are fhaken down fpite-fully on the earth, and are deuoured by fuch *Hoggiſh debters* before the true *Owners* can come to take them vp: and if fo, you are to be pittied and releeued. You tell me you will breake: do *Their good* fo, breake your neckes. But before you *name loft.* do fo, make this account, that you are as bad as halfe hanged; for you haue an ill, and a moft abhominable name: try elfe.

A *Bankrout,* that is to fay, a *Banker-out :* A *Who is a* Citizen that deales in mony, or had *Bankrout.* mony in *Banke,* or ;n ftocke, *He is out* (when he *Breakes :*) But me thinkes hee is rather *In.* I fée no reafon we fhould fay, *he breakes,* *The life of a* there is more reafon to cry out, *He* *Bankrout.* *makes all whole,* or *hee makes vp his* *mouth,* (as you haue done with my plums) or *he gets the diuell and all.* For what doe you, but lye grunting in your ftyes, like *Hogges,* and fat your ribbes with fruits of other mens labours. In my opinion you fhould feare the bread you eate fhould choke you, becaufe it is ftolne ; the drinke you fwallow fhould ftrangle you, becaufe you quaffe the bloud of honeft houfholders : and that the wine you carowfe fhould dam you, becaufe (with it) you mixe the teares of mothers, & the cries of children.

If a *Rogue* cut a purfe, hée is hanged ; if pilfer, hée is burnt in the hand : You are worfe then *Rogues* ; for you cut / many purfes : Nay, you cut many mens throats, you fteale from the husband, his wealth : from the wife her dowry : from children their portions. So that ouer your heads hang the curfes of Families : how then can you hope to profper? For to play the *Bankrout,* is to bid men to a Citty-rifling, where euery one puts in his money, and none wins but one, and that is the *Bankrout.*

The sinne of a Bankrout.

If all the water in the Thames were inke, and all the fethers vpon Swans backes were pens, and all the fmoky failes of weft- erne barges, were white paper, & all the Scriueners, all the Clarkes, all the Schoole-maifters, & all the Scholers in the kingdome were fet a writing, and all the yeares of the world yet to

The villany of Bankrouts cannot be expressed.

come, were to be imploied only in that bufineffe :
that inke would be fpent, thofe pens grub'd clofe
to the ftumps, that paper fcribled all ouer, thofe
writers wearied, and that time worne out, before
the fhifts, legerdemaines, conueiances, reaches,
fetches, ambufhes, traines, and clofe vnder-minings
of a *Bankrout* could to the life be fet downe.
This was the laft winter-plum the fad Comfit-
maker threw at their heads ; and fo left them,
and fo I leaue them.

> My Mufe that art fo merry,
> When wilt thou fay th'art weary ?
> Neuer (I know it) neuer,
> This flight thou couldft keepe euer :
> Thy fhapes which fo do vary,
> Beyond thy bownds thee cary.
> Now plume thy ruffled wings,
> Hee's hoarfe who alwayes fings.

Contigimus portum, quò mihi curfus erat.

FINIS. /